P9-BZO-639

TABLE OF CONTENTS
•••

CONTENTS

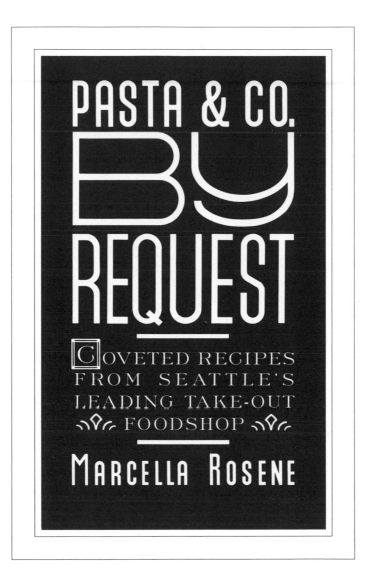

PASTA & CO. BY REQUEST

Coveted Recipes from Seattle's Leading Take-Out Foodshop

Marcella Rosene

Edited by Judy Birkland

Book Design: Kris Morgan
Cover Photographs: Kim Zumwalt
Art Direction: Jane Jeszeck
Copy Editor: Sally Anderson
Production: Sasquatch Books
Composition: Scribe Typography

Distributed by
Sasquatch Books
1931 Second Avenue
Seattle, WA 98101
(206) 441-6202

Library of Congress Cataloging-in-Publication Data

Rosene, Marcella, 1945–
    Pasta & co. by request : coveted recipes from Seattle's
leading take-out foodshop / Marcella Rosene.
        p.   cm.
    Includes index.
    ISBN 0-912365-49-8 : 13.95
    1. Pasta & Co.   2. Cookery—Washington (State)—Seattle.
I. Title.   II. Title: Pasta and Co. by request.
TX714.R67   1991
641.5'09797'792—dc20   91-5108
                                                           CIP

Published by Pasta & Co., Inc.
2640 NE University Village Mall
Seattle, Washington 98105

LOCATIONS:
University Village Store
2640 NE University Village Mall
Seattle, Washington 98105
(206) 523-8594

Bellevue Store
10218 N.E. 8th Street
Bellevue, Washington 98004
(206) 453-8760

Downtown Store
1001 Fourth Avenue Plaza
Seattle, Washington 98154
(206) 624-3008

DEDICATIONS
•••

. . . .

TO CHUCKMAN & SAM

As always

TO MY MOTHER

Who taught me to shop at the Pike Place Market

TO MY DAD

Who makes my herb garden grow

AND TO HARVEY

Who makes all good things seem possible.

IN MEMORIAM

DOROTHY BOLSTAD

Our first manager
So full of enthusiasm for our enterprise.

If Time, so fleeting, must like humans die, let it be filled
with good food and good talk, and then embalmed
in the perfumes of conviviality.
—M.F.K. Fisher, *Serve It Forth*

HOT PASTA:
THE SAUCES AND BAKED PASTA DISHES THAT ARE DAILY
FARE AT PASTA & CO.

OTHER HOT PASTA DISHES:
RECIPES FROM A MORE PRIVATE COLLECTION

HOT ENTRÉES:
MEANT TO BE REHEATED

DESSERTS AND BAKING:
FROM FRESH LEMON TARTS TO GROWN-UP GRANOLA

INDEX

ACKNOWLEDGMENTS
FROM PASTA & CO.'S
OWNERS
♦♦♦

We wish to thank all those who have had a part in the making of this book. Particularly, we think of customers who have continued to care about our products throughout a decade of business. And, we are grateful to employees — longtime and new — for whatever sustained, or fresh, enthusiasm they have contributed to our products.

We extend a special thank-you to Chad Haight, Jane Jeszeck, Kitty Harmon, and Sally Anderson at Sasquatch Books. Working with designer Kris Morgan, they steered us patiently through this project.

You will find pictured on the back flap of the book the staff members who have set the taste of Pasta & Co. foods. Jodelle Stith supplied the determination that, without a doubt, the book should go to press. She tested dozens of recipes, demanding clarity for the trusting cooks who might want to successfully use this book.

Judy Birkland — an outspoken and accomplished home cook, who has been with Pasta & Co. since its opening week — was our dauntless editor. There is hardly a recipe in this book (or in the last one) that does not in some way show her mark. Many of them she personally invented.

Jerry Malmevik, who runs our University Village kitchen, also tested dozens of recipes, as well as originating a number of the book's biggest sellers: Brown-Bottom Meat Loaf, Herb-Roasted Chicken, and The Big Blue.

At the downtown store, senior manager Charlie Leonard headed the team that tested all of our dessert and bakery recipes.

At the Bellevue store, Cory Vicens and Carolyn Flory perfected our baked pasta recipes, cutting them from batches that make dozens down to batches that make one. It was Andy Davis, our downtown assistant manager, who daily baked off the dishes, making certain all the cuts worked.

Food at Pasta & Co. has always been a group effort and, at times, maybe the only justification for running a fast-paced retail shop. After all, when the tortellini machine is broken, a third of the counter crew is out sick, the Cuisinart blade is missing, and the owners seem diabolically intolerable, there is still always something new to taste, to perfect, and then to tell others about. That is, indeed, the adventure and the pleasure of food.

Thank you all for sharing the food.

Harvey and Marcella Rosene
Seattle, Washington
September 1991

INTRODUCTION:
ABOUT OUR BOOK
AND OUR TIMES
◆◆◆

I n Pasta & Co.'s first cookbook, published in 1987, we wrote about the 1980s as "the most exciting period in our national culinary history." Now, at the start of the 1990's, we have achieved nothing less than what we and others predicted: "a new American standard of eating." Large numbers of us have learned to eat and drink with more discernment than ever before. To be sure, some of the exuberance of the eighties is gone. But then, so is some of the sheer silliness about food. There is much talk now about more sombre times, about an economy in trouble, and—ironically— about hunger. In this environment, cuisine has become more reasonable, more practical. Pasta & Co.'s own market has bent toward homier fare. It demands honest attention to nutrition and convenience. And the emphasis is on the pleasures of sharing food that is as wholesome and unpretentious as it is splendid and inventive. This, our second book, is intended to reflect all of the above. As the title implies, these are the recipes for foods that customers request day after day. As in our first book, the recipes have been exhaustively tested. Even more important, the food formulated in these pages, is what you will love to cook and serve.

Questions about nutrition? Watch for Notes from Nutrition Works. In a rush? Watch for recipes marked with a clock for "fast and easy."

Appetizers:

known

at

Pasta & Co.

as

"Conversation

Foods."

The start of a gathering is no place for boring foods. Appetizers should be "conversation foods"—foods which, because of their taste and appearance, intrigue guests. (Definitely do not overlook simple but startling foods, such as poppadums, page 21, and Hot Bread with Olive Oil and Vinegar, page 17.) ■ We also think appetizers should be prepareahead snaps that bode no last-minute terror for the host or hostess as guests arrive. ■ The recipes in this section are all for appetizers that will definitely get your guests talking. And they will ensure that you can listen in with leisure on what those guests are saying.

SPICED PUMPKIN SEEDS
OR ALMONDS

These snacky seeds and nuts definitely fill the bill for "conversation food." Guests will be intrigued with the novel, good taste of the spices and will be especially curious about the pumpkin seeds (see below), which you can buy at Pasta & Co. or health-food stores. **PREPARE-AHEAD/SERVING NOTES:** As long as you do not burn the seeds or nuts in the initial preparation, they are nearly indestructible. Bake them. Refrigerate them. Freeze them. Rewarm them. The cycle can go on for months before you lose any quality. You will love this appetizer because it is so handy to have around.

2 tablespoons plus 1 teaspoon ground cumin	3 cups hulled raw pumpkin seeds (see below) or blanched almonds
1 tablespoon sweet paprika	2 tablespoons pure olive oil
1½ teaspoons salt or to taste	1½ teaspoons very finely minced garlic
1 teaspoon cayenne	

Preheat oven to 350°F. Mix together cumin, paprika, salt, and cayenne. On a cookie sheet, toss pumpkin seeds or almonds with oil until well-coated. Then toss with spice mixture.

Place in oven and bake about 10 minutes until almonds turn golden or until seeds begin to puff (seeds will take approximately twice as long as nuts).

Remove from oven and toss with garlic. Serve warm or at room temperature.

MAKES 3 CUPS.

PUMPKIN SEEDS

We first discovered this intriguing ingredient when we were developing our Grown-up Granola (page 254), which also uses these nutty-flavored seeds. They are used traditionally in Mexican cooking, similar to the use of pine nuts in Italian cuisine. We like them spiced and roasted, as they are in the recipe above.

The pumpkin seeds used in these recipes are not straight from a Halloween jack-o'lantern. They are raw, hulled seeds, usually from China. Pasta & Co. and health-food stores sell them. Like all nuts and seeds, they store well frozen.

ROASTED BREADS

...

These crisp, roasted rounds of bread are so scrumptiously seasoned they can be eaten all by themselves; they can also be coupled with spreads, cheeses, or other appetizer foods. The only difficulty with this recipe is that when you make a large number (even the 65 that this recipe yields), tending the hot oven becomes tedious and the risk of burning your breads is high.

Our advice: Use this recipe for small — not large — dinner parties, but *definitely* make it. Also, feel free to alter the seasonings on the breads. When we serve the breads with smoked sturgeon, we brush them with only a tiny bit of mild olive oil and just a quick rub with the cut side of a garlic clove before roasting. To serve with the Purée of Highly Seasoned Tofu (page 20), we suggest using no garlic at all on the breads. **PREPARE-AHEAD/SERVING NOTES:** The good news is that once baked, these breads keep for weeks in an airtight tin. You can then serve them at room temperature or briefly rewarm them in the oven. **ESSENTIAL GEAR:** Mortar and pestle

1 heaping tablespoon Pasta & Co. House Herbs *OR* 10 grinds black pepper or pepper melange, 1½ teaspoons herbes de Provence, ½ teaspoon thyme, ½ teaspoon oregano, ½ teaspoon basil, and ½ teaspoon rosemary

¼ teaspoon salt

½ cup pure olive oil

1½ tablespoons garlic, put through a garlic press, *OR* 1½ tablespoons garlic purée (page 17)

8 ounces baguette-shaped bread, cut in ¼-inch–thick slices (a fun variation is to thinly slice larger loaves of peasant-style bread, which will give you large slices, particularly appealing for sit-down appetizer courses)

Preheat oven to 400°F. Line a baking sheet with parchment or foil.

Grind House Herbs (or the alternative selection of herbs) and salt together with a mortar and pestle. Whisk together herb/salt mixture, olive oil, and garlic. Here's where technique can help. The easiest method is this: Place the baking sheet on a counter next to your container of oil and the pile of sliced breads. Dip a pastry brush into oil mixture, stirring as you go so that you get a reasonable portion of herbs. Wipe off any extra oil on the side of the cup, as you would if you were painting. Then, holding the bread over the container of oil and herbs, brush one side of each slice and lay oiled-side-up on the baking sheet. The breads can be touching, but to bake evenly they should not overlap. Do not be too precise with either these or the pita chips in the next recipe. It is all right if one piece of bread has more oil and herbs than another. *Do not soak* the bread. You want just a light coating of oil.

Bake for 5 minutes. Rotate pan. Continue baking until golden brown. (And, oh yes — all the breads will not be evenly browned. No harm, as long as they are not burned.) Serve hot or cool.

MAKES 65 SLICES.

TO WEIGH OR NOT TO WEIGH

Weighing can be a much more reliable way of measuring ingredients than using cups and spoons. And when you think of the plethora of gadgets in most home kitchens, it is surprising that a small kitchen scale is usually not among them.

The advantage of having one is clear in the preceding recipe. Since the size of loaves and slices varies and it is not a simple matter to measure bread in cups and spoons, weight is the only means of producing somewhat predictable results.

We sometimes will include weights as well as measures. And we urge you to use a kitchen scale.

PURÉED GARLIC

Break garlic bulbs apart (do at least two heads at a time to make it worth your trouble). Peel the cloves, by first flattening them with the flat side of a heavy knife, then removing the skin. Place all cloves in a food processor fitted with a steel blade and drizzle with a small amount of olive oil. Process until garlic is puréed. Store for up to two weeks. *Refrigeration is essential.* The purée keeps longer if completely covered with olive oil. Discard the purée if any mold appears on the garlic. Use whenever a recipe calls for finely minced garlic or garlic put through a press.

A FAST, EASY, AND DAZZLING FIRST-COURSE IDEA

Coat the center of a plate with a thin layer of your best extra virgin olive oil (see page 106). Then pour a small amount of your best balsamic vinegar (see page 144) into the center of the olive oil. (The dark vinegar makes an attractive pattern floating in the olive oil. For high drama, we suggest you do the pouring at the table with your guests looking on.) Serve in place of butter with chunks of warm bread or focaccia (page 120).

PITA CHIPS
◆◆◆

. . . .

When you want chips and respectability all at once, you make these: triangular pieces of pita bread roasted to a crisp in olive oil, garlic, and herbs. Herbes de Provence, an herb blend that contains lavender, adds sunny flavor that will enhance most Mediterranean foods, but will be out of place in some menus. Use your judgment and season accordingly. The same goes for garlic and salt — use amounts that are appropriate for the foods that will accompany the chips. A caution: Not all brands of pita bread work equally well for chips. We suggest Salloum Bakery brand.

The Purée of Highly Seasoned Tofu (page 20) and the White Bean Hummus (page 24) are tailor-made to accompany these chips. **PREPARE-AHEAD/SERVING NOTES:** Serve warm from the oven or make them days ahead and store in an airtight tin.

12 ounces pita bread, Salloum Bakery brand

¾ cup pure olive oil

1 to 2 tablespoons garlic put through a garlic press OR 1 to 2 tablespoons garlic purée (page 17)

15 grinds black pepper or pepper melange

1½ teaspoons herbes de Provence

¾ teaspoon thyme

¾ teaspoon oregano

¾ teaspoon basil

¾ teaspoon rosemary

¼ teaspoon salt (you can add more if you want these to be truly addicting)

OR in place of all the seasonings listed, use 1 tablespoon Pasta & Co. House Herbs, 1½ teaspoons herbes de Provence, and ¼ teaspoon salt

Preheat oven to 400°F. Line two baking sheets with parchment or foil.

Cut pita bread into chip-size triangles, separating the bread into single-layer pieces. In a measuring cup, whisk together all other ingredients until well-blended. Use the method explained in the Roasted Bread recipe on page 16 to coat the pita bread pieces, being sure not to "soak" the pita in the oil. The pita pieces, unlike the bread slices, do not need to be in a single layer. Simply distribute them between two baking sheets that have been lined with parchment. Bake one sheet at a time for 5 minutes. Stir. Bake 5 more minutes each. Stir and check for doneness: Chips should be golden, but *not* browned. If necessary, bake for 2 more minutes. But remember: If the chips brown past "golden," the garlic becomes bitter. Remove from oven and place baked chips on paper towels to absorb excess oil. Proceed with second pan. Serve warm or at room temperature. If reusing pans for additional chips, be sure to clean off the browned drippings from each batch before baking more chips.

SERVES 8 TO 12.

BAKED CHEESE WAFERS

Beyond Parsley, a cookbook published by the Junior League of Kansas City, Missouri, in 1984, has inspired a couple of Pasta & Co. standbys. One is White Chili (page 220). The other is this ingeniously easy way of making paper-thin cheese wafers. What we have added is seasoning: hot paprika (see below) or a favorite dried herb. The cheese wafers are guaranteed to be easy and impressive. You will want to serve them time and time again — warm from the oven or at room temperature — either as an hors d'oeuvre or in place of bread with soup or salad. **PREPARE-AHEAD/SERVING NOTES:** The cheese wafers will keep for weeks in an airtight tin. However, what is easy to make in small quantities becomes tiresome when you make it for a large group. You may prefer to bake the wafers only for small dinner parties. **ESSENTIAL GEAR:** Nonstick cookie sheet

6 ounces Monterey jack cheese, cut into sixteen ¼-inch slices

1 heaping teaspoon Pasta & Co. House Herbs OR 1 heaping teaspoon herbes de Provence (with lavender) OR scant ½ teaspoon hot paprika

Preheat oven to 400°F. Place 8 cheese slices on a nonstick cookie sheet. Sprinkle with your choice of herbs or paprika. Bake exactly 10 minutes. Remove from oven, and with a long metal spatula, lift each cheese wafer onto a cooling rack covered with paper towels.

Repeat process with remaining 8 slices.

MAKES 16 CHEESE WAFERS.

PARIKA

Despite the ubiquity of sweet Hungarian paprika, there is another kind. It is simply called hot Hungarian paprika. It gives the same rosy hue as sweet paprika, but has a punch more like cayenne. We have used hot paprika in several recipes. It is available at all Pasta & Co. stores.

PURÉE OF HIGHLY SEASONED TOFU

In two places in this cookbook you will find recipes for incredibly good-tasting tofu, bearing no resemblance to the tasteless — though admittedly healthy — sponge it is. Here the tofu is turned into a nutritious concoction that easily replaces those calorie- and fat-laden dips and dressings we all love. Serve the Purée with Roasted Breads (page 16), Pita Chips (page 18), or, even easier — and sure to intrigue your guests — with freshly fried poppadums (see Insert, page 21). Also use the purée for vegetable crudites. Spread it on bread in place of butter or mayonnaise for sandwiches. Thin it with additional olive oil to turn it into a delicious salad dressing. **PREPARE-AHEAD/ SERVING NOTES:** The purée keeps for nearly a week in the refrigerator. **ESSENTIAL GEAR:** Electric food processor

¼ cup coarsely chopped yellow onion

5 green onions, green tops included, trimmed and coarsely chopped

2 to 3 cloves garlic, peeled

¼ cup extra virgin olive oil

¼ cup lemon juice

½ teaspoon hot curry powder

½ teaspoon cumin

½ teaspoon salt

3 grinds black pepper

1½ tablespoons black soy sauce

1½ tablespoons balsamic vinegar

½ teaspoon Tabasco or Jardine's brand Texas Champagne

1 (14-ounce) package "traditional" tofu, rinsed, drained, and dried with paper towels

Place all ingredients except tofu in food processor bowl equipped with a steel blade. Process until all ingredients are puréed and well-blended. Add tofu and process until smooth.

MAKES 2½ CUPS.

GARLIC AND OTHER HIGH SEASONINGS

We admit it. We tend to use an enormous amount of garlic in our recipes. And you will probably also notice that we are generally bold in our use of all seasonings, from cumin to vanilla extract. We have concluded that our customers like their food highly flavored. If they did not, these recipes would not have become the dependably good sellers that they are.

POPPADUMS

You must try these. The thin, crisp disks made from ground lentils usually come packed in small boxes containing about 20 poppadums. Deep-fry the poppadums in a bit of oil according to the easy directions on the package and serve them hot or at room temperature. Think of them as East Indian tortillas. They puff up and become very golden in cooking, making an exotic complement for soups or salads. Or they can accompany an appetizer, such as the Purée of Highly Seasoned Tofu (page 20). Once fried, the poppadums can be layered with paper towels in an airtight tin and held for days before serving. They are available at Pasta & Co. or specialty grocery stores and at some delis. We like Sharwood's brand, especially the one labeled "spiced."

SKI-BUS APPETIZERS

We first served this very combination on a ski bus as it rumbled down the road from Mount Rainier, but the fearless flavors of these easy-to-serve finger foods work for any casual gathering.

- Purée of Highly Seasoned Tofu (page 20)
- Poppadums (page 21), Roasted Breads (page 16), and Pita Chips (page 18)
- Spiced Almonds and Pumpkin Seeds (page 15)
- Imported Green Olives
- Bite-size pieces of Strata (page 23)
- Cold beer

MARINATED FRESH MOZZARELLA

O ver the past decade, our customers have become enamored of fresh Italian mozzarella cheese made from buffalo milk. The mild-flavored cheese bears no resemblance to its rubbery domestic namesake. The problem is that fresh buffalo mozzarella is very perishable. A number of domestic cheese makers now offer an alternative product, made with cow's milk, that has a longer shelf life but lacks the unique flavor and creaminess of the Italian cheese. This recipe marinates domestic fresh mozzarella to disguise some of its flaws and give you a tasty cheese to use on appetizer platters, salads, or pizza (page 116). During the summer, we toss the cheese and its marinade with fresh basil and vine-ripened tomatoes. **PREPARE-AHEAD/ SERVING NOTES:** The cheese holds well in its marinade for several days, though it may begin to discolor by the third day. If you refrigerate this dish, the oil will congeal. Just return the mixture to room temperature, toss the cheese with the oil, and it will be nearly as good as new.

1 pound fresh domestic mozzarella cheese

½ cup extra virgin olive oil

1 heaping teaspoon garlic, about 2 cloves put through a press

10 coarse grinds black pepper or pepper melange

⅔ teaspoon red pepper flakes

½ teaspoon oregano

⅛ teaspoon salt

Optional: 4 anchovy fillets, rinsed, well-drained, and finely minced

Drain cheese of all brine. Cut into desired-size slices or wedges. In a measuring cup, whisk together olive oil, garlic, black pepper, red pepper flakes, oregano, salt, and anchovy (if desired). Place cheese in a shallow dish, add dressing, and toss to coat.

MAKES ABOUT 4 CUPS.

A SUMMER ANTIPASTO MENU

■ Summer Green Beans and Tomatoes (page 54)

■ Marinated Fresh Mozzarella (page 22)

■ Alcazaba brand canned Spanish tuna in water (a couple of cans)

■ Bowls of imported olives and heaps of good crusty bread

■ A chilled dry rosé wine

STRATA

•••

For party after party, we cut this strata into bite-size squares, and it is always the first appetizer to disappear. Strata is also superb picnic food. **PREPARE-AHEAD/ SERVING NOTES:** Best served hot from the oven, but strata also keeps well for up to three days before being brought back to room temperature or reheated. **ESSENTIAL GEAR:** A shallow ovenproof pan (9 by 13 inches)

4 eggs

1½ cups milk

Optional: ½ teaspoon salt

¼ teaspoon pepper

4 cups Pasta & Co. croutons, purchased or made according to recipe on page 110

½ pound smoked Monterey Jack cheese, grated

¼ pound mozzarella cheese, grated

¼ pound prosciutto, cut into ¼-inch dice

¼ pound pancetta, cut into ¼-inch dice

½ cup thinly sliced chives or green onions

½ cup sun-dried tomatoes, drained of all oil and cut into strips

¼ cup Parmesan cheese, freshly grated

Preheat oven to 350°F. In a large mixing bowl (large enough to hold 10 cups), whisk together eggs, milk, salt (if desired), and pepper. Fold in croutons, jack cheese, and mozzarella. Set aside.

Sauté prosciutto and pancetta together until golden. Remove meat with a slotted spoon and drain on paper towels. Lightly coat a shallow pan (9 by 13 inches) with the meat drippings (there will not be many drippings, but there will be enough if you just swish a pastry brush around the sauté pan several times).

Thoroughly fold cooled meat into egg mixture, along with chives and sun-dried tomatoes, being sure that the ingredients are evenly distributed. Spoon into the prepared pan and pat down. The croutons should form a bumpy surface. Top with Parmesan. Bake for 35 to 40 minutes or until very browned.

Let cool 30 minutes, then cut and serve. Or cool completely, and refrigerate to store. When you want to serve, cut into bite-size squares and serve at room temperature, or quickly stir-fry in a sauté pan and serve warm.

MAKES ABOUT 48 BITE-SIZE APPETIZERS.

WHITE BEAN HUMMUS

❖❖❖

I f you have a bumper crop of fresh summer herbs, this recipe is for you. The versatility of this dish gives it many possibilities in a meal. It is equally good warm off the stove or at room temperature. Served with Pita Chips (page 18) or Roasted Breads (page 16), it is an inspired appetizer or picnic food. Use it as a side to lamb, beef, pork, or chicken, with or without the roasted peppers. **PREPARE-AHEAD/SERVING NOTES:** No matter how you use this bean dish, one of the niftiest things about it is that it can be prepared months ahead and frozen. In fact, the dish was created as a way to use up summer's fresh herbs. Cook and purée the beans with the fresh herbs, garlic, and olive oil. Freeze in convenient portions. Then finish off each batch as you need it, enjoying the taste of garden-fresh herbs even in mid-winter. **ESSENTIAL GEAR:** Electric food processor

TO MAKE THE HUMMUS:

1 pound navy beans or other small white beans

3 tablespoons salt

¾ cup extra virgin olive oil — best you have

1½ cups fresh herbs — whatever mix of rosemary, sage, thyme, oregano, and parsley is available — washed, dried, and stemmed (most of us urge you to go light on the rosemary)

8 cloves garlic, peeled — more if you like

2 teaspoons balsamic vinegar, or to taste

¼ teaspoon Tabasco or Jardine's brand Texas Champagne

Salt (about ½ teaspoon) and pepper to taste

TO FINISH THE HUMMUS:

For every 2 cups of hummus

¼ cup extra virgin olive oil

2 cups coarsely chopped yellow onions

2 ounces fresh goat cheese

Optional: Fresh herbs, finely minced

Optional: 2 red bell peppers, roasted (see Insert, page 25)

Sort through beans and discard any stones or debris. Presoak and cook beans according to directions on page 62. Near the end of cooking time, add sea salt to cooking water. (Don't be shy about the salt. Honestly, the beans will need this much.) When beans are tender, drain well and immediately toss with the ¾ cup olive oil.

Place herbs, garlic, vinegar, and Tabasco in a food processor bowl equipped with a steel blade. Process until herbs and garlic are well-chopped. Add half the beans and olive oil and process to a purée. Add remaining beans and olive oil and process until all ingredients are incorporated. Taste for salt and pepper.

This will yield approximately 6 cups of hummus — undoubtedly more than you will want to serve at one time, since the onions and cheese that complete the dish nearly double its volume. We suggest dividing the hummus into 2-cup portions. Refrigerate or freeze until ready to use.

Before serving, bring a 2-cup portion of the purée to room temperature. Place a sauté pan over low heat, add the ¼ cup extra virgin olive oil and the onions, and cook slowly until they are well-browned (about 20 minutes). Add bean purée and goat cheese and cook until cheese is melted. Taste for seasoning and texture — you may want to add more salt, pepper, or olive oil.

At this point, you can serve the hummus as an appetizer or side dish. Just sprinkle it with some freshly chopped herbs. Or you can proceed to "wrap" it in the roasted peppers, which add a wonderful taste dimension.

Line the sides of a straight-sided serving dish of appropriate size with the roasted bell peppers, letting 1 to 2 inches hang over the dish. Spoon in the hummus. Turn the ends of the peppers over the purée and serve with Roasted Breads (page 16).

EVERY 2 CUPS OF HUMMUS SERVES 6 AS AN APPETIZER OR SIDE DISH.

TO ROAST BELL PEPPERS

Keep the peppers whole. Char peppers evenly on all sides over a gas flame or under a hot broiler. Now place them in a paper bag. Close bag, letting peppers "steam" in the bag for 15 minutes. Then, holding each pepper under running cold water, rub off the charred skin. Stem and core the pepper and use its meat as you wish.

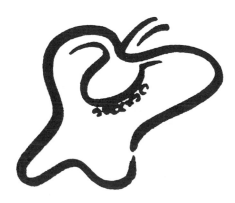

MARINATED BLACK OLIVES

These are the marinated olives we have been making since that day in March 1981 when we opened our first store. We call for them in sauces, such as Chèvre Sauce (page 170), and in salads, such as the Marinated Kielbasa (page 36). Keep a jar in your refrigerator. They are handy not only for cooking, but for a quick and sure-to-please appetizer. **PREPARE-AHEAD/SERVING NOTES:** Refrigerated, these marinated olives will keep at least two months.

2 (6-ounce) cans California black pitted olives (any size olive you prefer — small works as well as jumbo)

½ cup vegetable oil or mild-flavored extra virgin olive oil

¼ cup red wine vinegar

1 tablespoon oregano

1 teaspoon red pepper flakes

1 tablespoon garlic (approximately 3 large cloves), finely minced or put through a garlic press

Thoroughly drain the olives of brine. Meanwhile, in a large jar, mix together oil, vinegar, oregano, red pepper flakes, and garlic. When all the brine is off the olives, mix them into the marinade, making sure they are completely covered by the liquid. Refrigerate and let marinate at least 48 hours.

MAKES ABOUT 3 CUPS.

GARLIC

Garlic put through a garlic press, as a rule, has about twice the strength of garlic minced with a knife. We usually "press," but let your palate be the judge.

OUR PLETHORA OF OLIVES

For sheer range of taste, the olive is unmatched. Hundreds of varieties result from different soils, climates, and processing techniques. Though the preceding recipe here calls for the common California black olive — a bland relative of its high-spirited foreign cousins — Pasta & Co. has always sold many other kinds of olives, and each year, it seems, we discover more. One year we found California olives stuffed with jalapeño peppers and with garlic; another year, it was French and Moroccan oil-cured olives; our most recent discovery is Israeli olives. We use olives not only as pungent morsels to nibble before dinner, but also pitted and chopped, as flavorings for all sorts of dishes. We make the Marinated Black Olives (page 26) into a paste for dressing Tortellini in Olive Paste with Gremolata (page 94). We chop green olives and coat them with olive oil to finish off Pescine with Red Beans (page 195). We turn jalapeño-stuffed olives into a salad dressing to make Flageolet Beans and Macaroni with Green Olive Dressing (page 63). To top Pasta HDR (page 191), we chop pitted kalamata olives with tomatoes and onion to make a magnificent salsa. We add a bit of feta cheese to the same mixture for completing the Rigatoni in Lamb Sauce (page 197). The possibilities for lively and varied tastes are nearly endless. We think you will enjoy them.

TO PIT OLIVES

You need only a cutting board and a chef's knife.

Place olive on cutting board and lay knife blade flat on top of the olive (as you do when you skin a garlic clove). With one hand, hold the handle of the knife, and with the other, make a fist and firmly "whack" the flat side of the knife. Remove the knife and you will find that the pit easily pops out of the olive, leaving the olive meat fairly intact.

HOT OLIVES

Use these olives by themselves with bread (especially good is the focaccia, page 120) or as part of an assorted antipasto platter.

Put ⅓ cup extra virgin olive oil in a sauté pan, add 1 teaspoon of your choice of dried herbs (*Or* 1 to 2 tablespoons fresh herbs, finely minced), ¼ teaspoon red pepper flakes, and if you wish, a little finely minced garlic. Heat the mixture over low heat and add 1 cup of imported (pit-in) olives (a mixture of kinds and colors complete with a few stems and leaves is best). Continue heating until the olives are warm to the touch. Serve immediately with lots of bread to sop up the olive oil.

ONE MORE OLIVE APPETIZER NOT TO MISS

Serve dry Spanish sherry with imported green olives (the more pungent the better), rinsed of their brine and tossed with just enough extra virgin olive oil to barely make them shine. Very sophisticated…very Mediterranean.

Room-temperature foods:

for first courses, entrées, and side dishes.

We love room-temperature foods — both the freedom they imply and the flavors they deliver. No one need worry about dinner getting cold. These foods are easy eating. Prepare them hours, if not days, ahead of serving. Store them in the refrigerator. Return them to room temperature before eating. But do *not* serve them cold. Remember, while refrigeration protects food from bacterial growth, it rarely enhances its flavors or texture. (Admittedly, there are exceptions, such as salad greens, some fruits, some shellfish, some desserts.) ■Whether beef tenderloin or white fish, lentils or tortellini, the following foods — almost without exception — are to be served at room temperature.

PORK CHOP SALAD

♦♦♦

. . . .

Imagine the taste of pork chops browned and bathing in their own juices. Add a dose of extra virgin olive oil, red wine vinegar, and braised shallots, and you have this straightforward pork dish. And definitely use fresh sage, rosemary, and thyme in place of dried herbs, if you have them. **PREPARE-AHEAD/SERVING NOTES:** This dish will keep well for five days. Before serving, return to room temperature or re-heat very gently, toss in the dressing, and top with the raw shallots and parsley. See menu next page.

½ tablespoon Pasta & Co. House Herbs or your choice of dried or fresh herbs

Scant ¾ teaspoon salt

¼ teaspoon pepper

Big pinch allspice

2½ pounds boneless pork loin roast, cut into ½-inch to ¾-inch slices

½ cup pure olive oil

10 shallots, peeled and sliced

2 cloves garlic, put through a garlic press

¼ cup red wine vinegar

2 tablespoons extra virgin olive oil

TO TOP:

¼ cup finely chopped parsley

1 to 2 shallots, peeled and finely minced OR ½ cup red onions, cut in half-moons (page 37)

Mix together House Herbs, salt, pepper, and allspice. Season both sides of pork slices with this mixture, using it all.

In a large sauté pan, heat the pure olive oil to very hot. Add as many pork slices as will fit in the pan and brown thoroughly on both sides, being careful not to over-cook the meat. Remove slices to a large bowl as they are done and set aside. When pork has all been cooked, lower heat. Add shallots and garlic to the pan and cook un-til golden, taking care not to burn the garlic. Add vinegar, raise heat, and scrape up all meat drippings. Remove from heat and stir in the extra virgin olive oil. Let mix-ture cool while you cut pork slices into 1-inch to 2-inch pieces, returning them to the bowl and salvaging all meat juices. Toss pork with shallot mixture.

You may refrigerate the salad at this point, but when ready to serve, bring it back to room temperature or reheat gently. Spoon the salad onto a serving platter. Top with parsley and shallots.

MAKES 5 CUPS.

ROOM-TEMPERATURE MENU

■ Spiced Almonds (page 15)

■ Pork Chop Salad (page 31)

■ Spanish Bread Salad (page 72)

■ Green Beans in French Walnut Oil (page 55)

■ Italian Shortbread with Almonds, Brandy, and Lemon (page 246)

ROOM TEMPERATURE FOODS

THE MAKING OF STUNNING FOODS

Successful garnishing is more a matter of mastering a few simple concepts than of radish roses, parsley sprigs, and other such touches.

■ Sometimes it is nothing more than keeping the food looking shiny. Notice that when most dishes are first completed, they appear shiny. Food that is old, on the other hand, appears dry. Even food that sits untouched for as little as 30 minutes can acquire an unattractive pallor. All the shine literally drops to the bottom of the dish along with the juices. To make the food look fresh, turn it over in its juices so that the top shines once again. This is all the "garnishing" that dishes like Caponata (page 52) and Poached Chicken in Olive Oil, Garlic, and Green Peppercorn Sauce (page 40) need to look their best.

■ When shine alone is not enough, use clean, "redundant" garnishes to top the dish. Ever notice that when you fold the ingredients of a dish together, visually they blur? The result is that even the tastiest dish may have no eye appeal. We have learned that if you repeat a few key ingredients on the top of the dish, as we do with the peppers and red onions on the Salpicon of Shrimp and White Fish (page 38) or the raw shallots on Pork Chop Salad (page 31), the dish retains a clean, lively look.

■ Sometimes a dish needs contrasting, rather than redundant, garnishing. Both for taste and for appearance, you may decide to introduce a topping that is a radical departure from the rest of the dish. A case in point is the gremolata that tops the Tortellini in Olive Paste (page 94). The tortellini alone are tasty, but unattractive. With the contrasting flavors and colors of the gremolata, the tortellini become astonishingly good. We use salsas in the same way. In the French Green Lentils with Salsa (page 68) and in Pasta HDR (page 191), the salsa that tops the dish is an essential element, not only for appearance, but for taste. If you include the salsa ingredients in the main body of the dish, it becomes unattractive. If you introduce them as a salsa on top, the dish will dazzle both in taste and in looks.

MARINATED BEEF
TENDERLOIN

◆◆◆

. . . .

This extravagant beef dish will crown any room-temperature buffet. It also makes a sublime first course for a formal sit-down dinner. And, best of all, this is the meat used in Pasta HDR (page 191) — one of the best, most festive pasta sauces we have invented. **PREPARE-AHEAD/SERVING NOTES:** This recipe is a party-planner's delight. The meat can be cooked and marinated a full five days ahead of the event. Bring it back to room temperature, add the finishing touches of fresh arugula and garnishes, and serve. **ESSENTIAL GEAR:** Shallow metal pan just large enough to hold the tenderloin (you do not want the meat juices to spread out over a large pan and burn up, and the pan needs to take direct heat when you deglaze it at the end of the roasting)

1 beef tenderloin, 2 to 3 pounds, well trimmed of fat and gristle

1 tablespoon pure olive oil

2 teaspoons coarse salt

1 teaspoon freshly cracked black pepper or pepper mélange

1 cup homemade beef stock or canned consommé

2 ounces fresh herbs of your choice, washed, stemmed, and finely chopped with 1 teaspoon coarsely cracked black pepper and ½ teaspoon coarse sea salt (if you are sensitive to salt, you may want to

use less) **OR** 2 tablespoons Pasta & Co. House Herbs ground together with 1 teaspoon coarsely cracked black pepper and ½ teaspoon coarse sea salt

¼ cup extra virgin olive oil

FINAL ASSEMBLY:

Fresh arugula — enough to make a bed for the meat

Roasted bell peppers (page 25), for garnish

Shards of Parmigiano Reggiano (see Insert, page 35)

Preheat oven to 450°F. Brush tenderloin with the tablespoon of pure olive oil and rub with the salt and pepper.

Place meat in a shallow roasting pan just big enough to hold the tenderloin. Roast tenderloin until a meat thermometer inserted into thickest part registers 135°F — approximately 20 to 25 minutes. Remove pan from oven.

Remove meat to a plate and cover with plastic wrap. Refrigerate to facilitate slicing. Reserve all the meat juices in roasting pan. Return roasting pan to stove burner, and over medium heat stir in the stock or consommé, scraping up all meat drippings. Decant mixture into a container and save either for the next time you need good-quality beef stock or for making the sauce on page 191.

When meat is cold, remove from refrigerator and slice ⅛ inch to ¼ inch thick. In a shallow glass dish, layer meat slices with the herb, salt, and pepper mixture, the extra virgin olive oil, and any accumulated meat juices. Cover with plastic wrap and refrigerate for several hours or up to five days.

When ready to serve, bring to room temperature and arrange on a serving platter with arugula, peppers, and Parmigiano Reggiano. Be sure to spoon all the meat juices over the dish. Add a drizzle of additional olive oil if desired.

SERVES 4 TO 8.

You can use this same method of marinating with extra virgin olive oil, salt, pepper, and herbs with leftover grilled steak.

PARMIGIANO REGGIANO

Parmesan cheese comes in several grades, depending upon its origin, its age, and the way it has been processed. Our stores grate hundreds of pounds of Argentine Parmesan daily. And for most uses, this cheese is a good choice. However, Italian Parmigiano Reggiano — at roughly twice the cost — is the ultimate grade of Parmesan and worth the extra expense for certain dishes. The quality of this cheese is carefully regulated by the Italian government. You can tell Parmigiano Reggiano by its rind, which is covered with the cheese's name etched in small dots.

SHARDS OF PARMESAN

Parmigiano Reggiano is more than just a grating cheese. Though the dryness of the aged cheese makes it too crumbly for slicing, by using a carrot or potato peeler you can peel off paper-thin, rough-shaped pieces of the cheese that we call "shards." The texture of these pieces provides an attractive option for topping many dishes, from meats to pasta.

MARINATED KIELBASA

S erve this hearty room-temperature sausage-and-potato dish over a chiffonade (page 37) of fresh raw spinach leaves, and offer crunchy bread to wipe up the juices. You will have a complete meal that is a good candidate for picnics, in warm weather or cold. Choose your kielbasa carefully. Many brands are unacceptably fatty. We use Hillshire Farms Polska Kielbasa. **PREPARE-AHEAD/SERVING NOTES:** Combine the potatoes, kielbasa, and olives with the dressing up to four days before serving. Fold in the pickles, onion, and parsley close to mealtime.

1 cup cooking oil

½ cup extra virgin olive oil

1 cup plus 2 tablespoons red wine vinegar

3 tablespoons garlic, finely minced or put through a garlic press

1 tablespoon plus 2 teaspoons oregano

1 teaspoon basil

1 teaspoon red pepper flakes

1¾ pounds small red potatoes, boiled to tender and sliced about ¼-inch thick

1 pound kielbasa, cut on the diagonal into ¼-inch-thick slices

2 cups pitted and quartered black olives, well-drained

½ cup dill pickles, cut into ⅛-inch dice

1 red onion, cut into half-moons (see page 37)

1 cup finely chopped parsley

In a large tub, whisk together oils, red wine vinegar, garlic, oregano, basil, and red pepper flakes. Fold in sliced potatoes, sausage slices, olive wedges, dill pickle, and half of the red onion and parsley. Spoon onto a serving platter and top with remaining red onion and parsley. Serve at room temperature.

MAKES 12 CUPS.

CHIFFONADE

We know it sounds ostentatious, but chiffonade is the only word we know that means a ruffly pile of julienne-like pieces of vegetables — usually fresh greens, such as spinach, Napa cabbage, mustard greens, or even iceberg lettuce. They can be blanched or braised, but in most cases we suggest serving chiffonades raw for the texture and color they bring to dishes. The crispness of a chiffonade of raw greens adds an attractive contrast to pasta, and, used as a bed for the noodles, eliminates the need for an additional green vegetable. The same is true when a chiffonade is used along with grilled meats or fish. Best of all, chiffonades are low-calorie, no-fat entrée extenders — far better for weight watchers than a tossed green salad.

■ TO MAKE A CHIFFONADE OF LEAF GREENS, such as spinach: Make a stack of 6 to 10 washed and dried leaves. Fold them in half along their stems and cut across the stems every ⅛ inch to ¼ inch. Use the same technique for fresh herb leaves, such as basil.

■ FOR GREENS THAT COME IN HEADS, such as Napa cabbage: Cut thin slices crosswise through the head. Rinse with cold water and dry in a towel.

ONION HALF-MOONS

Repeatedly, we suggest cutting onions — especially red ones — into this shape. This is accomplished by cutting the onion in half from top to bottom, laying the cut side flat on a cutting board, and slicing into the onion along its grain lines. This produces little wedges which when cut apart look like half-moons (or, in reality, crescents). We have found that the shape and texture make a very desirable garnish for numerous dishes. If the taste of raw onion is too strong for you, place the half-moons in ice water for a few hours before using. Be sure to drain well.

SALPICON OF SHRIMP
AND WHITE FISH
♦♦♦

This is a prize of a seafood recipe. We made it first as a warm-weather dish, but it is just as stunning as part of a winter buffet. The lime juice tames the jalapeño peppers into a politely spicy dressing. Take care in poaching your fish (page 39), and we guarantee a dish to dazzle. **PREPARE-AHEAD/SERVING NOTES:** Dressing can be made a couple of days ahead. Assemble with fish no more than a few hours before serving.

½ cup soy oil

¼ cup rice wine vinegar

¼ cup freshly squeezed lime juice

1 tablespoon plus 1 teaspoon sugar

1 teaspoon marjoram

1 teaspoon salt

1 teaspoon freshly cracked black pepper

1 pound white fish, such as cod, poached rare (see page 39)

1 pound Chilean shrimp, cooked and drained

½ cup green bell pepper, cored, seeded, and cut into ¼-inch dice

¼ cup red bell pepper, cored, seeded, and cut into ¼-inch dice

¼ cup yellow bell pepper, cored, seeded, and cut into ¼-inch dice

3 tablespoons finely minced red onion

2½ tablespoons fresh jalapeño peppers (red, if possible), seeded, stemmed, and finely diced

TO TOP:

3 tablespoons snipped chives

2 tablespoons additional mixed peppers, cut into ⅛-inch to ¼-inch pieces

1 tablespoon finely minced red onion

Combine oil, vinegar, lime juice, sugar, marjoram, salt, and black pepper. Fold in fish, shrimp, bell peppers, red onion, and jalapeño peppers.

Immediately before serving, place on a shallow platter and top with chives, peppers, and red onion.

MAKES ABOUT 5 CUPS.

POACHING CHICKEN AND FISH

Over the years, we have done a lot of it. The standard for perfect poaching is meat that is neither undercooked nor overcooked. The meat should be satiny in texture, never dry. Because pieces of chicken and fish do not come in uniform thickness, poaching is not a question of timing, but rather of taking care.

■POACHING WHOLE PIECES OF FISH OR CHICKEN: Thoroughly rinse fish or chicken pieces in cold water and drain well. Trim off any excess fat on the chicken. Arrange pieces (skin-side-up, if there is skin) in a large sauté pan. For one pound of meat, add water just to cover, ¼ onion, ¼ stalk celery, 1 teaspoon dried basil or Pasta & Co. House Herbs, and 1 teaspoon salt. (If the chicken or fish is going into a strongly seasoned dressing, you may choose to poach it simply in salted water.) Place pan over medium heat.

When the water comes to a low simmer (not even bubbling), turn meat over, reduce heat, and continue to poach gently until the chicken meat just barely loses its pink color or the fish is barely opaque. If you are using an instant-read thermometer, the chicken will be done at 165°F, the fish at 150°F. Immediately remove meat from the cooking liquid. Remember that the meat will continue cooking from its own retained heat even when out of the broth. (If you have seasoned the poaching broth, you may want to strain and freeze it for use in stocks and sauces.)

■ IF YOU ARE GOING TO CUT UP THE PIECES OF CHICKEN OR FISH... the task is easier. Use the above method, but set a cutting board adjacent to the burner, and as each piece comes close to being done, remove it immediately to the cutting board. Cut breasts, in most cases, across the grain (see 41) into desired size. With chicken thighs, the connective tissues are such that you can pull the meat into bite-size pieces by hand. (You may want to run the thigh meat under cold water to make it cool enough to touch.) Flake fish pieces into large chunks to check for doneness. Return any undercooked pieces of chicken or fish to the simmering water for a few seconds and then recheck. Repeat the process until all the meat is evenly cooked to the desired degree.

POACHED CHICKEN IN OLIVE OIL, GARLIC, AND GREEN PEPPERCORN SAUCE

♦♦♦

You will want this very simple chicken dish again and again. You can eat it as is, at room temperature. You can serve it over a bed of greens and fresh tomatoes garnished with imported olives. You can gently reheat it and toss with pasta or blanched vegetables, such as asparagus or green beans. This is versatility at its best. **PREPARE-AHEAD/SERVING NOTES:** The dish is good and keeps getting better for at least five days after it is made. Refrigerate to store, but be sure to bring back to room temperature to serve. **ESSENTIAL GEAR:** Electric food processor

4 medium cloves garlic (or adjust garlic to taste, but do not skimp)

1 cup extra virgin olive oil

2 tablespoons green peppercorns, packed in brine, well-rinsed and drained

1 tablespoon plus 1 teaspoon fresh lemon juice

1 teaspoon sherry wine vinegar

1 teaspoon Pasta & Co. House Herbs or dried herbs of your choice

½ teaspoon red pepper flakes

¼ teaspoon salt

¼ teaspoon coarsely ground black pepper

2 pounds boneless chicken breasts and/or thighs

Place garlic in the food processor with ½ cup of the olive oil and process until garlic is very finely chopped. Decant the mixture to a large bowl.

Whisk in remaining ½ cup of olive oil, peppercorns, lemon juice, vinegar, dried herbs, red pepper flakes, salt, and black pepper. Place a cutting board and knife next to the stove. In a large sauté pan and in a single layer, poach the chicken in enough lightly salted water to cover the pieces. Follow poaching directions on page 39. As the pieces appear done, remove them to the cutting board. Cut breasts across the grain into 1-inch pieces. The thighs will separate along their own tissues. As you cut, anything that is too pink should be put back into the hot poaching water for just a few seconds.

As chicken finishes cooking, place pieces immediately in olive oil mixture. Let the cooking liquid cool to room temperature, then add ⅓ cup of it, strained, to chicken. Toss well to coat all the chicken pieces.

MAKES A GENEROUS 4 CUPS.

BREAST MEAT OR THIGH MEAT?
ACROSS THE GRAIN OR WITH THE GRAIN?

While these issues may seem inconsequential, we have found that they can determine the quality of room-temperature chicken dishes. First, as a general rule, boneless, skinless thigh meat holds up better in dressings containing vinegar or lemon than does the drier breast meat.

If, however, there is a preference for the milder flavor of breast meat, such as in Poached Chicken in Olive Oil, Garlic, and Green Peppercorn Sauce (page 40) or Chicken with Italian Prunes or Grapes (page 49), cutting the breast meat across the grain makes a more succulent meat than cutting with the grain, which emphasizes the natural fiber (almost stringiness) of white chicken meat. Occasionally, there will be a dish such as Penne with Torn Greek Chicken, Olives, and Fresh Lemon (page 96), in which the texture of the vertical fiber is desirable. Then, by all means, tear or cut with the grain.

basil
oregano
marjoram
thyme
rosemary
peppercorns
allspice

```
COOKING CHICKEN IN ITS OWN SALAD DRESSING
```

For the next couple of recipes, we cook the chicken in the ingredients that become the salad dressing itself. The method infuses flavor into the chicken at the same time as it incorporates all of the chicken juices into the dish. It is a nifty way to render moist, highly flavored chicken meat for room-temperature dishes.

CHICKEN AND RICE IN TARRAGON MUSTARD SAUCE

◆◆◆

When your backyard garden is producing more summer squash than you can bear, make this room-temperature entrée. Hopefully, you also have fresh tarragon to use (if not, dried works nicely). **PREPARE-AHEAD/SERVING NOTES:** The dish holds well for a couple of days. Top with the extra squash and parsley just before serving. **ESSENTIAL GEAR:** Electric food processor

3 cloves garlic, peeled

2½ tablespoons dried tarragon *OR* ¼ to ½ cup fresh tarragon, trimmed from stems

2 teaspoons whole fennel seed

1 teaspoon ground fennel

1 teaspoon red pepper flakes

½ tablespoon salt

½ cup sherry wine vinegar

¼ cup plus 2 tablespoons sweet mustard (we like Mendocino brand mustard)

1 tablespoon lemon juice

1¼ teaspoons Tabasco

1⅔ cups pure olive oil

2 to 3 pounds boneless chicken thighs

2 cups uncooked long-grain white rice

1¼ cups green zucchini, seeded and cut into ¼-inch dice

1¼ cups yellow zucchini or crookneck squash, seeded and cut into ¼-inch dice

⅓ cup finely chopped parsley

TO TOP:

⅓ cup yellow zucchini, seeded and
cut into ¼-inch dice

⅓ cup green zucchini, seeded and cut
into ¼-inch dice

2 tablespoons finely chopped parsley

Place garlic, tarragon, fennel seed, ground fennel, red pepper flakes, salt, vinegar, mustard, lemon juice, and Tabasco in food processor bowl equipped with a steel blade. Process until garlic is finely chopped and fennel seeds are well-broken. Then, with motor running, slowly drizzle in olive oil as if you were making mayonnaise. Reserve. Preheat oven to 350°F. Spread chicken on a baking sheet. Cover with the mustard mixture. Bake just until chicken is barely done (about 12 minutes) — juices should run clear, but do not overcook (the chicken will continue to cook as it cools). Let chicken cool in its sauce in the refrigerator. Cook the rice. Drain and reserve. When chicken is cool, tear into bite-size pieces (see page 39). (Some cooks like the chicken in this salad in tiny pieces, similar to the size of the squash pieces; others like it chunkier.) Being careful to scrape up all juices and drippings left from roasting the chicken, toss chicken and sauce with the rice, zucchini, and parsley. Place in serving dish and top with the additional zucchini and parsley to garnish. Serve at room temperature.

MAKES 10 TO 11 CUPS.

A SUMMER SUPPER

- Carrot Cilantro Soup (hot or cold) (page 140)
- Chicken and Rice in Tarragon Mustard Sauce (page 42)
- Fresh Tomatoes (thickly sliced)
- A chiffonade of washed, but undressed salad greens (page 37)
- Warm, crusty bread and sweet butter
- Apricot Mousse (page 248) and fresh summer fruits and berries — all in a pool of Pasta & Co. Chocolate Sauce (page 241).

CHICKEN BREASTS OVEN-POACHED GREEK-STYLE

♦♦♦

You will want this chicken for warm summer days. Bake it early in the morning and you are set for either picnics or patios — and you have no barbecue mess. The accompaniment of tomatoes, olives, and lemon wedges is important visually, as well as complementary in taste. Crusty breadsticks and cold beer or wine complete the meal. **PREPARE-AHEAD/SERVING NOTES:** The chicken can be cooked a couple of days before serving, as long as it comes back to room temperature before mealtime.

2 (6-ounce) jars Peloponnese Grapeleaf and Walnut Kopanisti

6 cloves garlic, put through a press

2 tablespoons extra virgin olive oil, preferably Greek

¼ teaspoon red pepper flakes

Olive oil to oil pan

1½ pounds boneless, skinless chicken breasts

TO TOP:

4 Roma tomatoes, well-ripened and coarsely chopped

1 cup kalamata olives, well-rinsed of brine

1 lemon, cut in wedges

Preheat oven to 350°F. In a small bowl, mix together the kopanisti, garlic, olive oil, and red pepper flakes.

Lightly oil a shallow baking dish just large enough to hold the chicken in a single layer. Lay chicken breasts to touch, but not overlap, in the pan. Spread kopanisti mixture over them. Cover pan tightly with foil.

Bake chicken 15 minutes and check for doneness. Chicken should be almost — but not quite — done. It will finish cooking as it cools in the mixture. Leave covered and place in refrigerator for 30 minutes.

Bring to room temperature and serve each breast with its share of the poaching juices, a generous dollop of chopped tomatoes, a handful of olives, and a couple of lemon wedges.

MAKES APPROXIMATELY 6 SPLIT CHICKEN BREASTS.

KOPANISTI

The premier line of imported Greek foods is under the Peloponnese label imported by Rockridge Trading Co. of Richmond, California. The line includes a product called Grapeleaf and Walnut Kopanisti. It is a paste made of grape leaves, walnuts, feta cheese, and olive oil. Right out of the jar, it is an unseemly concoction, salty-tasting and unpleasant-looking. We have found, however, that it makes an incomparable seasoning for chicken and pasta.

In this recipe, we bake boneless chicken breasts in the kopanisti. On page 96, we take the same baked-chicken mixture and toss it with pasta for one of our favorite room-temperature pasta dishes. We also love the kopanisti for seasoning ground lamb, as in the Rigatoni in Lamb Sauce (page 197). In case you cannot locate Peloponnese kopanisti in a store near you, we have included our formula for the mixture.

MOCK GRAPELEAF AND WALNUT KOPANISTI

2 cups extra virgin olive oil, preferably Peloponnese brand

12 cloves garlic, peeled

¼ cup plus 1 tablespoon capers, drained

¼ cup red wine vinegar

2 ounces feta cheese, coarsely crumbled

2 teaspoons oregano

40 grinds black pepper

2 (7-ounce) jars grape leaves with their brine

1 cup walnuts, coarsely chopped

½ onion, coarsely chopped

Note: Depending on the size of your food processor bowl, you may need to make this mixture in two or three batches.

Place olive oil and garlic in the work bowl of a food processor equipped with a steel blade. Process until garlic is chopped very fine. Add capers, vinegar, feta, oregano, and black pepper. Process very briefly (two or three short spurts).

Add grape leaves and their brine. (Do not bother to remove the stems from the grape leaves.) Again, process briefly. Add walnuts and onion and process until mixture is a finely textured purée.

MAKES ABOUT 3 PINTS. (THE RECIPE CAN EASILY BE HALVED. HOWEVER, THE MIXTURE ALSO FREEZES WELL AND IS HANDY TO HAVE READY-TO-USE.)

MARINATED CHICKEN BREASTS WITH ROASTED BELL PEPPERS

. . . .

ROOM TEMPERATURE FOODS

This is one of the best summer chicken dishes we know. Serve it over greens, letting the marinade double as your salad dressing. **PREPARE-AHEAD/SERVING NOTES:** Prepare the dish at least 24 hours before serving. The chicken can steep in the marinade for three or four days, ready at a moment's notice anytime you need a quick warm-weather meal. Do not hesitate to make lots; the recipe easily doubles.

1½ cups extra virgin olive oil

¼ cup sherry wine vinegar

2 cloves garlic, finely minced

1 teaspoon dried oregano, crumbled OR if you have fresh, use a couple of tablespoons finely chopped leaves

¾ teaspoon salt

¼ teaspoon pepper

1 red bell pepper

1 green bell pepper

2½ to 3 pounds split, bone-in chicken breasts

Water

1 stalk celery, cut in chunks

1 onion, halved and sliced

1 tablespoon basil

1 tablespoon salt

In a bowl large enough to hold all the chicken, whisk together olive oil, vinegar, garlic, oregano, salt, and pepper. Roast and peel the bell peppers according to directions on page 25. Cut the peppers in half lengthwise. Remove stems, cores, and seeds. Cut the halves into thirds, making strips about 1 inch wide. Place strips in the olive oil mixture.

Thoroughly rinse chicken in cold water and drain well. Trim off excess fat. Arrange the breasts skin-side-up in a large sauté pan. Add water just to cover and the celery, onion, basil, and salt. Cover and cook over medium heat until water begins to boil. Immediately reduce heat to low, and poach gently for approximately 12 minutes, turning the breasts over after about 6 minutes. Remove pan from heat and let the breasts stand in the poaching liquid for another 8 minutes. Remove breasts from the liquid and cool to room temperature. (The poaching liquid can be frozen for use in chicken stock.)

When chicken is cool, remove skin and place flesh-side-down in the olive oil marinade. Spoon marinade over chicken pieces, basting well. Cover and marinate in refrigerator for 24 hours.

To serve, arrange breasts on a serving dish, topping each with a strip of red and green pepper and an ample spoonful of the marinade.

MAKES 4 TO 6 MEDIUM CHICKEN BREASTS.

CHICKEN POACHED IN
ORANGE JUICE WITH
FRESH SAGE

♦♦♦

In spring, use this room-temperature chicken entrée with a side of fresh asparagus and the tiniest of boiled red potatoes. In winter, pair it at room temperature with steamy wild rice, your favorite winter green vegetable, and a spoonful of indubitably the best cranberry sauce you've ever tasted — Cranberry Sauce with Sour Cherries and Rum (page 48). The juices from the chicken will delicately season everything on the plate. **PREPARE-AHEAD/SERVING NOTES:** This is an easy dish to prepare and the makings of it can be prepared ahead, *but* it is best served within a few hours of assembly. Do not hold it overnight, except for tasty leftovers.

2½ to 3 pounds boneless, skinless chicken breasts

2 teaspoons salt

1 teaspoon freshly cracked black pepper

1 (½-ounce) package fresh sage leaves

1 cup orange juice, either freshly

squeezed or reconstituted from frozen concentrate

2 cups celery, thinly sliced on the diagonal

½ cup currants, rinsed and well-drained

3 tablespoons balsamic vinegar

1 cup walnut pieces, lightly toasted

Preheat oven to 375°F. Rinse chicken breasts and pat dry with a paper towel. Mix together salt and pepper. Season each chicken breast with the mixture and place them in a single layer in a shallow baking pan. Place a sage leaf under and on top of each breast. Pour orange juice over chicken. Cover with a sheet of waxed paper or parchment. The paper should fit inside the pan and rest directly on the chicken. Cook the chicken for about 12 minutes or until it registers 165°F on an instant-read thermometer inserted into the thickest part of the breast. (The breast will offer resistance when you apply firm pressure with the tip of your finger.) Be careful not to overcook.

While the breasts are in the oven, blanch the celery in a large volume of boiling water. Rinse in cold water and drain well. Rinse and drain the currants. (This step is not crucial, but it does result in plumper currants.)

When the chicken is done, remove it from the baking pan and arrange it on a serving platter. Discard the sage leaves. Whisk the balsamic vinegar into cooking juices and taste the mixture for seasoning. Pour the sauce over the chicken.

Scatter the celery, currants, and walnuts over the top of the chicken. Garnish with any remaining sage leaves. Serve at room temperature.

MAKES APPROXIMATELY 10 CHICKEN BREASTS.

PASTA & CO. CRANBERRY SAUCE WITH
SOUR CHERRIES AND RUM

This is the cranberry sauce we make every year from early November until late December. Experience shows us that even those who have spent a lifetime abhorring cranberries like this sauce. **PREPARE-AHEAD/ SERVING NOTES:** Refrigerated, the sauce keeps for at least three months. And since it easily doubles, you can make it once in early November and be stocked through the holidays.

> 1 (12-ounce) bag raw cranberries, washed, dried, and picked over
>
> ¾ cup dried sour cherries
>
> ⅓ cup sugar
>
> ⅔ cup (¾ of an 11-ounce jar) Pasta & Co. Red Currant Jelly (page 219)
>
> ⅔ cup water
>
> ¼ cup dark rum

In a large saucepan, combine cranberries, sour cherries, sugar, jelly, and water. Over low heat, bring to a low simmer and cook, stirring occasionally, about 5 minutes, or until cranberries begin to pop. (Cranberries should be tender, but not mushy. You may cook the sauce to your taste, from firm whole cranberries to softer ones that give off more pectin and make a thicker sauce.)

Remove sauce from heat. Stir in rum. Refrigerate at least overnight to thicken sauce. Return to room temperature to serve.

MAKES 3½ CUPS.

CHICKEN WITH ITALIAN
PRUNES OR GRAPES

◆◆◆

. . . .

Make this recipe when Italian prunes are in season and there is fresh tarragon in your herb garden. Off-season, make the salad when seedless grapes are at their best. Poaching the chicken in the same orange juice mixture as in the previous recipe produces a fragrantly flavored chicken meat that complements the fruit and nuts. **PREPARE-AHEAD/SERVING NOTES:** The salad does not hold well. Serve within a few hours of preparing.

4 skinless, boneless chicken breasts (approximately 1 pound)

1 teaspoon salt

½ teaspoon freshly cracked black pepper

½ cup orange juice, either freshly squeezed or reconstituted from frozen concentrate

¼ cup plus 2 tablespoons walnut oil

1 cup celery, thinly sliced on the diagonal and blanched

¾ cup lightly toasted walnuts

¼ cup fresh tarragon leaves, washed and stripped from their stems

1¼ pounds ripe Italian prunes, rinsed, pitted, and quartered OR 1 pound (3 cups) grapes, rinsed and halved

1 teaspoon lemon juice

¼ teaspoon salt

7 grinds black pepper

Preheat oven to 375°F. Rinse chicken breasts and pat dry with a paper towel. Mix together salt and pepper. Season each chicken breast with the mixture and place them in a single layer in a shallow baking pan. Pour orange juice over chicken. Cover with a sheet of waxed paper or parchment. The paper should fit inside the pan and rest directly on the chicken.

Cook the chicken for about 12 minutes or until it registers 165°F on an instant-read thermometer inserted into the thickest part of the breast. (The breast will offer resistance when you apply firm pressure with the tip of your finger.) Be careful not to overcook. Remove chicken to a cutting board and cool to room temperature. Discard cooking liquid.

Cut the chicken across the grain (page 41) into bite-size pieces. Toss with ¼ cup of the walnut oil, celery, and ½ cup of the walnuts. Finely chop three-quarters of the tarragon and stir into the salad. Leave remaining tarragon leaves whole and reserve for garnish. Toss the fruit with lemon juice, salt, and pepper. Stir fruit into chicken mixture.

Arrange the salad on a serving platter. Top with remaining walnuts. Drizzle on remaining walnut oil. Garnish with reserved tarragon leaves.

MAKES 6 CUPS.

GREAT AMERICAN POTATO SALAD

◆◆◆

- -

This is our idea of classic American potato salad: very tender potatoes dressed in a tangy coating of mayonnaise, sour cream, herbs, mustard, and hard-boiled eggs. With no regard to calories or cholesterol, this is the way the Fourth of July was meant to taste. **PREPARE-AHEAD/SERVING NOTES:** Best results come from making and serving the salad the same day. Immediately before serving, retoss the salad and add the celery seed and chive garnish. Serve slightly chilled.

2½ pounds white new potatoes, skins on, well-washed, and cut into 1-inch pieces

1 tablespoon salt

2 tablespoons vegetable oil

2 tablespoons white wine vinegar

½ teaspoon garlic, put through a press

¼ teaspoon salt

¼ teaspoon freshly cracked black pepper

¾ teaspoon brine from dill pickles

⅔ cup dill pickles, cut into ¼-inch dice

½ cup celery, cut into ¼-inch dice

½ bunch green onions, cleaned, trimmed, and sliced (use white parts only)

¾ cup plus 2 tablespoons Best Foods mayonnaise

¼ cup plus 2 tablespoons sour cream

½ bunch baby dill, washed, trimmed from stem, and coarsely chopped

1 teaspoon snipped fresh chives

¼ teaspoon tarragon

⅛ teaspoon chervil

½ tablespoon grainy mustard

4 eggs, hard-boiled, peeled, and cut into ¼-inch dice

Salt and pepper to taste

TO TOP:

Celery seed

Fresh chives, snipped

Place potatoes in a saucepan with water to cover, and the salt. Cook over medium heat until they are tender but still firm. While potatoes cook, mix together oil, vinegar, garlic, salt, black pepper, and pickle juice. When potatoes are done, drain and rinse with cold water. Drain very well and toss with oil-and-vinegar mixture. Refrigerate.

In a large bowl, fold together dill pickles, celery, green onions, mayonnaise, sour cream, dill, chives, tarragon, chervil, and mustard. Fold in eggs and the potato mixture. Salt and pepper to taste.

Spoon into a serving dish. Garnish with a light sprinkling of celery seed and chives.

MAKES 8 CUPS.

PATIO DINNER

- Strata (page 23) and Baked Cheese Wafers (page 19)
- Chicken or Burgers Grilled with the Great American Barbecue Sauce (page 222)
- Great American Potato Salad (page 50)
- Corn Salad (page 56)
- Heaps of undressed salad greens, such as butter lettuce, mizuna, and arugula — all ready for eating with the grilled meat and salads
- Alix's Chocolate Layer Cake (page 249)

CAPONATA

•••

T here must be dozens of eggplant recipes similar to this. Many of them end up with a tasty, but undeniably overcooked, grayish-looking porridge of vegetables. Not so with this version. It originated with Louise Hasson, who owns Bon Vivant Cooking School in Seattle. We love her recipe because it comes out a delectable dark red. Over the years we have contrived to make sure that the eggplant is cooked until it is so soft it almost becomes part of the sauce, while the other vegetables remain quite firm. The result has sold successfully day after day at all three of our stores.

The recipe makes a chunky, saucy dish that is good as a side to meats or over pasta. If you want it to spread easily for serving with bread as an hors d'oeuvre, process it a few seconds in a food processor. Remember, just a couple of seconds. You do not want to purée it. **PREPARE-AHEAD/SERVING NOTES:** Most of the time, this dish keeps well refrigerated for three or four days. Occasionally, however, something about the seasonal variations in the eggplant shortens the dish's shelf life to only a couple of days. Freeze only as a last resort.

1 eggplant, unpeeled, cut into 1-inch cubes	**1 cup celery, cut on the diagonal into ½-inch pieces**
1 tablespoon salt	**½ green bell pepper, cored and cut into ¾-inch pieces**
2 tablespoons sugar	
3 tablespoons red wine vinegar	**½ red bell pepper, cored and cut into ¾-inch pieces**
2 tablespoons tomato paste	**7 black pitted olives, halved**
⅓ cup pure olive oil	**1 cup Paradiso brand crushed tomatoes in purée**
½ large onion, coarsely chopped	

In a large colander, toss eggplant with salt and allow to drain for 30 to 60 minutes. Rinse eggplant with water and drain well. Mix together sugar, vinegar, and tomato paste. Reserve. Cover bottom of a large sauté pan with the olive oil. Place pan on medium-high heat. When olive oil is sizzling, add eggplant and sauté until it begins to glisten and soften. Add onions and continue cooking until eggplant begins to get very soft. Lower heat and add remaining vegetables. Cover and steam until peppers and celery are tender but crisp (about 5 to 10 minutes). Remove from heat and toss with tomato paste mixture, olives, and tomatoes.

MAKES APPROXIMATELY 5 CUPS.

ARTICHOKE SALAD WITH OLIVES, PEPPERS, AND FETA CHEESE

◆◆◆

I t seems that no matter how expensive canned artichoke hearts become, this salad remains popular with our customers. **PREPARE-AHEAD/SERVING NOTES:** The artichokes and olives benefit from being in the marinade for a couple days. Add the remaining ingredients, however, shortly before serving.

2 (9-ounce) cans quartered artichoke hearts

½ cup extra virgin olive oil

½ cup white wine vinegar

⅛ teaspoon salt

8 grinds black pepper

1 garlic clove, put through a garlic press

1 cup imported (pit-in) olives, drained of brine

1 red bell pepper, cored, seeded, and cut into ¾-inch diamonds

1 green bell pepper, cored, seeded, and cut into ¾-inch diamonds

½ pound Greek feta cheese, cut into ½-inch cubes

⅓ red onion, cut into ¼-inch–thick half-moons (page 37)

1 tablespoon finely chopped parsley

Thoroughly drain artichokes of brine. In a large bowl, whisk together olive oil, vinegar, salt, black pepper, and garlic. Fold in artichoke hearts, olives, and one-third of the red and green bell peppers.

When ready to serve, spoon mixture with dressing into a serving dish. Top with remaining bell peppers, cheese, onion, and parsley.

MAKES 8 CUPS.

SUMMER GREEN BEANS AND TOMATOES

♦♦♦

Ever dressed wonderfully fresh green beans in a vinaigrette only to have the beans turn an unappetizing olive drab? Scratch the vinegar from the vinaigrette, ice the beans immediately after blanching, and you will produce a brilliantly green dish every time. **PREPARE-AHEAD/SERVING NOTES:** This dish is best served within a few hours of preparation.

1 tablespoon and 1 teaspoon salt

1½ pounds fresh string beans, green or a mix of green and yellow, trimmed of strings and cut on the diagonal into 2-inch pieces

4 Roma tomatoes, cut into ½-inch pieces, saving all juices

4 tablespoons extra virgin olive oil

1¼ cups onions, sliced into half-moons (page 37)

3 cloves garlic, finely minced

Freshly cracked pepper

Boil water in a large kettle. Add the 1 tablespoon salt and return to boil. Have ready a large bowl of ice water. Drop beans into boiling water and cook just until tender. Immediately drain and submerge in ice water. When well-chilled, drain well and reserve. Toss tomatoes with the 1 teaspoon salt and reserve. In a medium-size sauté pan, heat 2 tablespoons of the olive oil over medium heat. Add onions and cook just until they begin to color. Add garlic and remove from heat. Immediately fold in remaining olive oil and the tomatoes. Toss tomato mixture with beans. Season with freshly cracked black pepper to taste. Serve at room temperature.

MAKES 6 CUPS.

AN ALTERNATIVE FOR ROOM-TEMPERATURE GREEN BEANS

If you want a more basic treatment for fresh beans, blanch them as above, then simply toss them with enough French walnut oil to coat. Taste for seasoning. They may need more salt and will quite likely need freshly cracked black pepper. For a more festive look, top the beans with a sprinkling of whole pink peppercorns.

And definitely try using the same treatment for asparagus spears.

■ A FEW WORDS ABOUT WALNUT AND OTHER NUT OILS... The French ones are usually the most flavorful. They are expensive; they are perishable; and they are superb ingredients. Buy them in as small a quantity as you can. Store them refrigerated. Use them frequently to sauce pasta (see Fresh Sage and Hazelnut Pesto, page 175), to dress greens or fresh fruit — even use them in baking. They are a marvelous way to achieve a nutty flavor without the calories of the nuts themselves. Two teaspoons of nut oil will give you the flavor of 1 cup of nuts at about one-tenth the calories.

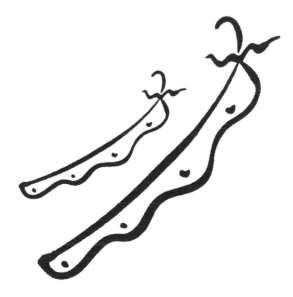

CORN SALAD

•••

This is easy. You will want the salad to serve with grilled burgers or chicken in the summertime or to brighten a buffet of room-temperature dishes all year long. Served as a side, it makes even a grilled-cheese sandwich stylish. **PREPARE-AHEAD/SERVING NOTES:** Save yourself last-minute hassle and make the dressing days before you need it. Just refrigerate. If you want to make the salad more than a few hours before serving, reserve the peppers and green onions and toss them in just before putting in a serving bowl. No matter what, be sure to add the garnish immediately before serving.

¼ cup vegetable oil

3 tablespoons freshly squeezed lime juice

2 tablespoons finely chopped parsley

1 teaspoon chili powder

½ teaspoon oregano

½ teaspoon ground coriander

½ teaspoon hot paprika

¼ teaspoon salt

1½ cups Pasta & Co. Marinated Olives (purchased or made from recipe on page 26) — remove from marinade with slotted spoon (reserve marinade for another purpose)

1 (16-ounce) bag frozen corn (about 3½ cups), thawed

1 red bell pepper, cut into ⅛-inch dice

1 green bell pepper, cut into ⅛-inch dice

1½ cups grated Cheddar cheese

½ cup canned garbanzo beans, well-drained

4 green onions, sliced (use both green and white parts)

TO TOP:

2 green onions, thinly sliced on the diagonal

2 tablespoons red bell pepper, cut into ⅛-inch dice

2 tablespoons green bell pepper, cut into ⅛-inch dice

In a large bowl, whisk together oil, lime juice, parsley, chili powder, oregano, coriander, paprika, and salt. Set aside. Halve the olives and add them along with the corn, red pepper, green pepper, Cheddar, garbanzo beans, and green onions to the dressing. Toss well. Place in serving dish and top with garnish.

MAKES 8 TO 9 CUPS.

HOUSE RICE SALAD

♦♦♦

For years, Pasta & Co. has sold a popular blend of wild rice, California brown basmati, and a long-grain brown rice called "House Blend Rice." The combination of rices makes a very attractive dish with a unique texture that comes from cooking together rices with varied cooking times. Our instructions are intended to give you brown rice that is very tender and basmati or wild rice that is just slightly crunchy.

If you cannot get the House Blend Rice or if you prefer a more evenly cooked rice, use ¾ cup long-grain white rice and ½ cup wild rice, each cooked separately to desired doneness, drained, and tossed together with the dressing and other ingredients.

Either way you choose to make this recipe, the salad's fresh, lemony flavor makes it a well-liked room-temperature side dish all year round — as good with a winter bird as it is with barbecued steaks or chicken. **PREPARE-AHEAD/SERVING NOTES:** The dish keeps up to four days refrigerated.

1¼ cups Pasta & Co. House Blend Rice **OR** see alternative above

2 tablespoons pure olive oil

1 (14.5-ounce) can chicken broth

¼ cup water

¼ cup extra virgin olive oil

1½ tablespoons fresh lemon juice

1 teaspoon Pasta & Co. House Herbs

chives

½ teaspoon garlic, finely minced or put through a press

¼ teaspoon freshly ground black pepper

1 (8.5-ounce) can quartered artichokes in brine (*not* marinated in oil and herbs), well-drained

1 tablespoon capers, rinsed and drained

¼ cup chopped parsley, plus some additional for optional garnish

In a heavy, flat-bottomed saucepan, sauté rice in the 2 tablespoons olive oil over medium heat for about 5 minutes. While rice is sautéing, heat chicken broth and water in a separate saucepan.

Pour hot broth over rice, stir briefly, and cover with tight-fitting lid. Lower heat and simmer for 35 minutes, stirring once or twice during cooking period. After 35 minutes, remove pan from heat, and let rice sit an additional 10 minutes with lid still in place.

While rice is cooking, whisk together in a large stainless bowl the ¼ cup olive oil, lemon juice, Pasta & Co. House Herbs, garlic, and black pepper. Set aside.

The rice is done when the lighter grains are thoroughly cooked, and the darker grains are slightly crunchy. When the rice is cooked, pour it and any remaining cooking liquid into the bowl with the dressing. Toss and set aside to cool for about 10 to 15 minutes.

Add artichokes and capers. Toss again. Stir in freshly chopped parsley. Spoon the salad into a serving bowl and garnish with additional chopped parsley if desired.

MAKES 4 MAIN COURSE SERVINGS OR 6 SIDE SERVINGS.

A ROOM TEMPERATURE BUFFET FOR ANY TIME OF YEAR

- Start with Vichyssoise (hot or cold) (page 126) and Roasted Breads (page 16)
- House Rice Salad (page 57)
- Marinated Beef Tenderloin (page 34)
- Caponata (page 52)
- Summer Green Beans and Tomatoes (page 54) or do green beans, asparagus, or sugar snap peas in walnut oil (page 55)
- Apricot and Sour Cherry Bread Pudding (page 247) with a side of barely sweetened whipped cream

MEXICAN GREEN RICE

For a change, make this room-temperature rice dish part of your next Mexican menu, or just serve it as a side to grilled meat or seafood. It is superb. **PREPARE-AHEAD/SERVING NOTES:** The dish keeps well refrigerated for up to three days. Bring to room temperature to serve.

3 tablespoons vegetable oil

1½ cups Uncle Ben's converted rice

½ cup finely minced onion

1 green Anaheim chile, roasted, peeled, seeded (see Roasted Bell Peppers, page 25), and finely chopped

2 cloves garlic, put through a press

½ teaspoon salt or to taste

½ tablespoon cumin

½ teaspoon hot paprika

2¾ cups homemade chicken stock or canned broth

2 cups (about 1 bunch) lightly packed cilantro, washed, dried, and finely chopped

⅓ pound Monterey jack cheese, grated

¼ cup pumpkin seeds, lightly toasted (page 15)

In a large saucepan, heat oil over medium heat. Add rice. Cook, stirring constantly, until rice turns opaque — about 3 minutes. Add the onion and sauté about 2 minutes. Add chile, garlic, salt, cumin, and paprika and sauté another 30 seconds. Add stock. Mix well. Heat over high heat to boiling. Reduce heat to low and cover, cooking until rice is tender (about 10 minutes — you may need to add a small amount of broth). When rice is tender, remove from heat, toss with a fork, and let cool.

When cooled to room temperature, toss with cilantro, cheese, and pumpkin seeds.

MAKES 7 CUPS.

DUFFY CLARKE'S MINTED
TUNA AND RICE SALAD
◆◆◆

We first had this salad when Duffy Clarke, a friend and customer, brought it to a summer potluck. Among a couple dozen salads, it was such a standout that we became aggressively acquisitive. We were lucky. She has been making the dish for years, adjusting it here and there, and graciously shared the recipe with us. Now it is a customer favorite for warm summer days. (And yes, this is one — because of the mayonnaise — that you may want to serve slightly chilled.) **PREPARE-AHEAD/SERVING NOTES:** Though leftovers are good eating for a couple of days, plan to serve this within a few hours of preparation. Any longer and the peas will yellow.

1 cup uncooked long-grain white rice

1 teaspoon grated lime peel

¼ cup plus 2 tablespoons fresh lime juice (2 to 3 limes)

¼ cup finely chopped fresh mint

4 (6.5-ounce) cans solid white albacore packed in water, thoroughly drained

2 cups Best Foods brand mayonnaise

½ cup buttermilk

1 tablespoon plus 1 teaspoon sugar

2 teaspoons Dijon mustard

2 teaspoons Tabasco

2 cups thinly sliced celery

2 cups frozen baby peas, thawed

¼ cup sliced green onions

¼ cup finely chopped parsley

Cook rice according to package directions. When tender, drain of any liquid, fluff with a fork, and let cool to room temperature.

In a large bowl, combine lime peel, lime juice, and chopped mint. After making sure the tuna is well-drained of can juices, flake it into large bite-size pieces and toss with lime mixture. Fold in rice and reserve. Combine mayonnaise, buttermilk, sugar, mustard, and Tabasco. Pour over rice mixture. Then fold in celery, peas, green onions, and parsley.

MAKES 8 CUPS.

ROOM TEMPERATURE FOODS

CHOPPED TOFU WITH BLACK BEANS

♦♦♦

. . . .

You will love this dish for its surprise ingredient: protein-rich tofu never tasted so good. We like it served alongside our Chinese Vermicelli (page 80), as a side to numerous grilled meats or chicken dishes, and especially accompanied by fresh or sun-dried tomatoes and hot bread. **PREPARE-AHEAD/SERVING NOTES:** This dish keeps well for up to three days.

1¼ cups black beans, picked over for stones and rinsed

1½ to 2 teaspoons salt

1 bay leaf

2 cloves garlic, peeled

1 teaspoon cumin

½ to 1 teaspoon salt

¼ teaspoon freshly cracked pepper

2 tablespoons extra virgin olive oil

1 tablespoon sherry wine vinegar

1 teaspoon Worcestershire sauce

1 clove garlic, peeled and put through press

1 (14-ounce) package *firm* tofu

2 tablespoons extra virgin olive oil

2 tablespoons garlic, finely chopped or puréed (as on page 17)

1 cup finely chopped parsley

¼ cup Best Foods brand mayonnaise

2 tablespoons freshly squeezed lemon juice

1½ teaspoons salt

½ teaspoon white pepper

Cook beans according to directions on page 62. After 45 minutes of cooking, add salt, bay leaf, and garlic. As beans continue to cook, mix together in a medium-size bowl the cumin, salt, pepper, 2 tablespoons olive oil, vinegar, Worcestershire sauce, and garlic.

When beans are very tender (just beginning to pop their skins), drain and rinse very well; the water will run clear, with no black residue. Toss beans with dressing and allow to marinate overnight. Drain tofu well. Wrap in a thin kitchen towel or 4 layers of cheesecloth and squeeze to remove any additional moisture. Unwrap the tofu, chop roughly, and place in a large bowl. In a small skillet, heat additional olive oil over low heat. Add chopped or puréed garlic and cook just until golden but not browned, about 3 minutes. Add chopped or puréed garlic to the bowl with the tofu. Add parsley, mayonnaise, lemon juice, salt, and white pepper. Mash with a fork until fine. To assemble, gently mix marinated beans into tofu mixture. Serve at room temperature.

MAKES ABOUT 4 CUPS.

ABOUT COOKING
DRIED BEANS

Cooking beans is deceptively easy. Yes, the proverbial pot of beans does cook nearly unattended. However, for these homely pellets to reach their full culinary potential, they need the same vigilant judgment as does the most expensive meat. Properly cooked dried beans are creamy on the inside; ready to pop their skins, but still intact; neither crunchy nor mushy.

There are numerous methods for cooking beans. This is the one that gives us the best results:

Sort through beans and discard any pebbles or debris. Be thorough. Rinse.

Place the beans in a saucepan large enough to hold them after they have cooked (they usually expand to two to three times their dried volume). Add warm water to about 3 inches over the beans. With a lid on the pan, bring beans to a boil over low heat (this can take nearly 30 minutes, depending on the amount of beans you are cooking). Let the beans boil for 1 minute. Remove from heat. Let sit, covered, for 1 hour (up to 3 hours is fine).

After this pre-soak, drain beans and cover with enough fresh water or chicken stock to be 1 inch above beans. (Many veteran cooks insist on using chicken stock. But unless you plan to turn the bean broth into soup, in most cases this is unnecessarily extravagant. Also, there is a prevailing theory that the salt present in most broths will toughen the beans in the early stages of cooking.) Cover pot, keeping lid ajar, and bring beans to a boil over medium-high heat. Keep them at a low boil for the entire cooking time. If the water level drops below the beans, add more liquid.

Do *not* add salt to the cooking liquid when you first put the beans on to cook, since it tends to toughen the beans and inhibit their cooking. Rather, add salt after 45 minutes of cooking. Use approximately 1 tablespoon salt per cup of dried beans. This seems like a lot, but beans are stubbornly bland, especially when they are to be served at room temperature.

The only way to know when beans are done is to taste them periodically during their cooking. Most dried beans will take at least 1 hour to cook. Some kinds will take much longer. The beans should feel creamy on your tongue and a few in the pot will begin to split before the batch is done.

When at last the beans are done, drain well, rinse in cold water, and proceed with your recipe.

— *Excerpted from* Pasta & Co. — The Cookbook.

FLAGEOLET BEANS AND
MACARONI IN A GREEN
OLIVE DRESSING

◆◆◆

Beans and pasta — the Italian classic of *pasta e fagioli* or *pasta fazul* — is a combination that should appear more often in American food. Nutritionally, the two together make an almost balanced diet in themselves, providing protein and carbohydrates without cholesterol or fat. What they almost always lack, however, is bold flavoring. Here we get it by making the dressing with jalapeño-stuffed olives (use half plain green olives, if you want less fire) and a big dose of garlic and herbs. Admittedly, we add fat with the olives and olive oil. At least it is unsaturated fat. **PREPARE-AHEAD/SERVING NOTES:** The salad holds well for a couple of days, but if possible, add the red onion and parsley close to mealtime. **ESSENTIAL GEAR:** While you could chop the olives and herbs by hand, an electric food processor makes it much easier.

1 cup uncooked flageolet beans (page 64)

2 teaspoons salt

8 cloves garlic

40 jalapeño-stuffed olives OR 20 jalapeño olives and 20 pitted green olives

3 tablespoons oregano

1 teaspoon thyme

¼ cup plus 1 tablespoon white wine vinegar

1 cup extra virgin olive oil

1 (16-ounce) can kidney beans

1 (10-ounce) package frozen corn

½ pound tubetti, or any similar good-quality, small, dried salad macaroni

⅔ cup red onion, cut into in ⅛-inch dice

⅔ cup finely chopped parsley

Pick through beans and discard any stones or debris. Cook beans according to directions on page 62, adding the 2 teaspoons salt near the end of the cooking time.

While beans cook, peel garlic and process in food processor until fine. Add olives, oregano, thyme, and vinegar, and process in short spurts until olives are finely minced. (Do not process too long or the mixture will turn into a paste.) Remove dressing to a large mixing bowl, stir in olive oil, and let the flavors blend.

Rinse and drain kidney beans and add to the dressing. Pour frozen corn into a strainer. Let thaw and drain.

When flageolet beans are tender, drain well and add to the dressing in the bowl. Stir to coat. Cook the tubetti or salad macaroni until tender in a large volume of boiling, lightly salted water. Drain and stir into the beans and dressing. Let salad cool to room temperature. Add corn. Stir again. Reserve 2 tablespoons each of the red onion and parsley. Toss remaining onion and parsley into the salad.

Remove salad to a serving bowl and garnish with reserved red onion and parsley.

MAKES 12 CUPS.

THE "NEW" BEANS

Over the past decade, the American cook's enthusiasm for unusual ingredients has spawned a new, albeit tiny, agricultural movement in the United States: the growing of specialty foods, such as fresh herbs and baby vegetables. One of the most promising results of this new agriculture is the cultivation of rare varieties of dried beans. Due in large part to an Idaho company, Potage U.S.A., there is now on the market a wide selection of dried beans with strange-sounding names, such as "Jackson Wonder," "Tongues of Fire," "Rattlesnake," and "Flageolet" (the small, pale green, delicately flavored bean that historically has been imported from France, but is now grown domestically).

We urge you to try some of these beans. Their various shapes, sizes, and colors combine in wonderful ways. Flageolet Beans and Macaroni in a Green Olive Dressing (page 63), Chopped Tofu with Black Beans (page 61), Christmas Limas in Chutney Vinaigrette (page 65), Pescine and Red Beans (page 195), and Cowboy Beans (page 217) are all incredibly tasty examples of what you can do with the "new beans." They are available under either the Potage U.S.A. or the Dean & Deluca label.

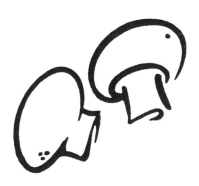

CHRISTMAS LIMAS IN
CHUTNEY VINAIGRETTE
◆◆◆

. . . .

One of our favorites of the new beans (page 64) is a big, mottled bean called the Christmas lima. It tastes a bit like a chestnut, and since it retains its great markings even after cooking, it makes a handsome dish. This recipe is equally tasty made with flageolet beans, or a mixture of Christmas limas and flageolets. **PREPARE-AHEAD/SERVING NOTES:** The salad can be made up to a day ahead, but prepare the topping of parsley and red onions immediately before serving.

1 pound dried Christmas limas or flageolet beans

1 tablespoon plus 1 teaspoon salt

1 teaspoon basil

1 teaspoon oregano

14 cloves garlic, peeled and put through a garlic press OR 3 tablespoons garlic purée (page 17)

½ cup extra virgin olive oil

⅓ cup Cinnabar brand tomato chutney (page 66)

¼ cup red wine vinegar or balsamic vinegar

½ teaspoon salt

¼ teaspoon dry mustard

Freshly cracked black pepper to taste

1 pound boneless chicken-thigh meat, cooked and torn into bite-size pieces, according to directions on page 39

TO TOP:

½ red onion, cut into half-moons (page 37)

Parsley or other fresh herb, finely minced

Cook beans according to instructions on page 62. After 45 minutes of cooking, add salt, basil, oregano, and garlic. (Flageolets may require as much as 1½ hours to cook; Christmas limas, 2½ hours.) While beans cook, whisk together in a large bowl olive oil, chutney, vinegar, salt, dry mustard, and black pepper.

Thoroughly drain cooked beans, making sure all liquid is drained off. Add beans and cooked chicken to dressing and toss. Just before mealtime, stir well, spoon into a serving dish, and top with red onions and the parsley or other fresh herb. Serve at room temperature.

MAKES 8 CUPS.

JARRED CHUTNEYS

On the whole, jarred chutneys are overcooked, overspiced, and over-priced concoctions of overripe fruits and vegetables. Then there are the Cinnabar brand chutneys. They have been formulated with authentic Indian seasonings and processed with small-batch care that makes them a quality addition to any number of dishes. We recommend these chutneys for use not only as condiments, but as flavorings for dressings as we have in Christmas Limas in Chutney Vinaigrette (page 65). Here we use the Cinnabar tomato chutney, but you could just as well use Cinnabar pear cardamom, peach, or mango chutneys. Any one of these full-bodied products will provide the kind of taste heft that room-temperature foods — particularly bland ones, such as beans or pasta — typically require.

USE CHUTNEY TO FLAVOR YOUR NEXT GREEN SALAD

Even when you have a superb chutney, such as Cinnabar, the tendency is to use a bit and let the rest sit in the refrigerator for months. Remember, good chutney is not only a condiment for meat and egg dishes. It is, first and foremost, a seasoning. That is how we use it in the Christmas Limas in Chutney Vinaigrette. Try a similar dressing for a green salad:

¼ cup extra virgin olive oil

¼ cup vegetable oil

¼ cup red wine vinegar

3 tablespoons Cinnabar chutney (any flavor)

¼ teaspoon dry mustard

¼ teaspoon salt

Pinch white pepper

Salad greens — especially sturdy ones, such as romaine, spinach and curly endive — rinsed and patted dry

Imported feta cheese — just a bit, to crumble over greens

Freshly cracked black pepper

Whisk together oils, vinegar, chutney, dry mustard, salt, and white pepper. Toss with greens to coat. Top with the feta and cracked pepper. Extra dressing will keep a couple of weeks in the refrigerator.

BLACK-EYED PEAS WITH MUSTARD GREENS AND GRUYÈRE

•••

M ake this no-meat salad in the spring or fall, when fresh mustard greens are at their best. It makes a lively light meal all by itself or as a side dish to grilled meats or roasted ham. The snappy mustard-and-tarragon vinaigrette sets off the earthiness of black-eyed peas and the slightly bitter taste of these sturdy greens. **PREPARE-AHEAD/SERVING NOTES:** You can marinate the beans in the dressing for a couple of days before serving, but toss with remaining ingredients as close to mealtime as possible so that the greens do not wilt. **ESSENTIAL GEAR:** Electric food processor

¾ cup dried black-eyed peas

2 teaspoons dried tarragon

1 teaspoon fennel seeds

¼ teaspoon salt, heaping

¼ teaspoon red pepper flakes

2 tablespoons plus ½ teaspoon sherry wine vinegar

1 tablespoon sweet mustard (we use Mendocino brand mustard)

½ cup less 1 tablespoon extra virgin olive oil

¾ cup coarsely grated Gruyère cheese

⅔ cup thinly sliced green onions

Freshly cracked black pepper to taste

3 ounces (about 4 cups lightly packed) fresh mustard greens, washed, dried, and trimmed of any coarse stalks

2 tablespoons finely chopped fresh tarragon

Cook peas according to our directions for cooking beans on page 62. While peas cook, place dried tarragon, fennel seeds, salt, red pepper flakes, vinegar, and mustard in food processor equipped with a steel blade. Process just until mixture is well-blended and fennel seeds are crushed. Add olive oil all at once and process long enough to blend but not emulsify. Decant dressing into a large bowl.

When beans are tender (just beginning to pop their skins and taste very creamy — about 25 to 30 minutes), drain well and toss with the dressing. Let cool completely.

Immediately before serving, toss beans with Gruyère, green onions, black pepper, and mustard greens. Top with fresh tarragon and serve.

MAKES 4 TO 5 CUPS.

FRENCH GREEN LENTILS
WITH SALSA

This is one of two recipes we have developed to showcase green lentils (see page 69). It is also a prime example of what we mean when we refer to "contrasting" garnish and the use of salsas, on page 33. If the salsa ingredients were tossed into the lentils, the dish would lose its eye appeal. By using the ingredients on top of the lentils in the form of a salsa, we get the advantage of not only their flavor and texture, but of their color. Try the stunning combination of peppers, tomatoes, red onion, goat cheese, vinegars, and walnut oil as a condiment to other dishes, such as roasted chicken or lamb. **PREPARE-AHEAD/SERVING NOTES:** The lentils can be cooked and dressed with the broth several days before serving. The salsa, however, should not be prepared until hours ahead of mealtime.

1 pound French green lentils

1 tablespoon salt

2 cups homemade beef stock or canned broth

FOR SALSA:

3 Roma tomatoes, cut into ¼-inch dice, including all juices

1 yellow bell pepper, cut into ¼-inch dice

1 red bell pepper, cut into ¼-inch dice

1 cup red onion, cut into ¼-inch dice

1 tablespoon of your best balsamic vinegar (see page 144)

1 tablespoon red wine vinegar

1 teaspoon salt

Freshly cracked black pepper to taste

¼ pound goat cheese such as Montrachet, cut into bite-size pieces

2 tablespoons French walnut oil (see page 55)

Rinse but do not soak lentils. Cover with cold water and cook about 20 minutes at a simmer — just until tender but not mushy. Season during the last 10 minutes of cooking with the 1 tablespoon salt. Place beef stock in a large sauté pan and bring to a boil over high heat. Cook until broth is reduced to 1 cup. Remove from heat and reserve. When lentils are done, drain well and toss with the reduced broth. Place in serving dish. If preparing ahead, cover and refrigerate, but return to room temperature before serving. To make salsa, toss together tomatoes and juices, bell peppers, red onion, vinegars, salt, and black pepper. Immediately before serving the lentils, top them with the salsa and goat cheese. Drizzle walnut oil over all. Serve at room temperature.

SERVES 8 TO 10 AS A SIDE DISH.

FRENCH GREEN LENTILS

The box will be labeled *Lentilles vertes du puy*. This is a lentil that currently is grown in commercial quantities only overseas, mostly in France. There is no comparison to domestic lentils in taste and texture. In fact, the green lentil is so desirable for cooking that U.S. legume farmers (the bulk of whom are in Eastern Washington's Palouse country) are attempting a commercial crop. Until they succeed, the imported variety commands a premium price, but we think you will agree that in dishes where the lentils are *not* to be puréed, the green lentil should be used. In French Green Lentils with Salsa (page 68), the lentils are served at room temperature. Do not miss, however, using them simply cooked in a flavorful broth and served hot as a side to roasted meats and vegetables. They are an inspired change from potatoes, rice, or pasta.

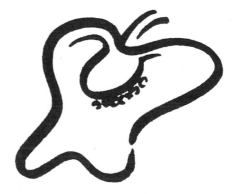

WHOLE WHEAT COUSCOUS
AND FRENCH LENTILS
◆◆◆

This second green lentil recipe (page 69), seasoned with lemon and mint, is reminiscent of tabouli. It is wonderfully nutritious — whole wheat couscous combined with the high-fiber lentil makes the dish a source of high-quality protein, even though it is vegetarian. If you must, substitute the more common brown lentil for the French green lentil. The dish will have a softer texture and a paler appearance. **PREPARE-AHEAD/SERVING NOTES:** The dish keeps well for a day or so, but add the vegetables and mint as close to serving time as possible.

½ cup plus 2 tablespoons extra virgin olive oil

½ cup plus 2 tablespoons fresh lemon juice

1½ tablespoons garlic, finely minced or put through a press

¾ tablespoon oregano

2 teaspoons marjoram

½ tablespoon cumin

½ teaspoon salt

2 teaspoons grainy mustard

2 tablespoons olive oil

1 cup whole wheat couscous

1 cup French green lentils

½ teaspoon salt

1½ cups cucumber, unpeeled and cut into ⅛-inch dice

⅔ cup green bell pepper, cut into ⅛-inch dice

½ cup chopped fresh mint

5 ounces feta cheese, well-drained of brine and chopped very fine

20 grinds freshly cracked pepper

TO TOP:

½ cup quartered cherry tomatoes (do not seed)

¼ cup chopped cucumber

¼ cup finely diced green bell pepper

In a large bowl, whisk together the extra virgin olive oil, lemon juice, garlic, oregano, marjoram, cumin, salt, and mustard. In a saucepan, bring to a boil 1½ cups water and the 2 tablespoons olive oil. Add whole wheat couscous. Stir, cover, and reduce heat to low. Cook for 5 minutes. Remove from heat and fluff with a fork. Then toss with dressing and let cool. Rinse lentils, place in a saucepan with the salt and enough water to cover. Bring to a boil and let simmer uncovered for about 15 minutes, until tender but not mushy (they should maintain their shape). When tender, rinse lentils with cold water, drain very well, and toss with couscous mixture. This can be made a day ahead.

Before serving, bring the dish to room temperature and toss with cucumber, bell pepper, mint, feta, and cracked pepper. Place in serving dish and top generously with the tomatoes, cucumber, and bell pepper.

MAKES 8 CUPS.

COUSCOUS

No one agrees on exactly what couscous is, so we have come up with our own definition. We call it a tiny granular Moroccan pasta made with semolina flour or — in the case of whole wheat couscous — whole wheat flour. It is definitely an ingredient worthy of attention. Our Black Bean and Couscous (page 66 of *Pasta & Co. — The Cookbook*) is a long-time daily big seller in our stores. Also popular is the Whole Wheat Couscous and French Lentils (page 70). Sometime try cooking just the couscous, according to the directions in either of these recipes, and serving it hot as an alternative to rice or potatoes with a juicy meat or seafood entrée.

Experts on Moroccan cooking insist on a complicated and tedious cooking method, but we have had fine results using the quick and simple technique specified in the recipe for Whole Wheat Couscous and French Lentils (page 70). Casbah and Tipiak are a couple of the couscous brands that Pasta & Co. stores use and sell.

BREAD SALADS

Bread has become extraordinarily good and extraordinarily expensive in recent years. Some loaves in our stores now retail for nearly $4 apiece. With that kind of bounty frequently on our day-old list, we decided to do a little research, and found that for years cooks have been making wonderful concoctions out of stale bread. We knew about bread puddings (see our version on page 247), but there are also bread soups and — our favorites — bread salads. The notion is a simple one: good olive oil, good vinegar, and good bread make for plain good taste. (See the essence of the idea in the first-course suggestion on page 17.) We have perfected three of these salads: Spanish Bread Salad, page 72; Summer Bread Salad, page 74; and Winter Bread Salad, page 75. So, when you have leftover, stale bread, do as we do: Freeze it until you have accumulated enough to make it into a salad.

SPANISH BREAD SALAD
♦♦♦

Processing the bread until it has the texture of coarse bread crumbs gives you a salad that will hold for a day or two. **PREPARE-AHEAD/SERVING NOTES:** The bread and onion should be prepared a day ahead of serving. Add the vegetables as close to mealtime as possible. **ESSENTIAL GEAR:** Electric food processor

14 ounces stale, heavy-crusted bread (about 12 cups cubed)

¾ cup red wine vinegar

½ red onion, cut into ⅛-inch dice

½ cup extra virgin olive oil

3 large cloves garlic, peeled

Optional: ½ cup basil leaves, washed and dried

1 cup green bell peppers, cut into ⅛-inch dice

1 cucumber, unpeeled, seeded, and cut into ⅛-inch dice and allowed to drain

Salt and pepper to taste

TO TOP:

1½ cups fresh tomatoes, cut into very small dice and drained

To prepare bread crumbs (at least one day before serving), preheat oven to 350°F. Coarsely cube bread, leaving crusts on. Spread bread on a large shallow roasting pan and toast in preheated oven for 20 minutes or until very golden brown. Remove from oven. Add vinegar and toss to evenly coat. Cover and let stand overnight at room temperature. Meanwhile, place red onion in ice water and refrigerate.

The next day, place olive oil, garlic, and basil leaves (if desired) in the work bowl of a food processor equipped with a steel blade. Process until basil leaves and garlic are finely chopped. Decant and reserve.

Add vinegar-soaked bread to the processor in three batches, adding some of the oil mixture to each batch. Process each batch until texture is that of coarse, moist bread crumbs. Remove batches to a large mixing bowl. When done processing the bread, fold in any remaining olive oil mixture. If crumbs seem dry, add olive oil to taste.

Thoroughly drain water off red onion. Fold onion, bell peppers, and cucumbers into bread mixture. Season with salt and pepper to taste. Place in serving dish and top with tomatoes.

MAKES 10 CUPS.

SUMMER BREAD SALAD

♦♦♦

ROOM TEMPERATURE FOODS

Make this bread salad with summer's best fresh basil and tomatoes. **PREPARE-AHEAD/SERVING NOTES:** While this is one of our staff's favorite salads, it has little more shelf life than a tossed green salad. After about 2 hours, you will find that the basil turns black and limp and the croutons get soggy. So serve this salad right away.

¾ cup extra virgin olive oil

3 tablespoons red wine vinegar

⅓ cup finely chopped basil

1½ teaspoons garlic, finely minced or put through a garlic press

¼ teaspoon salt

⅛ teaspoon black pepper

4 to 5 cups tomatoes (5 Roma tomatoes OR 3 beefsteak tomatoes), cut into ½-inch dice OR 6 cups cherry tomatoes, halved

2¼ cups (about 1½ cucumbers) English cucumber, seeded but not peeled (unless peel is bitter), cut into ½-inch dice

1⅛ cups green bell pepper, cut into ¼-inch dice

¾ cup small imported black olives (Niçoise olives are best; kalamatas are too large)

¼ cup capers, rinsed and well-drained

½ pound (about 4 cups) croutons, purchased from Pasta & Co. or made according to recipe on page 110 — make sure the bread is cut no larger than ½-inch cubes

1 cup additional basil leaves, washed, dried, and cut into very coarse chiffonade (page 37)

TO TOP:

½ cup red onion half-moons (page 37)

In a large bowl, mix together olive oil, vinegar, basil, garlic, salt, and pepper. Add tomatoes, cucumber, bell pepper, olives, capers, croutons, and additional basil leaves. Toss to blend. Place in a serving bowl and top with a few red onion half-moons. Let sit for about 30 minutes before serving.

MAKES 11 CUPS.

WINTER BREAD SALAD
(A.K.A. PASTA & CO. STUFFING)

♦♦♦

This recipe has many uses. It makes a fine room-temperature side to grilled or roasted meats, especially if the meat juices seep into the bread. If you prefer, the dish can be heated with great appeal. Our favorite use for the recipe is as a stuffing for any roasting bird (not just the holiday turkey). It is truly a great stuffing recipe any time of the year. **PREPARE-AHEAD/SERVING NOTES:** You can prepare this the day before for any of the above-mentioned uses.

1 (2-pound) loaf heavy-crusted peasant-style bread

½ cup extra virgin olive oil

10 shallots, peeled and thinly sliced

3 cloves garlic, put through a press

⅓ cup finely chopped sage leaves

1 tablespoon Pasta & Co. House Herbs or your choice of dried herbs, to taste

⅔ cup homemade chicken stock or canned broth

⅔ cup extra virgin olive oil

⅓ cup plus 1 tablespoon dry white wine

⅓ cup red wine vinegar

⅓ cup dried currants, plumped in red wine vinegar — drain off vinegar before using currants

⅓ cup walnuts, lightly toasted

Salt and freshly cracked pepper to taste

Preheat oven to 350°F. Cut or tear bread into irregular cubes no bigger than ½ inch.

Place bread on a baking sheet and toss with one-half of the ½ cup olive oil. Place in oven and bake for 20 minutes or until bread is just golden. Remove from oven and reserve.

In a medium-size sauté pan, heat remainder of the ½ cup olive oil over medium heat. Add shallots, garlic, sage, and House Herbs. Cook until translucent, then toss with bread. In a small bowl, whisk together chicken stock, the ⅔ cup olive oil, white wine, and vinegar. Fold into bread mixture along with drained currants and walnuts. Season to taste with salt and pepper.

MAKES 12 TO 14 CUPS.

Pasta

salads:

at room

temperature,

of course.

With a name like ours, it is not surprising that we make a lot of pasta salads. We have discovered a few important rules (page 79), but beyond these guidelines there is room for experimentation. Start by thinking of pasta salads as pasta dishes to eat at room temperature, either as appetizers, side dishes, or entrées. ■ Pasta salads lend themselves to a sense of camp. For instance, one of our biggest sellers, Chinese Vermicelli (page 80), is a culinary parody of a classic Oriental noodle dish. ■ There is also opportunity for sophistication. Tortellini in Olive Paste with Gremolata (page 94) makes a classy appetizer. And for a distinguished supper entrée, you cannot top the Pasta with Seafood (page 99). ■ Maybe the reason pasta salads are so popular is that they can be made and served in so many ways. They are a whole class of dishes intended to be fun for the cook.

EIGHT PASTA SALAD RULES NEVER TO BE BROKEN

■ Combine ingredients that complement each other in size, texture, and color.

■ Prepare ingredients hours ahead, but assemble the salad no more than 2 hours before serving.

■ Make dressing *before* cooking the pasta, and make it zesty.

■ Cook pasta with care in boiling *salted* water.

■ Drain very well. Depending on the particular salad, you may or may not need to rinse the cooked pasta with cold water. For instance, usually you will rinse long noodles, since that removes extra starch, which can cause them to cling together in salads. Also rinse with cold water any pasta going into a dressing with cream or raw egg in it. Short pasta going into a vinaigrette, however, does not need to be rinsed.

■ Toss drained pasta immediately with about 1½ cups dressing per pound of pasta.

■ Set the pasta aside to cool to room temperature. Hot pasta will wilt and discolor other ingredients, such as vegetables.

■ Once cooled, toss the pasta with the remaining ingredients and serve at room temperature.

CHINESE VERMICELLI

◆◆◆

Over the past decade, just about every establishment that sells prepared foods has put a spicy cold noodle dish on the menu. We were one of the first, and to this day, we probably make more Chinese Vermicelli than any other pasta dish we sell. Our particular formula was inspired by a recipe called Orchid's Tangy Cool Noodles, published in an unusually instructive book on Chinese cooking, *The Modern Art of Chinese Cooking*, by Barbara Tropp. **PREPARE-AHEAD/SERVING NOTES:** This dish keeps well for up to two days, but add the green onions only shortly before serving.

¼ cup sesame oil

¼ cup black soy sauce

2 tablespoons sugar

2 tablespoons hot chili oil

2 tablespoons black vinegar or balsamic vinegar

1 ¼ pounds fresh vermicelli

½ cup sesame seeds, toasted

1 cup green onions, thinly sliced on the diagonal, for garnish

In a large bowl, whisk together sesame oil, soy sauce, sugar, chili oil, and vinegar.

Cook vermicelli in boiling water until barely tender (probably less than a minute). Drain, rinse with cold water, and drain again. With your hands, immediately toss the pasta with the dressing, making sure pasta is completely and evenly coated. Add seeds and continue folding dressing through the pasta, literally "wiping" the bowl with the vermicelli. Remove to a shallow platter, top with green onions, and serve at room temperature.

MAKES 8 CUPS.

PASTA SALADS

POTSTICKER SALAD

♦♦♦

Italian ravioli's similarity to the Chinese potsticker inspired this salad's name. Here we take a fiery dressing very similar to that used in Chinese Vermicelli (page 80) and toss it with fresh pork-sausage–filled ravioli. Generous amounts of vegetables, sesame seeds, and pine nuts provide plenty of texture and a pleasant foil to the spiciness of the dressing. **PREPARE-AHEAD/SERVING NOTES:** Prepare the dressing days ahead. Toss the ravioli with the dressing up to one day ahead, but add the vegetables, seeds, and nuts just before serving.

¼ cup sesame oil

¼ cup black soy sauce

2 tablespoons sugar

2 tablespoons hot chili oil (less if you want a milder salad)

2 tablespoons black vinegar or balsamic vinegar

1 pound meat-filled fresh ravioli

2 cups broccoli flowerets

½ carrot, peeled and julienned

1 stalk celery, julienned

½ red bell pepper, julienned

¼ cup sesame seeds, toasted

¼ cup pine nuts, toasted

TO TOP:

¼ cup green onions, thinly sliced on the diagonal

Additional sesame seeds and pine nuts

In a large bowl, mix together sesame oil, soy sauce, sugar, chili oil, and vinegar. Cook ravioli until very tender. Drain well; toss with the dressing. Let cool to room temperature.

Meanwhile, blanch broccoli flowerets for a couple of minutes in boiling water, then drain well and plunge into ice water.

When ravioli has cooled, toss with carrot, celery, bell pepper, sesame seeds, and pine nuts. Place in a serving bowl. Thoroughly drain broccoli. Arrange broccoli flowerets down the middle of the salad. Scatter green onions and additional sesame seeds and pine nuts over the top.

Serve at room temperature.

MAKES 6 CUPS.

MING VEGETABLES
WITH ORZO

◆◆◆

We developed this beguiling green-and-pink dish because we needed a lunchtime accompaniment to our Chinese Vermicelli (page 80). Full of crunchy vegetables and speckled with tiny orzo pasta, fresh cilantro, and baby shrimp, this is one of the few pasta salads that benefits from being served slightly chilled.

Caution: Choose your shrimp carefully. Pale-colored, anemic-tasting shrimp destroy this dish. We have the best results using Chilean shrimp. **PREPARE-AHEAD/ SERVING NOTES:** Serve within a few hours of preparing. Next-day Ming Vegetables are a sorry sight.

½ cup cooking oil

3 tablespoons rice wine vinegar

½ tablespoon hot chili oil

½ teaspoon garlic, put through a press

Salt and pepper to taste

½ cup uncooked orzo pasta

1 cup celery, sliced diagonally into ¼-inch pieces

1 cup snowpeas or sugar snap peas, sliced diagonally in half and blanched 30 seconds in boiling water

1 cup English cucumber, seeded, sliced diagonally into ¼-inch pieces, and allowed to drain for 15 minutes

1 cup green onions, sliced diagonally into ¼-inch pieces

1 cup daikon radish, cut into ¼-inch by 2-inch matchsticks

½ pound cooked Chilean shrimp, well-drained

½ cup finely chopped parsley

⅓ cup cilantro, well-washed, dried, and finely chopped

In a large bowl, combine cooking oil, vinegar, chili oil, garlic, salt, and pepper. Reserve.

Cook orzo in boiling salted water until tender. Rinse with cold water, drain well, and toss with dressing. Allow to cool at least 30 minutes.

When pasta is at room temperature, fold in celery, snowpeas, cucumber, green onions, daikon, shrimp, parsley, and cilantro. Chill slightly and serve.

MAKES 8 CUPS.

THE GREAT AMERICAN
MACARONI SALAD
◆◆◆

. . . .

We like to take much-maligned dishes and bring them up to today's standards. We have done it with such recipes as macaroni and cheese (page 181), meat loaf (page 225), potato salad (page 50), and, here, with macaroni salad. We tried several different sizes and shapes of pasta for this salad before settling on a tiny, ribbed macaroni called *maccheroncini rigati*. The rib on the pasta adds a sturdy texture to the salad. This, of course, is a fine point, but after all, we do intend for this to be the best macaroni salad you have ever eaten. It has all the time-honored components — including the paprika on top. **PREPARE-AHEAD/SERVING NOTES:** The salad holds well for a couple of days.

1 pound *maccheroncini rigati* pasta (Pasta LaBella brand)

1¼ cups Best Foods brand mayonnaise

⅓ cup sour cream

1½ tablespoons white wine vinegar

1 tablespoon garlic, put through a garlic press

1 teaspoon dry mustard

½ teaspoon salt

½ teaspoon freshly cracked black pepper or to taste

½ teaspoon sweet paprika

½ teaspoon Tabasco or Jardine's Texas Champagne

2 cups green bell pepper, cored and cut into ¼-inch dice

1½ cups celery, cut into ⅛-inch dice

1 cup cucumber, seeded, cut into ⅛-inch dice, and drained

1 cup sliced or coarsely chopped pimiento-stuffed green olives

½ cup sliced or coarsely chopped pitted black olives

⅓ cup red onion, cut into ⅛-inch dice

1 (4-ounce) jar pimiento strips, including all juices

6 ounces extra sharp Cheddar cheese, cut into ¼-inch cubes

½ cup finely chopped parsley

TO TOP:

Additional sweet paprika

Cook pasta in boiling salted water until tender. Rinse with cold water and let drain thoroughly.

While pasta cooks, mix together mayonnaise, sour cream, vinegar, garlic, dry mustard, salt, black pepper, paprika, and Tabasco in a large bowl. When pasta has cooled to room temperature, toss with the dressing. Fold in bell pepper, celery, cucumber, green and black olives, red onion, pimiento and juices, cheese, and one-third of the parsley. Spoon into serving dish and top with remaining parsley and additional paprika. Serve at room temperature.

MAKES 12 CUPS.

PASTA: THE FUN OF IT ALL IS SHAPES AND SIZES

Part of the appeal of pasta is that it comes in a myriad of shapes and sizes. In the 15 pasta salads in this section, we call for 13 different shapes of pasta, from tiny orzo to the long corkscrews we've dubbed "phone cord." Feel free to substitute your own favorites.

FRESH PASTA VS. DRIED

Pasta & Co. makes and sells over a ton of fresh pasta products a week. We make a dozen different shapes of fresh pasta and supplement them with top-quality dried pasta in the cuts that are not feasible for us to produce.

In short, we use both fresh and dried pasta. And we hasten to point out that "fresh" does not automatically mean better. There is now a slew of premium-priced fresh pasta products on the market that are no better than — if as good as — dried pasta. Only if the pasta is made with the proper flours and fresh eggs, and if moisture and other variables are controlled, will it be a superior-quality product. Then, especially for basic long noodles, lasagne, and filled pasta, fresh pasta offers enormous advantages over dried. Otherwise, top-quality dried pasta made with 100% semolina flour may be preferred.

AT&T PASTA SALAD
◆◆◆

When we started making a pasta salad with *fusilli lunghi*, we were struck by the resemblance between the pasta and the spiral cord used on telephones. So we called the pasta "phone cord" and the salad we make with it "AT&T." You will love its sunny flavor and versatility. We recommend it as a side dish to grilled meats and seafood.

Though the fresh basil dressing can be used on other kinds of pasta, we have yet to find one that is better for this particular dish than "phone cord." For ease of eating, break the spirals into 2-inch to 3-inch pieces. Otherwise, when you pick the pasta up with a fork, it literally springs off the plate, flinging ingredients every which way. Try this indisputably lively pasta, not only in this dish, but as a fun substitute for spaghetti to be served with meat sauce. **PREPARE-AHEAD/SERVING NOTES:** Despite the salad's odd name, it has become a perennial best seller. To take advantage of the summer basil crop, we make huge batches of the dressing during basil season and freeze it for dressing pasta all winter long. You can do the same. **ESSENTIAL GEAR:** Electric food processor

2 cups lightly packed fresh basil leaves, washed, dried, and stemmed (see page 86)

¾ cup freshly grated Parmesan cheese

¼ cup freshly grated Romano cheese

⅓ cup pine nuts

4 cloves garlic, put through a garlic press

½ cup extra virgin olive oil

1 pound dried *fusilli lunghi* pasta

TO TOP:

12 to 15 sun-dried tomatoes, drained of oil and julienned

⅓ cup pine nuts, lightly toasted

½ cup freshly grated Parmesan cheese

Place basil, Parmesan, Romano, pine nuts, and garlic in a food processor bowl equipped with a steel blade. Process until well-blended. Then, with the processor running, drizzle in olive oil until ingredients are well-combined.

Break pasta into thirds. Cook in boiling salted water until tender. Rinse with cold water and drain well.

Toss pasta with basil mixture. When ready to serve, place in a serving bowl. Top with sun-dried tomatoes, toasted pine nuts, and the additional Parmesan. Serve at room temperature.

MAKES 8 CUPS.

TO STORE FRESH BASIL

Having stored literally tons of freshly picked basil over the past 10 years, we have perfected the storage technique. The best method is to place the basil, on the stem and unwashed, in a plastic bag closed with a twist tie, then refrigerate. This will give you crisp green leaves for at least three or four days. Immediately before using the basil, wash, dry, and stem the leaves.

"HOMEMADE" SUN-DRIED TOMATOES

The best sun-dried tomatoes in olive oil now sell for over $20 a pound. A more economic alternative is to buy dried tomatoes and reconstitute them yourself. Pasta & Co. stores sell both. The latter come with complete directions for reconstituting.

THE HOUSE PASTA

This is the "basic black dress" of pasta salads. Though heavily spiked with garlic, the salad goes with nearly everything. Try topping it with blanched vegetables, poached seafood, or fresh tomatoes. Or use it as is, alongside grilled or roasted meats. You can use any pasta you wish, but our favorites by far are *creste gallo* — a rooster-tail–shaped pasta (the Italian name means "cockscomb") — and *chitarra*, a square spaghetti. **PREPARE-AHEAD/SERVING NOTES:** The dish keeps well for at least two days.

1 cup extra virgin olive oil

½ cup plus 1 tablespoon cream

2 tablespoons Pasta & Co. House Herbs OR dried or fresh herbs of your choice and to your taste

½ teaspoon Tabasco

¼ teaspoon salt

3 cloves garlic, put through a garlic press

¼ cup fresh lemon juice

1 pound *creste gallo*, *chitarra*, or other dried pasta of your choice (if you are using fresh pasta, use up to 2 pounds)

1 cup freshly grated Romano cheese

TO TOP:

Parsley, finely chopped

Freshly ground black pepper

In a large bowl, whisk together olive oil, cream, House Herbs, Tabasco, salt, and garlic. When well-mixed, whisk in lemon juice. Cook pasta in boiling salted water until tender. Rinse immediately under cold water and drain thoroughly. Add to olive oil mixture and toss until well-coated. Add Romano and toss again. Place in serving dish and top with parsley and black pepper.

MAKES 8 TO 9 CUPS.

RADIATORE AND CHICKEN IN A YOGURT MUSTARD-SEED MAYONNAISE

◆◆◆

. . . .

Here is a perfect example of a dish made superb by matching the cut of the pasta to the other ingredients. *Radiatore* is a short pasta filled with little crevices, just the right size to pick up the couple of hundred mustard seeds in the recipe and produce a fun taste and texture. Follow exactly the instructions for popping the mustard seeds and you will not be disappointed. Do *not* substitute the more common yellow mustard seeds (page 89). Serve the dish for a summer luncheon or supper with a side of the season's best fruits and berries and freshly fried poppadums (page 21). As with all dishes containing cooked chicken, be cautious in your poaching technique (page 39). **PREPARE-AHEAD/SERVING NOTES:** The mayonnaise for the dish can be made a day or two before serving and the rest of the ingredients prepared several hours ahead. Assemble the salad within an hour or two of mealtime. Be sure to serve at room temperature. **ESSENTIAL GEAR:** Medium-size nonstick sauté pan with lid to fit

6 tablespoons peanut oil	1 pint plain yogurt
2 tablespoons black or brown mustard seeds (available at Pasta & Co. and at Middle Eastern grocery stores)	⅓ cup freshly squeezed lemon juice
	1½ cups golden raisins
1 tablespoon plus 1 teaspoon cumin seeds	½ cup currants
	¾ pound *radiatore* pasta
2 tablespoons (about 7 medium cloves) garlic, finely minced or put through a garlic press OR 2 tablespoons garlic purée (page 17)	2½ pounds skinless, boneless chicken-thigh meat, poached and pulled into large pieces (page 39)
1 tablespoon finely grated fresh ginger	2½ cups sweetened coconut, toasted to golden brown
2 teaspoons hot paprika	¾ cup shelled peanuts, preferably dry-roasted
1 teaspoon turmeric	½ cup green onions, thinly sliced on the diagonal
1½ teaspoons salt	
1 teaspoon red pepper flakes	

Have all your ingredients premeasured and ready by the stove. Heat oil in a medium, nonstick sauté pan over medium-high heat. Have ready a lid that fits the pan. Add mustard seeds. They will begin to pop immediately, so cover with lid and leave on heat until popping slows. Shake the pan as you do to pop popcorn. This will keep the seeds from burning.

When popping slows way down, reduce heat to very low and add cumin seeds. Stir until golden (about 1 minute). Add garlic and stir about 5 seconds. Add ginger, stir another 5 seconds, and remove from heat. (The challenge here is that if you undercook these ingredients, the sauce will be underflavored. If you overcook them, the sauce will taste bitter.)

Stir in paprika, turmeric, salt, and red pepper flakes. Let cool and mix with yogurt and lemon juice. Reserve.

Cover raisins and currants with boiling water. Let steep 30 minutes. Drain very well.

Cook pasta in boiling salted water until tender. Rinse with cold water and drain. When all liquid has drained off the pasta, toss with yogurt mixture. Add drained raisins and currants, chicken, and one-third of the coconut.

Spoon onto serving plate and top with remaining coconut, peanuts, and green onions. Serve at room temperature, and do not forget to accompany with poppadums (page 21).

MAKES 12 CUPS.

"POPPED" BLACK MUSTARD SEEDS

Not really black, but rather a dark rust color, these tiny seeds are valuable for the color and texture they add to vegetable and pasta dishes. Somewhat smaller and less pungent than the more common yellow mustard seeds, they are frequently called for in East Indian cooking. They can be used raw, but "popping" them in hot oil (using the procedure detailed in the recipe for Radiatore and Chicken in a Yogurt Mustard-Seed Mayonnaise, page 88) turns them deliciously nutty. Once you have mastered the technique so that you do not burn the seeds (giving them a bitter taste), you will want to use popped black mustard seeds in any number of inventions. In the radiatore dish, the seeds tuck into the crevices of the radiatore pasta, adding tiny specks of crunch to each mouthful. Another favorite combination includes blanched and marinated vegetables, such as the Tuscan Vegetables on page 49 of our first cookbook.

You can find black mustard seeds at Pasta & Co. stores and at Middle Eastern grocery stores.

SPAGHETTI WESTERN SALAD

This salad combines Southwest and Mexican food flavors with pasta. Do not stop there. While it is great as a side to barbecued burgers, it will also be a Texan star served along with refried beans and your best corn chips or tortillas.

The spiciness of the dish depends on the salsa you choose. We suggest Jardine's Hot Texacante Salsa for its excellent quality and its mid-range firepower. If you want the dish milder, use Mild Texacante. **PREPARE-AHEAD/SERVING NOTES:** The salad can be made a day ahead and refrigerated, but return to room temperature, retoss, and top with tomatoes and green onions right before serving. If, after refrigeration, the salad seems dry, season to taste with a little additional oil and/or vinegar.

1 pound *cavatappi* or *serpentini* pasta

1 tablespoon cooking oil

1 (14.5-ounce) can peeled tomatoes in juice, cut into ¼-inch dice, including all juices

1 (12¾-ounce) jar Jardine's brand Hot Texacante Salsa

1 cup Quark (nonfat or low-fat) or sour cream

2 tablespoons red wine vinegar

2 cloves garlic, put through a garlic press

2¾ cups grated sharp Cheddar cheese

2 cups pitted black olives, well-drained and quartered

¾ cup green bell pepper, cut into ⅛-inch dice

1 cup cilantro, well-washed, dried, and finely chopped

9 Roma tomatoes, cut into ¼-inch dice

1 cup green onions, sliced ¼-inch thick on the diagonal, to top

Cook pasta in boiling salted water until tender. Rinse with cold water, drain well, and toss with oil. Set aside.

In a large dish, mix together canned tomatoes and juice, salsa, Quark, vinegar, and garlic. Fold in the cooked pasta; then add cheese, olives, bell pepper, cilantro, and half the Roma tomatoes. If salad seems dry, toss with an additional tablespoon of oil. Spoon salad into a serving dish and top with the green onions and remaining tomatoes.

MAKES 16 CUPS.

THIS GREAT STUFF CALLED "QUARK"

We suggest substituting Quark in any dish calling for sour cream — even a plump, steamy baked potato. We originally used sour cream in this dish, but found that we could very successfully substitute nonfat or low-fat Quark, a soft cheese with the texture and taste of sour cream. The wonderful news about Quark is that even the low-fat version uses only 50% fat, compared with 86% for sour cream. The calorie count for 4 ounces of low-fat Quark is 140; for nonfat, 71; for sour cream, 243. The cholesterol count for 4 ounces of low-fat Quark is 14 milligrams; for nonfat, 4.8; for sour cream, 50. And yes, it tastes far better than yogurt.

SESAME-ROASTED
CHICKEN AND RAMEN
♦♦♦

. . . .

We haven't a clue what "ramen" really is. We know about the curly noodles with seasoning packets one buys at a grocery store. But we have discovered marvelous ramen noodles (no seasonings included) that are made with buckwheat, whole wheat, or brown rice flour. These are the noodles that make this stunning Oriental-style pasta salad a meal in itself. **PREPARE-AHEAD/SERVING NOTES:** The salad keeps well for a couple of days. Bring to room temperature before serving.

1⅓ pounds skinless, boneless chicken thighs, cut into ¾-inch pieces

1 teaspoon cayenne

¼ cup sesame oil

2 tablespoons plus 2 teaspoons soy sauce

2 tablespoons honey

1 tablespoon sherry vinegar

¼ teaspoon allspice

¼ cup plus 2 tablespoons vegetable oil

2 tablespoons sesame oil

6 to 7 ounces ramen noodles (made with either buckwheat, whole wheat, or brown rice flour) — available at Pasta & Co. and some health-food stores

⅔ cup carrots, sliced very thin on the diagonal and then cut in half lengthwise

⅔ cup celery, sliced very thin on the diagonal and then cut in half crosswise

⅔ cup daikon radish, cut into juliénne

¼ cup slivered almonds, toasted

½ cup halved cashews, toasted

½ cup green onions, sliced very thin on the diagonal

Preheat oven to 350°F. Arrange chicken in a shallow roasting pan. Whisk together cayenne and the ¼ cup sesame oil and drizzle mixture over the chicken. Bake chicken for 14 minutes or until it is just firm to the touch (be careful not to overcook).

Drain off all the juices from the chicken into a measuring cup and reserve.

In a large bowl, whisk together soy sauce, honey, vinegar, and allspice. Gradually add vegetable oil, the 2 tablespoons sesame oil, and 2 tablespoons of the reserved cooking juices, whisking constantly. Add the reserved chicken to this mixture and set aside.

Cook ramen until just barely tender (usually by the time the ramen "pad" has broken apart, it is done — it overcooks easily). Rinse ramen with cold water and drain well. Toss with chicken mixture.

PASTA SALADS

Blanch carrots and celery until barely tender. Rinse with cold water and drain well.

To assemble, place ramen mixture in a large serving bowl. Top with the blanched vegetables, daikon, roasted nuts, and green onions. Serve at room temperature.

MAKES 8 CUPS.

USE TORTELLINI IN OLIVE PASTE AS
A STYLISH APPETIZER

Think of it. There are 100 tortellini in a pound, and each is a bite-size hors d'oeuvre. All you need is a thick dressing that does not drizzle (you have it in the recipe for olive paste on the next page and also in Pasta Bruta — page 127 of our first cookbook) and some good-looking Japanese toothpicks (available at Pasta & Co. stores). Use these recipes the next time you need finger food for appetizers. (In fact, a Pasta & Co. catering standby is to fill a large platter half with the shiny black Tortellini in Olive Paste with Gremolata and half with the rusty red Pasta Bruta. Very attractive.)

TORTELLINI IN OLIVE
PASTE WITH GREMOLATA
♦♦♦

This quick recipe turns tortellini into a spirited salad or a handy room-temperature appetizer (page 93). This is one of those dishes we talk about in "The Making of Stunning Foods," on page 33. Though the tortellini are tasty by themselves, both for visual and taste considerations they require a topping. Here we use a classic from Italian cuisine: gremolata. The mixture is traditionally used to top the veal shanks in osso bucco. However, it is such a tasty combination that you should look for other ways to use it, such as for seasoning chicken or tossed green salad. **PREPARE-AHEAD/SERVING NOTES:** The tortellini and olive paste can be prepared up to two days before serving, as can the gremolata. Assemble the dish shortly before serving. **ESSENTIAL GEAR:** Electric food processor

1 cup Pasta & Co. Marinated Black Olives — purchased or made according to recipe on page —— (include at least ½ cup of the marinade)

½ pound fresh tortellini — pesto-filled, if possible

3 tablespoons freshly grated Parmesan cheese

GREMOLATA:

2 tablespoons coarsely chopped parsley

Zest of 1 lemon

1 clove garlic, peeled and coarsely chopped

Place olives and marinade in food processor bowl equipped with steel blade. Process to a very coarse purée. Remove to a bowl large enough to hold olives and the tortellini and reserve.

Cook tortellini until very tender. (The tortellini will toughen as they cool in the salad, so be sure they are tender.) Drain well and toss with olive mixture. Let cool to room temperature. Then toss with Parmesan.

To prepare the gremolata: Chop together (with a knife; quantity is too small for a full-size food processor) parsley, lemon zest, and garlic until very fine. Reserve.

Just before serving, retoss the tortellini and top with gremolata. Serve at room temperature.

MAKES ABOUT 4 CUPS, OR APPROXIMATELY 50 APPETIZERS.

FILLED PASTA TOSSED
WITH A CHUNKY ITALIAN
SALSA

◆◆◆

. . . .

We do not know the origin of salsa, but as you may have noticed, we use the notion of a chunky, sprightly flavored condiment a lot (see pages 68, 193, and 198). This recipe uses a Mexican-style salsa with Italian seasonings tossed with ravioli or tortellini for a room-temperature pasta dish that has been a hit in our stores. **PREPARE-AHEAD/SERVING NOTES:** The dish can be prepared without its topping a day ahead, but it is imperative to bring it back to room temperature (you can reheat it gently in a sauté pan to get the chill out of it), toss well, and then add the mozzarella and green onions immediately before serving.

2 (14.5-ounce) cans S&W brand Diced Tomatoes in Purée (using exactly this product is essential in this recipe)

⅔ cup Pasta & Co. Marinated Olives (purchased or made with recipe on page 26), halved, including their marinade

⅓ cup finely minced onion

¼ cup extra virgin olive oil

2 tablespoons red wine vinegar

¼ cup finely chopped parsley

1 tablespoon oregano

1 tablespoon garlic, put through a garlic press

1 teaspoon red pepper flakes

Salt to taste

1 pound filled fresh pasta: meat ravioli or veal- or cheese-filled tortellini

TO TOP:

2 cups grated mozzarella cheese

2 green onions, thinly sliced on the diagonal (use green parts also)

In a large bowl, fold together tomatoes with all their juices, olives and their marinade, onion, olive oil, vinegar, parsley, oregano, garlic, and red pepper flakes. Taste for salt and set aside.

Cook pasta in boiling salted water until very tender. (Be sure it is tender; filled pasta will toughen as it cools in the salad.) Rinse with cold water and drain well. Toss pasta with a couple of tablespoons of the salsa and let cool to room temperature. Fold in remaining salsa. Spoon into a serving dish. Top with mozzarella and green onions. Serve at room temperature.

MAKES 8 CUPS.

PENNE WITH TORN GREEK CHICKEN, OLIVES, AND FRESH LEMON

ere we use the kopanisti mixture from page 45 to season the chicken and make the dressing for the pasta. This is also one of the few recipes where we prescribe tearing the chicken along the grain instead of cutting it across the grain (see page 41). "Torn" chicken, in this case, better absorbs the flavors of the dressing and complements the shape of the penne.

This is a marvelously flavored room-temperature dish, but as we mentioned earlier, kopanisti has an unappealing color. Here is where our "clean" garnishing (page 33) comes in. A topping of paper-thin lemon slices and roasted red peppers adds to the flavor of the dish while making the whole look as good as it tastes. **PREPARE-AHEAD/SERVING NOTES:** The salad can be prepared ahead without its toppings. Return it to room temperature, toss well in the dressing, and top with the lemon, peppers, and parsley just before serving.

1½ pounds boneless, skinless chicken breasts, cooked with kopanisti, garlic, olive oil, and red pepper flakes (see page 44)

½ pound dried penne pasta

Juice of 1 lemon

2 cups black olives (preferably kalamata or Moroccan), pitted (see page 27)

Freshly cracked black pepper to taste

Additional olive oil to taste

TO TOP:

1 lemon, thinly sliced and seeded

1 to 2 red bell peppers, roasted (see page 25) and cut into diamonds or strips

¼ cup finely chopped parsley or other fresh herbs

When the chicken has been cooked with the kopanisti, garlic, olive oil, and red pepper flakes, refrigerate in the sauce for 30 minutes. Then tear it into long strips along the grain, coating it in the sauce as you work. Leave the torn chicken in the pan with all the sauce.

Cook penne until very tender (it is easy to undercook penne). You will need to stir almost constantly to prevent the penne from sticking together. Drain pasta well and place in a large bowl. Toss with lemon juice. Fold in chicken mixture and olives. Season with freshly cracked black pepper to taste. If the dish seems a little dry, toss with a small amount of additional extra virgin olive oil.

Spoon into serving dish. Immediately before mealtime, retoss pasta and chicken in its dressing and top with lemon slices, bell peppers, and the parsley or fresh herbs. Serve at room temperature.

MAKES 10 CUPS.

DELI BEAN & PASTA SALAD

•••

. . . .

Beans and pasta have at least one thing in common: They respond well to strong-flavored but well-balanced dressings. This dressing comes from customer and local food commentator Mauny Kaseburg. We combine it with beans and pasta for a homey room-temperature dish that will remind you ever so slightly of deli-counter three-bean salads. The similarity is fleeting. The salad is great for backyard barbecues. **PREPARE-AHEAD/SERVING NOTES:** Marinate the beans for several hours or days. Finish off with the pasta and other ingredients just before you are ready to serve. Serve at room temperature, not cold. **ESSENTIAL GEAR:** Electric food processor

1 teaspoon salt

½ teaspoon sugar

¼ teaspoon black pepper

2½ tablespoons red wine vinegar

1 tablespoon fresh lemon juice

2 teaspoons Worcestershire sauce

1½ teaspoons Dijon mustard

1 large shallot, peeled and quartered

1 to 2 cloves garlic, smashed and peeled

¼ cup extra virgin olive oil

¼ cup salad oil

1 tablespoon finely chopped parsley

1 tablespoon chopped fresh basil
OR ½ teaspoon dried basil

1 (16-ounce) can kidney beans, rinsed and drained

1 (16-ounce) can garbanzo beans, rinsed and drained

⅓ to ½ pound fresh pescine

2 (2¼-ounce) cans sliced ripe olives, drained

3 large Roma tomatoes, cut into ½-inch dice

⅔ cup yellow bell pepper, cut into ½-inch dice

⅔ cup red onion, cut into ¼-inch dice

Additional 1 tablespoon finely chopped parsley

Combine salt, sugar, black pepper, vinegar, lemon juice, Worcestershire sauce, and mustard in measuring cup and set aside.

Using a food processor equipped with a steel blade, with machine running, drop shallot and garlic through feeder tube onto spinning blade. With machine still running, slowly pour vinegar mixture through feeder tube. Add oils slowly through feeder tube, then drop in parsley and basil. As soon as oil is well-blended, stop machine.

In a large bowl, toss rinsed and drained beans with the dressing and let marinate for at least a few hours.

Cook pescine in a large volume of salted water for 3 to 4 minutes. When tender, drain well. Toss with the beans and dressing.

Stir in half the olives, half the tomatoes, half the bell pepper, and half the red onion.

Place salad in serving bowl and garnish with remaining olives, tomatoes, bell pepper, red onion, and parsley.

MAKES 8 CUPS.

PICNIC FARE

■ Baked Cheese Wafers (page 19)

■ Herb-Roasted Chicken (at room temperature) (page 224)

■ Deli Bean Salad (page 97)

■ Great American Potato Salad (page 50)

■ Italian Shortbread with Almonds, Brandy, and Lemon (page 246)

PASTA AND SEAFOOD

♦♦♦

. . . .

This is it: the best dressing we have found for combining pasta with any kind of seafood, from canned albacore to smoked scallops. It brings boldly scented olive oil up against the taste of great seafood. And it works every time. Serve the dish along with crusty breadsticks, fresh tomatoes, and Niçoise olives. **PREPARE-AHEAD/ SERVING NOTES:** While the salad keeps quite well for a couple of days, in most versions you are using expensive seafood that does not improve with age. Plan to vigorously consume this salad within only 2 or 3 hours of making it.

¾ cup extra virgin olive oil — your best

3 tablespoons fresh lemon juice — maybe a little extra to taste

2 tablespoons plus 2 teaspoons garlic, finely minced or put through a garlic press OR 2 tablespoons plus 2 teaspoons garlic purée (page 17)

1 tablespoon freeze-dried green peppercorns, coarsely crushed with back of a large knife blade (as with garlic or olives — see page 27)

1½ teaspoons red pepper flakes

¼ to ½ teaspoon salt (depending on saltiness of the seafood)

1 pound fresh pescine OR ¾ pound dried penne

1 pound cooked seafood in bite-size pieces — you can use smoked sturgeon, smoked salmon, smoked sea bass, poached white fish (see page 39), or canned albacore (including can juices)

2 cups green onions, sliced thinly on the diagonal

In a large bowl, whisk together olive oil, lemon juice, garlic, peppercorns, red pepper flakes, and salt. (If you are doubling the recipe, you can use whole cloves of garlic and whole green peppercorns and place them in a food processor bowl equipped with a steel blade, along with ¼ cup of the olive oil, the red pepper flakes, and salt. Process until you are certain all the garlic and peppercorns have been finely minced. Remove mixture to a large bowl and whisk in remaining olive oil.)

Cook pescine until tender, rinse with cold water, and drain well. Toss with the dressing. Fold in seafood of your choice and half the green onions. Spoon into a serv-ing dish and top with remaining green onions. Serve at room temperature.

MAKES 14 CUPS.

A FUN VARIATION FOR PASTA AND SEAFOOD (PAGE 99)

Season the dressing with a little diced anchovy to taste. Cook ½ cup dried navy beans until very tender. Drain well and marinate in the dressing overnight. To assemble the salad, use 3 (3.9-ounce) cans Spanish albacore tuna, including the can juices. Use only ¾ pound of fresh pescine or ½ pound dried penne. Use the same amount of green onions as above or substitute a favorite fresh herb. Highest recommendation for a meal of a salad!

MENU FOR A SUMMER EVENING

■ Roasted Breads (page 16) with White Bean Hummus (page 24)

■ Pasta with Seafood (page 99) (choose the best smoked or grilled fish you can afford — do not use the bean variation), served on a bed of fresh arugula

■ Dark Chocolate Mousse (page 237), topped with Fresh Caramel Sauce (page 242) and accompanied with fresh fruit and berries.

PENNE WITH FRESH
FENNEL AND TUNA

◆◆◆

This recipe is just as good as the Pasta and Seafood (page 99), but, with its fresh fennel and golden raisins, it is not as versatile. Nevertheless, if you want a truly remarkable room-temperature pasta dish, make this recipe with 12 or 13 ounces of grilled fresh tuna or other firm-fleshed white fish. Cook the fish on the rare side, dress it in a little olive oil, and reserve for this salad. When it is time to assemble the dish, cut the fish in thin strips across the grain, or flake (depending on the fish and how well-cooked it is). Toss the fish with the pasta and other ingredients. If grilling fresh fish is out of the question, settle for the best canned tuna you can afford, and the dish will still be an impressive entrée for a warm-weather lunch or dinner. Serve it on a bed of fresh greens — arugula, if you have it, or Napa cabbage cut into a chiffonade (page 37). **PREPARE-AHEAD/SERVING NOTES:** This dish is best served immediately after it is made. However, you can successfully prep all the ingredients hours before serving, except for the fennel, which begins to turn brown soon after it is cut. If you are prepping ahead, just hold out the tuna and the fennel until right before you serve.

¾ cup extra virgin olive oil

¼ cup freshly squeezed lemon juice

3 tablespoons freshly squeezed orange juice

4 large cloves garlic, put through a garlic press

½ teaspoon red pepper flakes

¼ teaspoon salt

Pepper to taste

3¼ cups fresh fennel bulb, sliced thinly and cut into pieces no longer and no wider than 1 inch

2 (6.5-ounce) cans solid white tuna in oil, including all juices OR 13 ounces grilled fresh tuna or other firm white fish (see notes above)

1 cup golden raisins, steeped in boiling water and drained

⅔ pound dried penne pasta

1 tablespoon extra virgin olive oil

⅔ cup pine nuts, lightly toasted

1 cup green onions, very thinly sliced

3 tablespoons finely minced parsley

TO TOP (OPTIONAL):

Fresh tomato, juiced, seeded, and minced

Imported black olives, pitted and finely chopped

Paper-thin slices of orange and lemon

In a large bowl, whisk together olive oil, lemon juice, orange juice, garlic, red pepper flakes, salt, and pepper to taste. Fold in fennel bulb, tuna and its juices, and raisins.

Cook the pasta until very tender (you will need to stir the penne frequently to keep it from sticking together). When pasta is done, rinse with cold water, drain well, toss with olive oil, and let cool to room temperature. When cooled, fold into the other ingredients, along with pine nuts, green onions, and parsley. If you are using grilled fresh tuna, you may need to add a little extra olive oil to the dish. Spoon into a serving dish and top with any or all of the garnishes, if desired. Serve immediately at room temperature.

MAKES 12 CUPS.

WARM-WEATHER PASTA

■ Roasted Breads (page 16) with Purée of Highly Seasoned Tofu (page 20)

■ Penne with Fresh Tuna and Fennel (page 101)

■ Summer Green Beans and Tomatoes (page 54)

■ Fresh strawberries served with Pasta & Co.'s Chocolate Sauce (page 241)

Makings
for green
salads:
here is
where
cold and
crisp
come in.

Unlike our room-temperature foods with their make-ahead ease, green salads need to be crispy-cold and eaten immediately after they are tossed together. ■ Over the years, we have formulated the makings for several green-salad classics. Every one of them has become a best seller: The Greens Dressing, a basic but bold and balanced vinaigrette; The Big Blue, a thick blue-cheese dressing made with Gorgonzola; Pasta & Co. Mayo, as good for making coleslaw as for dressing celery root; Easy Caesar, a clone of that timeless taste of egg, anchovy, garlic, and extra virgin olive oil; and Pasta & Co. Croutons, a dazzling use for stale bread. ■ We think you will find good use for all of these recipes.

THE GREENS DRESSING

Years ago, we aspired to make a vinaigrette that would be well-balanced yet full-bodied. The mixture of herbs we finally chose to season the vinaigrette worked so well that we now package and sell it as the "House Herbs" — a blend of basil, oregano, marjoram, thyme, rosemary, peppercorns, allspice, and (take note) no salt. **PREPARE-AHEAD/SERVING NOTES:** The dressing keeps well for weeks in the refrigerator.

2 to 4 tablespoons red wine vinegar, depending on your taste and what kind of salad greens you are using

2 tablespoons Pasta & Co. House Herbs OR your choice of mixed dried herbs OR up to ½ cup mixed fresh herbs, finely minced

1 clove garlic, put through a garlic press

1 teaspoon grainy mustard

¾ cup extra virgin olive oil

Whisk together vinegar, herbs, garlic, and mustard. Drizzle in olive oil while continuing to whisk.

MAKES ABOUT 1 CUP.

THE GREENS THEMSELVES

Many uncommon varieties of salad greens have become popular in recent years. Most of them are still too perishable to find with any dependability at a grocery store, but if you have any backyard garden whatsoever, do grow a few plants of arugula, oak leaf lettuce, mizuna, and any other of the less common greens that strike your fancy. The only trick is to keep slugs and snails from eating the tender green shoots before you do.

ABOUT OLIVE OIL

Buying and using olive oil is much like buying and using wine. Since good olive oils can differ widely in flavor and intensity, one selection may not meet all cooking needs. With experience, cooks come to favor particular olive oils for particular dishes. In most of our recipes, we do not specify a particular brand, but rather just "pure" or "extra virgin."

As a general rule, if you are cooking with the oil, we suggest pure olive oil. This is a lesser-quality oil and is usually priced accordingly. If, however, the oil is to be used in a marinade, dressing, or sauce, where the flavor of the olive oil is critical to the taste of the dish, use extra virgin. In addition, if you are just gently heating the oil (as is done in Hot Olives, page 28, or when tossing pasta with olive oil), use extra virgin. The term "extra virgin" describes oil taken from the first cold pressing of the olives. Extra virgin oils have the lowest level of acidity and the highest level of flavor.

But remember, there is great variation even among extra virgin oils. Buy in the smallest quantities available. Taste before buying whenever possible. And experiment with the oils. Generally, the best olive oils are imported. In recent years, Italian and French oils have become almost prohibitively priced. Spanish, Greek, and Israeli oils have represented better values. Also, California oils have found a following. Some of these oils have very full-bodied flavors that can dominate a dish. This can be desirable as, in the Black Olive and Tomato Salsa (page 193), which depends on the very distinctive flavor of Santa Barbara Olive Oil for its character. However, should you find an oil too full-bodied for a particular dish, cut it with some good-quality vegetable oil.

PASTA & CO. MAYO

We created this recipe originally to dress our coleslaw (page 43 of *Pasta & Co. — The Cookbook*). It is such a tasty mayonnaise, however, that we have found numerous other uses for it. Try spreading the mayo on turkey sandwiches or tossing it with julienned and blanched celery root. **PREPARE-AHEAD/SERVING NOTES:** The mayonnaise keeps for months refrigerated. **ESSENTIAL GEAR:** Electric food processor

1 tablespoon sugar

1½ teaspoons salt

¾ teaspoon coarse black pepper

3 tablespoons cooking oil

2 tablespoons extra virgin olive oil

1 tablespoon Chinese hot oil

3 tablespoons balsamic vinegar

1½ teaspoons prepared mustard

1½ cups mayonnaise — homemade or Best Foods brand

In a food processor bowl equipped with a steel blade, combine sugar, salt, black pepper, cooking oil, olive oil, hot oil, vinegar, and mustard. Process to blend. Then add mayonnaise and process until it is folded into the other ingredients.

Decant and refrigerate until ready to use.

MAKES ABOUT 2 CUPS.

THE BIG BLUE

•••

O ne food critic described this blue-cheese dressing as "chunky enough to serve as a dip." We concede that the dressing violates everything we all strive for in regard to fats in our diet. If you find it intolerably thick and rich, thin to taste with red wine vinegar and extra virgin olive oil. **PREPARE-AHEAD/SERVING NOTES:** Dressing keeps for at least a month refrigerated.

1 cup sour cream

1 cup Best Foods brand mayonnaise

½ cup buttermilk

6 ounces Gorgonzola cheese (not too ripe), coarsely crumbled

1 large clove garlic, finely minced

1 teaspoon coarsely ground black pepper

¼ teaspoon salt

Gently fold all ingredients together. Refrigerate to store.

MAKES 3 CUPS.

THE PASTA & CO. BURGER

On each serving plate, make a bed of salad greens (leaf lettuce, romaine, or raw spinach is a good choice). Top with a sizzling hamburger patty and piles of sliced raw mushrooms, chopped red onion, and ripe tomatoes. Finalize with a dollop of the Big Blue. (Catsup is optional.) What calories you save from not eating a hamburger bun you can more than make up for with the Big Blue.

EASY CAESAR DRESSING

Caesar salad is a perennial favorite that usually comes with its own very personal ritual of preparation. With all due respect to this time-honored creation, here is a dressing that makes a Caesar salad far better than most and has the advantage of keeping in your refrigerator for up to a month. Once the dressing is made, all you need worry about is cold and crisp romaine (please, without too many of those tough center veins), croutons (dependably made with the recipe on page 110 or purchased from Pasta & Co.), and a generous supply of Parmesan cheese (preferably Parmigiano Reggiano, page 35) to grate over the top. **PREPARE-AHEAD/SERVING NOTES:** Prepare at your convenience, and store refrigerated for up to a month. **ESSENTIAL GEAR:** Electric food processor

1 cup Best Foods brand mayonnaise

9 anchovies, rinsed and drained

1½ tablespoons garlic, peeled and coarsely chopped

¼ cup plus 1 tablespoon freshly squeezed lemon juice

1 tablespoon sherry wine vinegar

1 teaspoon grainy mustard

½ cup extra virgin olive oil

1 teaspoon Tabasco or Jardine's brand Texas Champagne

25 grinds black pepper, coarsely ground

Place mayonnaise, anchovies, garlic, lemon juice, vinegar, and mustard in a food processor bowl equipped with a steel blade. Process until anchovies and garlic are puréed. With motor running, drizzle in olive oil and Tabasco. Stir in black pepper. Decant into a storage jar and refrigerate until needed.

MAKES ABOUT 2 CUPS — ENOUGH FOR AT LEAST 2 HEADS OF ROMAINE.

PASTA & CO. CROUTONS

••••

Nothing, it seems, disappoints customers more than if we are out of these croutons. Regulars buy them as much for snacking as for salads. Here is how we make them. **PREPARE-AHEAD/SERVING NOTES:** Since the croutons keep well a couple of weeks in a covered jar, we suggest making a fairly large batch.

½ cup pure olive oil

1 tablespoon finely minced garlic

1 tablespoon Pasta & Co. House Herbs or your choice of dried herbs and cracked pepper

2 quarts day-old bread, crusts trimmed and cut into ½-inch to ¾-inch cubes

Preheat oven to 425°F.

Mix together oil, garlic, and herbs in a large bowl. Add bread to mixture and *immediately* and *quickly* toss with the oil mixture to evenly coat (if you dawdle here, you will not get an even distribution of the oil mixture on the bread).

Spread bread in a single layer on a cookie sheet and bake for 5 minutes. Stir croutons and bake for another 5 minutes. Repeat process until croutons are toasted and golden. Cooking time will vary. Watch closely. These burn easily.

MAKES 8 CUPS.

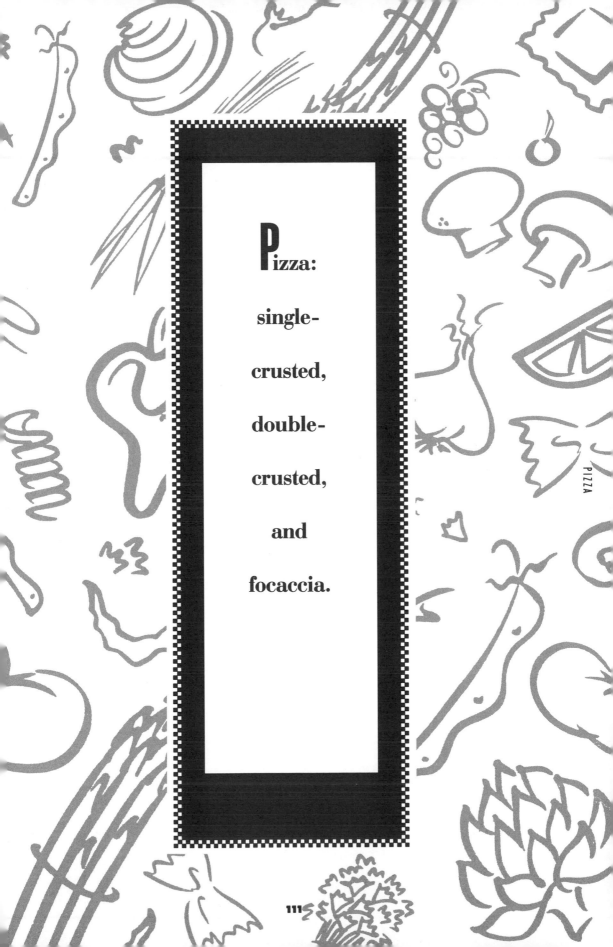

Pizza:

single-
crusted,
double-
crusted,
and
focaccia.

We at Pasta & Co. became intrigued with pizza when one of our former managers, Bonita Atkins, convinced us that making pizza was a snap using her dough recipe. We were so impressed that we started making and selling Bonita's pizza dough. Naturally, with all that pizza dough around, we had to try our hand at toppings. ■ The next few recipes — especially the double-crusted pizzas and the focaccia — are prime material for appetizers, buffets, and picnics. While day-old pizza is not necessarily desirable, it tends to be wonderfully tasty for at least a couple of hours after it leaves the oven. So there is no need to fuss about serving time.

PIZZA WITH FRESH SPINACH, TOMATOES, AND BRAISED ONIONS

•••

....

s much as we still love domestic mozzarella or provolone cheese hanging in strings from our pizza slice, we have found that other cheeses do make inspired pizza toppings. In this recipe, we use Fontina (the best you are inclined to afford) to set off the taste of browned onions, garlic, and fresh spinach. Hardy greens, such as spinach or arugula, by the way, "wilt" wonderfully on a pizza crust. The trick is to make them the bottom layer (well-covered with cheese) so that the other ingredients protect them from too much charring. **PREPARE-AHEAD/SERVING NOTES:** As with all our pizza recipes, allow plenty of time for the frozen pizza dough to thaw (about 4 hours at room temperature). The finished pizza is at its prime for as long as 2 hours after baking. **ESSENTIAL GEAR:** Heavy-weight cookie sheet, pizza pan, or pizza stone. **CAUTION:** If you make your dough into a thicker and smaller pizza than the 13 inches called for in the recipe (and some people do prefer a crust thicker than ⅛ inch to ¼ inch), you will want to reduce the amount of toppings accordingly.

2 tablespoons pure olive oil

3 cups onions, sliced and separated into rings

2 teaspoons Pasta & Co. House Herbs OR your choice of dried or fresh herbs to taste

1 teaspoon sugar

5 cloves garlic, put through a garlic press

½ teaspoon red pepper flakes

1 pound Pasta & Co. frozen pizza dough, thawed in bag and at room temperature

Cornmeal

1 teaspoon pure olive oil

2 cups fresh spinach leaves, washed, dried, stemmed, and cut into a rough chiffonade (page 37)

1¼ cups fresh tomato, chopped into ¼-inch dice, including about ½ the juices

Optional: 3 kabanossi or pepperoni sausages, finely chopped OR ½ pound Italian sausage, cooked, drained of grease, and crumbled

4 ounces Fontina cheese, grated (Swiss Fontina is adequate; Italian is better.)

3 tablespoons freshly grated Parmesan or Romano cheese

Preheat oven to 500°F.

In a medium sauté pan, heat the 2 tablespoons olive oil and add onions, herbs, and sugar. Cook over low heat until onions begin to get very brown and caramelized. Add garlic and red pepper flakes and continue to cook for about 30 seconds. Remove from heat.

Press pizza dough down to a thickness of about ½ inch. Lightly dust pan with cornmeal. Place dough on prepared pan and press or roll with a rolling pin to a thickness of ¼ inch to ⅛ inch. You should have a diameter of roughly 13 inches. Do not be concerned if dough resists. Stop for a few seconds, then continue pressing. Be assured. It will work. And do not fret if the dough is not a perfect round or rectangle. This is meant to be rustic food. Brush the dough with the 1 teaspoon olive oil. Top with spinach, sautéed onions, tomatoes, and meats (if desired). Sprinkle Fontina and Parmesan over everything, being sure to cover spinach and tomatoes.

Bake on lowest shelf at 500°F for 10 minutes. Check for doneness: toppings and crust should be golden. Remove to a cooling rack and let sit for about 10 minutes before cutting.

MAKES ONE 13-INCH PIZZA TO SERVE 2 TO 4.

SAVE YOUR OLIVE OIL

For a long time we thought it was necessary to oil the baking sheet or pizza pan before sprinkling it with cornmeal and laying on the dough. Not so. Cornmeal alone is enough to keep the dough from sticking.

PASTA & CO.'S INCREDIBLE PIZZA DOUGH

This Pasta & Co. frozen pizza dough that Bonita taught us to make is truly remarkable. It stands up to freezing, thawing, rebaking, reheating, and even to inexperienced pizza bakers. Recipes in this chapter all call for balls of this dough. Though we are hopelessly biased, feel free to substitute your own choice of dough. (Bonita also teaches classes in making pizza dough.)

PIZZA: UPGRADED OR EXPLOITED?

Pizza, perhaps more than any other food, is symbolic of what has happened to cooking in America over the past decade. The ordinary pizza pie underwent an extraordinary transformation, somewhere between upgrading and exploitation.

Yes, many of us learned what really good pizza crust tasted like. We also tasted what fresh tomatoes and herbs and other unadulterated makings could do that the average pizza sauce could not. We experienced a marvelous opportunity for experimental cooking. But soon, pizza came to mean barbecued chicken and duck sausage and caviar; for a short while, all our mouths watered for "designer pizza."

Now, pizza, like most of the other foods we "played with" over the last decade, has returned to being a bit more sensible. Fun and extravagant toppings still have their place, but a topping's perennial appeal comes from summery-tasting, rustic ingredients that are indigenous to pizza's origins.

PIZZA WITH MARINATED
FRESH MOZZARELLA

◆◆◆

. . . .

Essential to this pizza is the Marinated Fresh Mozzarella on page 22. It is the gutsy marinade of good olive oil, a bounty of garlic, red pepper, and (if you choose) good-quality anchovies that makes for a memorably flavored pizza. Using fresh mozzarella cheese (instead of the stringy-textured mozzarella that has become synonymous with American pizza) makes this pizza so deceptively light you almost cannot stop eating it. Do not squander it on the kids. This one is for adults. **PREPARE-AHEAD/SERVING NOTES:** Be sure to let cheese marinate for at least two days before making the pizza, and allow sufficient time for the frozen pizza dough to thaw (about 4 hours at room temperature). The pizza is at its prime for as long as 2 hours after baking. **ESSENTIAL GEAR:** Heavy-weight cookie sheet, pizza pan, or pizza stone. **CAUTION:** See page 113.

1¼ cups marinated fresh mozzarella cheese (purchased or made according to recipe on page 22, if what you purchase does not have chopped anchovies in it, add them to taste)

1 pound Pasta & Co. frozen pizza dough, thawed in bag and at room temperature

Cornmeal

2 cups fresh spinach leaves or a combination of fresh spinach and basil leaves, washed, dried, stemmed, and cut into a rough chiffonade (page 37)

1¼ cups fresh tomato, chopped into ¼-inch dice, including about ½ the juices

⅓ cup imported black olives, any kind, pitted (see page 27) and roughly quartered

Optional: 2 Italian sausages, cooked, skinned, and crumbled

Parmigiano Reggiano, shaved (see page 35), or freshly grated Parmesan cheese (about 2 ounces)

Cut mozzarella into ¼-inch–thick slices. Reserve. Preheat oven to 500°F.

Lightly dust pizza pan with cornmeal and prepare pizza dough as in Pizza with Fresh Spinach, Tomatoes, and Braised Onions (page 113). Then, with a pastry brush, coat pizza dough with the cheese marinade, being sure to get ample garlic, herbs, and anchovies onto the dough. Layer spinach, tomatoes, olives, and sausage (if desired) over dough. Top with mozzarella, again making sure to include as much of the marinade seasoning as possible with the cheese. Finish with a generous layer of Parmigiano Reggiano shaved with a carrot peeler, as on page 35.

Bake on lowest shelf at 500°F for 10 minutes. Check for doneness: Toppings and crust should be golden. Remove to a cooling rack and let cool for about 10 minutes before serving.

MAKES ONE 13-INCH PIZZA TO SERVE 2 TO 4.

DOUBLE-CRUSTED PIZZA
WITH FRESH SPINACH,
COPPA, OLIVES, AND FETA
◆◆◆

. . . .

The following two pizzas are two of the most dazzling and versatile in our reper-toire. Bonita Atkins, who formulated our pizza dough, introduced these double-crusted wonders to us. Incredibly, this is an easy recipe, especially if you use frozen pizza dough. And indisputably, it is a recipe you will want to use over and over: warm out of the oven, at room temperature hours or even days later, for an ap-petizer, for buffet luncheons and dinners, for picnics, and with many variations on the filling. **PREPARE-AHEAD/SERVING NOTES:** The filling can be prepared up to a day ahead of using. Allow at least 4 hours at room temperature for the frozen dough to thaw. The pizza itself needs to sit approximately 1 hour after it comes out of the oven for ease of serving, and it is excellent served day-old at room tempera-ture. **ESSENTIAL GEAR:** Medium-weight cookie sheet or pizza pan (since this pizza cooks longer at a lower temperature, do not use the same heavy-weight pans called for in the single-crusted pizzas)

1 teaspoon pure olive oil

1 cup coarsely chopped red onion

3 cloves garlic, finely minced

2 teaspoons oregano

1 cup ricotta cheese

2 eggs

4 ounces (about 3 cups) spinach leaves, trimmed, washed, dried, and coarsely chopped

1 pound coppa (or other spicy Italian salami), thinly sliced and cut into juliénne

½ pound feta cheese, crumbled

¼ pound mozzarella cheese, grated

1 cup kalamata olives, pitted (see page 27)

¼ cup freshly grated Parmesan cheese

1 tablespoon finely chopped parsley

Salt and pepper to taste

2 (l-pound) balls Pasta & Co. frozen pizza dough, thawed in bag and at room temperature

Cornmeal

Additional pure olive oil

1 egg, lightly beaten

½ teaspoon basil

To make filling, heat the 1 teaspoon olive oil over medium heat in a small sauté pan. Add onion, garlic, and oregano. Cook until onion is translucent. Remove from heat and let cool. In a large bowl, whisk together ricotta and eggs. Fold in spinach,

117

coppa, feta, mozzarella, olives, Parmesan, and parsley. Add cooled onion mixture. Taste for salt and pepper.

Preheat oven to 350°F.

Lightly sprinkle cornmeal over the baking sheet. Place one of the balls of dough on the prepared baking sheet and press or roll into a ½-inch–thick round. Then press or roll into a 13-inch roughly shaped circle, about ¼ inch to ⅛ inch thick. Brush dough lightly with additional olive oil. Spoon filling onto dough, leaving a 1-inch rim all around. Press or roll second ball of dough into another 13-inch circle. Brush edges of the first circle with egg. Place second circle of dough over the filling and pinch edges of the two rounds together securely (as you would a pie crust). Brush top of crust with additional olive oil and sprinkle with basil. With scissors, cut six small air vents into crust.

Bake at 350°F on bottom shelf of oven for 50 minutes or until filling begins to bubble through vents and crust is golden brown. Let cool on a rack for at least 30 minutes before cutting.

MAKES 16 APPETIZER-SIZE WEDGES.

DOUBLE-CRUSTED PIZZA WITH FRESH SPINACH, SAUSAGE, SUN-DRIED TOMATOES, FONTINA, AND OLIVES

◆◆◆

. . . .

See notes to previous recipe, page 117.

1 cup ricotta cheese

2 eggs

4 ounces (about 3 cups) spinach leaves, trimmed, washed, dried, and coarsely chopped

¾ cup sliced green onions

2 tablespoons finely chopped parsley

3 cloves garlic, finely minced

½ pound Fontina cheese, grated or crumbled (Swiss Fontina is fine)

¼ pound mozzarella cheese, grated

⅓ cup grated Parmesan cheese

1¼ cups Pasta & Co. Marinated Black Olives (purchased or made according to recipe on page 26), quartered

1 cup sun-dried tomatoes, drained and julienned ("homemade" — see page 86 — is fine)

1½ pounds Isernio hot Italian sausage, cooked, drained, cooled, and crumbled into ½-inch pieces

Salt and pepper to taste

2 (1-pound) balls Pasta & Co. frozen pizza dough, thawed in bag and at room temperature

Cornmeal

Pure olive oil

1 egg, lightly beaten

½ teaspoon basil

To make filling, whisk together ricotta and eggs in a large bowl. Add spinach, green onions, parsley, garlic, Fontina, mozzarella, Parmesan, olives, sun-dried tomatoes, and cooled sausage. Salt and pepper to taste.

Preheat oven to 350°F.

Lightly sprinkle cornmeal over a medium-weight (not steel) baking sheet. Place one of the balls of dough on the prepared baking sheet and press or roll into a 13-inch circle, about ¼ inch to ⅛ inch thick. Brush dough lightly with olive oil. Spoon filling onto dough, leaving a 1-inch rim all around. Press or roll second ball of dough into another 13-inch circle. Brush edges of the first circle with egg. Place second circle of dough over the filling, pinching edges of the two rounds together securely (as you would a pie crust). Brush top of crust with additional olive oil and sprinkle with basil. With scissors, cut six small air vents in top crust.

Bake at 350°F on bottom shelf of oven for 50 minutes or until filling begins to bubble through vents and crust is golden brown. Let cool on a rack for at least 30 minutes before cutting.

MAKES 16 APPETIZER-SIZE WEDGES.

FOCACCIA WITH SHALLOTS
AND HOUSE HERBS

◆◆◆

. . . .

There seem to be infinite versions of the flatbread Italians call focaccia. We have quite arbitrarily decided that pizza has a thin crust; focaccia, on the other hand, though it uses the same dough, is allowed to rise to make a chewy, thicker bread. The result — again, using our "incredible" frozen pizza dough — compares favorably with any focaccia on the market that we have tasted. It is easy, handsome, and delectable all at once.

For an impressive appetizer, serve this focaccia warm from the oven with a good red wine and nothing else. Your small effort will be rewarded. **PREPARE-AHEAD/ SERVING NOTES:** Be sure to allow enough time for the dough to thaw thoroughly (4 hours at room temperature) and for it to rise (about 1½ hours). Plan to serve the focaccia within a few hours of baking. If you need to hold it longer, reheat before serving. **ESSENTIAL GEAR:** Heavy 12-inch ovenproof skillet

1 pound Pasta & Co. frozen pizza dough, thawed in bag and at room temperature	**½ teaspoon Pasta & Co. House Herbs OR 1 to 2 tablespoons coarsely chopped fresh herbs**
Cornmeal	**¼ teaspoon salt (omit if you use the olives)**
Olive oil	**½ teaspoon coarsely ground black pepper**
½ cup peeled and sliced shallots	
Optional: ⅓ cup imported black or green olives, pitted (page 27) and coarsely chopped	**5 tablespoons extra virgin olive oil**

Sprinkle a breadboard lightly with cornmeal. Roll out dough to form an 8-inch circle about ½ inch thick. Brush lightly with olive oil, cover with a cloth tea towel, and let rise 1½ hours in a warm spot.

In a small bowl, toss shallots, olives (if desired), herbs, salt (if olives are not used), and black pepper with 4 tablespoons of the extra virgin olive oil, making sure to separate the shallots into rings. Reserve.

Preheat oven to 425°F.

When dough is nearly 1 inch thick, place a heavy 12-inch ovenproof skillet over high heat for 1 minute. Add remaining 1 tablespoon of extra virgin olive oil. When oil is shimmering, remove from heat and carefully lay the dough in the pan. Using your fingertips, make indentations in dough. Spread with shallot mixture and olives (if desired). Bake in upper third of the oven at 425°F for about 20 minutes, or until golden brown. When done, remove focaccia from pan and let cool on a rack. Cut into wedges to serve.

MAKES 8 TO 12 WEDGES.

Soups:

with

cream

and

without.

At Pasta & Co. stores, soup-making is a daily event. Each store kitchen makes an average of two soups a day year-round. Our soups are all sturdy ones; with only a little care, they rewarm without a hitch. And while some of our most legendary ones, such as Wild Rice (page 123) or Sherried Brie and Mushroom (page 124), are rich with cream, we also have an impressive collection of soups that are relatively low-fat.

WILD RICE SOUP

◆◆◆

. . . .

This is the queen of our soups — one we have made for years; one that is a perennial favorite despite its extravagant, calorie-loaded ingredients; and one that customers rely on for everyday eating as well as for special events. **PREPARE-AHEAD/SERVING NOTES:** The soup keeps well for days refrigerated. Some quality is lost in freezing.

1½ cups water

½ teaspoon salt

½ cup uncooked wild rice

3 tablespoons butter

2 small leeks, split lengthwise, then quartered and thoroughly rinsed of all grit

1½ cups mushrooms (about ¼ pound), ends trimmed and halved

1 tablespoon flour

¾ teaspoon basil

¾ teaspoon salt

¾ teaspoon freshly cracked black pepper

¼ teaspoon ground nutmeg

½ cup dry sherry

1 tablespoon lemon juice

1 quart plus ½ cup homemade or canned chicken stock, heated

¼ teaspoon Tabasco or Jardine's brand Texas Champagne

1 cup (about ¼ pound) carrots, peeled and grated

2 cups cream, heated — do not boil

In a heavy, flat-bottomed saucepan with a tight-fitting lid, bring water and salt to a boil over high heat. Add rice to boiling water. When water returns to boil, cover and reduce heat. Simmer 30 to 45 minutes or until rice is barely tender (it will continue to cook in the soup). Check rice a couple times during its cooking to make sure it does not cook dry. Add more liquid if necessary. Set aside when done.

In a 4-quart kettle, sauté leeks in the butter over medium heat until limp. Add mushrooms and cook briefly. Add flour and basil, salt, black pepper, and nutmeg, making sure flour thoroughly combines with butter. Do *not* brown this roux mixture. Add sherry and lemon juice. Stir thoroughly so no lumps form. Stir in hot stock and Tabasco.

Drain off any liquid that remains in the rice. Add cooked rice to the soup. Bring soup to simmer and cook approximately 15 minutes. Add grated carrots and hot cream. Simmer another 5 minutes.

MAKES 8 CUPS.

SHERRIED BRIE AND
MUSHROOM SOUP
♦♦♦

A nother rich and festive soup, this may well be the best mushroom soup you will ever taste. We highly recommend it as a first-course soup for an "event" of a meal. **PREPARE-AHEAD/SERVING NOTES:** The soup keeps well refrigerated for several days. Reheat over low heat and be sure not to boil. Freeze only as a last resort.

2 cups dry sherry

1½ tablespoons butter

1 pound mushrooms, sliced

½ cup shallots, peeled, trimmed, and minced

1 tablespoon freshly squeezed lemon juice

2 tablespoons flour

1 quart homemade beef stock or canned beef broth (we like Sexton brand beef consommé)

1 pound Brie cheese, trimmed of its rind and roughly torn into 2-inch pieces (it is easy to trim rind if you first place cheese in the freezer for an hour or two)

1¾ cups half-and-half

½ teaspoon pepper

½ cup snipped chives, for garnish

Additional salt and pepper to taste

In a small saucepan, boil sherry until it is reduced to 1 cup. Reserve. In a 4-quart saucepan, melt butter. Stir in mushrooms, shallots, and lemon juice. Cook over medium-high heat, tossing the mixture constantly for about 4 minutes. Remove from heat and stir in flour, blending until incorporated. Return mixture to the heat and stir in beef stock and reserved sherry. Bring mixture to a boil. Reduce heat and simmer about 15 minutes. Add trimmed Brie, stirring until the cheese melts. Add half-and-half and the ½ teaspoon pepper and continue to simmer without boiling for 5 minutes. Salt and pepper to taste.

Garnish with chives to serve.

MAKES 8 CUPS.

SOUPS

SMOKED-TROUT CHOWDER

◆◆◆

This is the kind of soup to serve on Christmas or New Year's Eve (an alternative to the James Beard ritual of oyster stew). We originally made the soup with heavy cream; now we use half-and-half — a small sign of the times. **PREPARE-AHEAD/SERVING NOTES:** The soup holds in the refrigerator for several days, but rewarm very gently so as not to overcook the fish. Ideally, make the soup up to the point of adding the white fish. Then, immediately before serving, finish off with the two kinds of fish and fresh dill. Freeze only as a last resort.

3 (9.6-ounce) cans S&W brand clam juice

¼ cup dry white wine

¼ cup butter

⅔ cup onion, cut into ⅜-inch dice

⅓ cup celery, cut into ⅜-inch dice

⅓ cup carrot, cut into ⅜-inch dice

3 tablespoons flour

½ teaspoon thyme

¼ teaspoon black pepper

¼ teaspoon white pepper

1 small bay leaf

½ pound white boiling potatoes, unpeeled, cut into ⅜-inch dice

2 cups half-and-half

¼ pound white fish, such as cod, cut into ½-inch pieces

3 ounces smoked trout, trimmed of skin and bones

1 tablespoon chopped fresh dill

Boil clam juice and wine together for 3 minutes. Set aside. In a soup pot, melt butter. Add onions, celery, and carrot and sauté until vegetables are soft. Add flour, thyme, black pepper, white pepper, and bay leaf and stir 1 minute, being very careful not to let the roux burn. Add reduced broth/wine mixture and bring to a simmer.

Add potatoes and cook until they are tender (stir often or potatoes will stick). Carefully monitor potatoes for overcooking. While potatoes cook, heat half-and-half.

When potatoes are tender, add half-and-half and white fish. Simmer slowly over low heat for 10 minutes or just until fish is barely cooked. Add smoked trout and dill. Remove from heat, taste for salt (it probably needs some), and serve.

MAKES 7 CUPS.

VICHYSSOISE

◆◆◆

....

Hardly anyone puts vichyssoise on their menu these days. It is an indulgently rich soup, but when done right, it is one that awakes cravings even years after you have had your first bowl. It follows a deceptively simple formula. Good-quality chicken stock is essential (Swanson's canned stock is adequate — see page 127), as is the balance between potato and cream and the right amount of cayenne, nutmeg, and fresh chives. Hot or cold, vichyssoise makes an exquisite first course or a meal by itself with crusty warm bread, sweet butter, and wine. Repent another day if necessary, but do treat yourself to this soup. (We did, at least, eliminate the butter from the recipe.) **PREPARE-AHEAD/SERVING NOTES:** If serving the soup chilled, allow sufficient time to get it very cold (4 to 6 hours). The soup keeps refrigerated for at least three days and rewarms over low heat without a flaw (just stir occasionally so that the puréed potato does not stick). **ESSENTIAL GEAR:** Electric food processor

see page 127

2 teaspoons olive oil

3 small leeks (white parts only), sliced and well-washed

5 medium White Rose potatoes (approximately 1¾ pounds), peeled and thinly sliced

2½ cups homemade chicken stock or canned chicken broth

2 cups half-and-half

2 cups cream

1 teaspoon salt

½ teaspoon white pepper

Pinch freshly grated nutmeg

⅛ teaspoon cayenne

½ cup snipped chives, for garnish

Heat olive oil in a large saucepan over medium heat. Add leeks and cook until soft. Add potatoes and chicken stock. Bring mixture to a simmer and cook, stirring occasionally, until potatoes are tender (about 15 minutes). Ladle mixture into the work bowl of a food processor equipped with a steel blade. Purée until smooth. Decant into a large bowl. Whisk in half-and-half, cream, salt, white pepper, nutmeg, and cayenne. Refrigerate until very cold or serve hot.

Spoon soup into serving bowls, topping each portion with chives.

MAKES 8 CUPS.

A GRAND SOUP SUPPER

- Marinated Beef Tenderloin, served on a bed of fresh arugula and roasted bell peppers (page 34)
- Big bowls of Vichyssoise (page 126), served steamy hot or icy cold
- Warm bread with sweet butter
- Italian Shortbread with Almonds, Brandy, and Lemon (page 246)

CANNED CHICKEN BROTH

The regrettable truth is that if we insisted on wonderfully brewed homemade stocks for our recipes, few of them would ever get made. If you have time, definitely make and use your own stocks. If you do not have time, be assured that canned broths will work satisfactorily in most recipes. Be aware, however, that canned broths tend to be salty — especially when used in reductions. Season accordingly.

SWEET PEA SOUP

This clever soup makes frozen peas taste as sweet and delicate as fresh ones. Use it in spring and summer when you are hankering for the taste of fresh asparagus soup but want to spend neither the time nor the money to make it. This Sweet Pea Soup is easy to make, especially if you take advantage of the prewashed fresh spinach available now at most grocery stores. (Just be sure you are getting dark green, small to medium-size leaves, not the yellowed, overgrown ones that sometimes are packed for our presumed convenience.) Leaf-lettuce leaves are an acceptable substitute, but make for a shallower flavor. **PREPARE-AHEAD/SERVING NOTES:** The soup reheats well, so you can make it a day ahead of serving, but do use care. High heat or long periods of heat ruin the soup's pale green color. **ESSENTIAL GEAR:** Electric food processor

⅓ cup butter

1 cup coarsely chopped onion

1 tablespoon flour

3¼ cups homemade chicken stock or canned chicken broth

1 (10-ounce) package frozen peas

2 cups packed fresh spinach leaves, washed, stemmed, and dried OR 3 ounces frozen chopped spinach

½ teaspoon (heaping or to taste) hot curry powder

½ teaspoon salt, or to taste

¼ teaspoon white pepper, or to taste

1 cup half-and-half, heated

¼ to ½ teaspoon lemon zest

Optional: Fresh mint leaves, to top

In a 2-quart saucepan, melt butter. Add onion and sauté until soft. Stir in flour and cook over low heat for a couple of minutes, being careful not to burn. Whisk in chicken broth and bring to a boil, stirring flour off the bottom of the pan. Add peas, spinach, curry powder, salt, and white pepper. Simmer a couple of minutes. Decant soup into a food processor bowl equipped with a steel blade. Purée briefly. Return to saucepan and add heated half-and-half. Season with lemon zest to taste. Top with mint leaves, if desired.

MAKES 5 CUPS.

TOMATO CHEDDAR SOUP

This is one of our favorite homey soups. Words are superfluous. Try it once, and you will make it again and again. **PREPARE-AHEAD/SERVING NOTES:** One of this soup's many virtues is that it freezes well. So make a big batch. Your family and guests will thank you.

3 tablespoons butter

½ cup onion, roughly chopped into ½-inch pieces

1 (28-ounce) can Paradiso brand pear tomatoes in juice, chopped into ¼-inch pieces, including all juices

1¼ cups chicken stock, homemade or canned

1¼ cups water

½ cup sour cream

¼ teaspoon white pepper

7 ounces sharp Cheddar cheese, grated

Salt and freshly cracked pepper to taste

In a 3-quart saucepan, melt butter over medium heat. Add onions and sauté until soft. Add tomatoes and their juices, chicken stock, and water. Bring to simmer, then remove from heat. Let cool 10 minutes.

Add one-half of the sour cream. Whisk until well-blended, then add remaining sour cream. Stir in white pepper and cheese to blend. Salt and pepper to taste. Gently reheat to serve.

MAKES 6 CUPS.

CLAM CHOWDER
♦♦♦

. . . .

Granted, there are already more than enough versions of clam chowder. And now we have added another — one that we rank with the best. Note that it uses canned baby clams, a product we discovered when we first made clam sauce for sale in our stores. As a rule, this product has all the advantages of fresh baby steamer clams, without any of the hassle. If the clams appear sandy, rinse them well and run the juice through a paper coffee filter. **PREPARE-AHEAD/SERVING NOTES:** The soup keeps well for up to five days in the refrigerator. It also freezes well, especially in serving-size quantities.

4¼ cups canned clam juice

1 (10-ounce) can baby clams, including all juices

1¼ pounds white-skinned potatoes, washed, not peeled, and cut into ¼-inch dice

¾ cup celery, cut into ¼-inch dice

¾ cup carrot, peeled and cut into ¼-inch dice

¼ pound salt pork, trimmed of rind and coarsely cubed

2 cups onion (about 1 medium onion), peeled and cut into ¼-inch dice

⅔ cup flour

3 cups whole milk, heated

2 cups cream, heated

¼ cup finely chopped parsley

2 tablespoons butter

Salt and pepper to taste

Put clam juice in a 2-quart saucepan. Add drained juice from clams into the saucepan. Pick through clams and discard any bits of shell you may find. Reserve clams. Heat clam juice to a simmer. Add potatoes, celery, and carrot. Cook over medium heat until tender. Drain vegetables, reserving clam juice.

In a food processor bowl equipped with a steel blade, process the salt pork until very finely ground (or chop by hand until very, very fine). Place ground salt pork in a 4-quart saucepan. Heat over medium heat, add onion, and cook until onion is translucent. Add flour and cook, stirring, for 5 minutes, making sure flour does not brown. Add reserved clam juice and cook until smooth and thick. Fold in reserved vegetables, reserved clams, milk, cream, and parsley. Stir in butter and adjust seasoning.

MAKES 12 CUPS.

CHICKEN SOUP WITH
MACARONI
◆◆◆

We have lost count of how many chicken soups we tried, looking for the very best of that taste we crave when we are feeling a little under-the-weather. We finally settled on this recipe to give us the richly flavored stock we were seeking. **PREPARE-AHEAD/SERVING NOTES:** You can keep this soup in the refrigerator for days and reheat as you need. Freeze only as a last resort because of the vegetables and pasta (see Insert, page 132).

TO MAKE STOCK:

1 whole chicken, rinsed

3 quarts water

6 cups homemade chicken stock OR 1 (50-ounce) can chicken broth

1 tablespoon Lawry's brand seasoned salt

2 teaspoons sage

2 teaspoons thyme

1 teaspoon whole black peppercorns

1 bay leaf

3 stalks celery with tops, cut in 3 or 4 pieces

2 carrots, cut in 3 or 4 pieces

1 large onion, quartered

1 clove garlic, smashed

TO FINISH SOUP:

3 cups carrots, cut into ¼-inch slices

3 cups celery, cut into ¼-inch dice

2 cups onions, diced small, and 2 cloves garlic, minced, lightly browned together in small amount of olive oil

2 tablespoons Worcestershire sauce

½ to 1 teaspoon coarsely ground black pepper, to taste

½ pound tiny uncooked macaroni (about 1¾ cups — we use Federici Elbows No. 72)

SOUPS

Remove the fat from neck and tail cavities of chicken. With a cleaver or heavy chef's knife, break open backbone, chest cavity, and leg bones just enough to allow the bone marrow and juices to seep into soup (this is an old Chinese technique Jerry Malmevik recently incorporated into our soup-making operations).

Place chicken in a stockpot with water and chicken stock. Bring to a boil over high heat. As water begins to boil, skim off the scum that rises to the surface. Continue skimming until scum no longer forms. Add seasoned salt, sage, thyme, peppercorns, bay leaf, celery pieces, carrot pieces, onion, and garlic and simmer, covered, for about 30 minutes. The chicken will be done when you can pull the drumstick out of its socket.

Remove from heat. Remove chicken from stock and let sit until cool enough to handle. While chicken is cooling, strain stock, discard vegetables, wash the stockpot, and return stock to the clean pot. By this time you should be able to remove the chicken meat from the bones. Discard bones and skin and tear the meat into bite-size pieces. Reserve the meat.

Bring strained stock back to a simmer and add the diced carrots, celery, onion/garlic mixture, Worcestershire sauce, and black pepper. Simmer for 5 minutes. Add macaroni. Simmer 8 to 10 additional minutes, or until vegetables and macaroni are done. Taste for seasoning. Add reserved chicken and serve.

MAKES ABOUT 20 CUPS.

A NOTE ABOUT PASTA & SOUP

Chicken noodle soup is a nice idea, but we all know what happens to pasta — especially thin noodles — when it sits in liquid: It becomes soft as a soggy sponge, or worse.

If you really want "noodles" — long, eggy ribbons — in your soup, use fresh fettuccine noodles and add just enough for the meal to the boiling soup. Serve as soon as the noodles are cooked. (By the way, this can be a wonderfully low-calorie way of eating pasta. The Italians call it "en brodo," and tortellini or ravioli cooked similarly in broth is a long-time favorite.)

However, if you want a soup with pasta that you can reheat, we have found that a small, firm dried pasta made with 100% semolina flour is best. In the Chicken Soup with Macaroni (page 131), we use a good brand of tiny macaroni; in Chicken Soup with House Rice and Orzo (page 133) and Pasta & Co.'s Minestrone Genovese (page 135), we use the rice-shaped orzo.

CHICKEN SOUP WITH HOUSE RICE AND ORZO

◆◆◆

. . . .

This is a chicken soup dressy enough to serve to company, yet soothing enough to seemingly cure the common cold. It is also substantial enough to serve as luncheon or supper fare, served by itself with hot bread and lots of freshly grated Parmesan to top the soup. Do not be discouraged by the length of the recipe. It is not difficult. **PREPARE-AHEAD/SERVING NOTES:** The soup refrigerates well for up to five days and freezes without a flaw.

1 whole chicken, rinsed

3½ quarts water

6 cups homemade chicken stock OR 1 (49-ounce) can chicken broth

1 tablespoon Lawry's brand seasoned salt

2 teaspoons sage

2 teaspoons thyme

1 teaspoon whole black peppercorns

1 bay leaf

3 celery stalks with tops, cut in 3 or 4 pieces

2 carrots, cut in 3 or 4 pieces

1 large onion, quartered

1 clove garlic, smashed

2 tablespoons olive oil or butter

¾ cup Pasta & Co. House Rice (see House Rice Salad, page 57)

½ cup dry sherry

¼ cup butter

2 cups celery, cut into ½-inch dice

2 cups onions, cut into ½-inch dice

3 cloves garlic, finely minced

1 teaspoon basil

1 teaspoon oregano

½ teaspoon salt

½ teaspoon black pepper

¼ teaspoon African bird pepper or cayenne

½ cup fresh bread crumbs

½ cup finely chopped parsley

½ cup orzo

Freshly grated Parmesan or a wedge of Parmigiano Reggiano, for garnish

Remove the fat from neck and tail cavities of chicken. With a cleaver or heavy chef's knife, break open backbone, chest cavity, and leg bones as in the recipe for Chicken Soup with Macaroni (page 131).

Place chicken in a stockpot with water and chicken stock. Bring to a boil over high heat. As water begins to boil, skim off the scum that rises to the surface. Continue skimming until scum no longer forms. Add seasoned salt, sage, thyme, peppercorns, bay leaf, celery pieces, carrot pieces, onion, and garlic clove. Simmer, covered, for about 30 minutes. The chicken will be done when you can pull the drumstick out of its socket.

Remove from heat. Remove chicken from stock and let sit until cool enough to handle. While chicken is cooling, strain stock, discard vegetables, wash the stockpot, and return stock to the clean pot. Measure out 1 cup of the stock and set aside.

By this time you should be able to remove the chicken meat from the bones. Discard bones and skin and tear the meat into bite-size pieces. Reserve the meat.

Heat the 2 tablespoons olive oil or butter in a heavy 4-cup flat-bottomed saucepan. Add the House Rice and sauté over medium heat for 3 to 4 minutes. Add the reserved 1 cup of hot stock and the dry sherry. Bring mixture to a simmer, cover with a tight-fitting lid, and let rice cook for 35 minutes over lowest heat. After 35 minutes, remove saucepan from heat and let sit an additional 10 minutes, covered.

While rice is cooking, melt the ¼ cup butter in a large sauté pan and cook diced celery and onions over medium heat. When onions are translucent, add minced garlic and sauté 1 or 2 minutes longer. Stir in basil, oregano, salt, black pepper, African bird pepper, bread crumbs, and parsley. Sauté 1 or 2 minutes longer and remove from heat.

When rice has finished cooking, stir it into the vegetable-and-herb mixture and reserve.

Return stock to a simmer. Add orzo to the simmering stock and let simmer for 10 minutes. Test for doneness.

When orzo is done, add rice-and-vegetable mixture and the reserved chicken to the stockpot. Taste for seasoning.

Pass around a bowl of freshly grated Parmesan for garnish — or better yet, provide a wedge of Parmigiano Reggiano and a hand grater and let guests grate their own right into the hot soup.

MAKES 20 CUPS.

MINESTRONE GENOVESE

♦♦♦

This was the first soup Pasta & Co. ever sold. It is vegetarian, quite possibly the best vegetarian soup ever. We call it minestrone, yet it has little in common with those famed vegetable porridges distinguished by their rich, long-cooked flavors but appalling for their overcooked vegetables and pasta. By contrast, you will eat this soup for its precisely cooked vegetables and its heady flavor, which comes from seasoning with fresh basil, garlic, tomato, and olive oil, much like the French make their legendary *pistou*. **PREPARE-AHEAD/SERVING NOTES:** Since the beauty of this soup is in its perfectly cooked vegetables and vine-fresh flavors, this is not a freezer soup. Refrigerated, however, it will hold for up to five days.

⅓ to ½ cup basil leaves, washed, dried, and finely chopped

⅓ cup freshly grated Parmesan cheese

¼ cup tomato paste

3 cloves garlic, put through a garlic press

¼ cup extra virgin olive oil

½ cup orzo or melonseed pasta

½ cup freshly grated Romano cheese

6 cups water

2 teaspoons salt

2 cups carrots, peeled and cut into ¼-inch dice

1 cup onion, cut into ¼-inch dice

1 cup celery, cut into ¼-inch dice

2 cups red potatoes, skins on and cut into ½-inch dice

½ cup green bell pepper, cut into ¼-inch dice

½ cup zucchini, unpeeled, cut into ¼-inch dice

¼ cup best-quality unflavored bread crumbs

½ teaspoon hot paprika

10 grinds black pepper

Optional: Very small pinch saffron

2 cups water

1 (8-ounce) can kidney beans, well-rinsed and drained OR 3 cups fresh green beans, washed and cut diagonally into 1-inch pieces

1 (14.5-ounce) can S&W Diced Tomatoes in Rich Purée OR 2 cups fresh tomatoes, cut into ¼-inch pieces, including all juices (see Insert, page 136)

½ cup frozen peas or corn (add to soup frozen) — do *not* use if using fresh green beans, unless you incorporate fresh corn cut from the cob)

½ cup finely chopped parsley

Parmesan cheese, grated by hand at the table — Parmigiano Reggiano, if possible (see page 35), to top

In medium bowl, whisk together basil, Parmesan, tomato paste, and garlic into a thick paste. Slowly drizzle in olive oil until it is incorporated. Set aside.

Cook orzo in a large amount of boiling water until tender. Drain well and fold into olive oil mixture. Fold in Romano and set aside.

In a large soup pot, bring the 6 cups water and the salt to a boil. Add carrots, onion, and celery and cook 5 minutes. Add potatoes and cook 5 minutes more. Add bell pepper, zucchini, bread crumbs, paprika, black pepper, and saffron (if desired) and cook 5 minutes more.

Turn off heat and ladle a couple of cups of the soup into orzo mixture. Stir well and pour back into the soup pot. Add the 2 cups water, kidney beans, tomatoes, frozen peas or corn, and parsley.

Stir to mix. Serve topped with additional freshly grated Parmesan.

MAKES 13 CUPS.

MAKE THIS MINESTRONE DURING
HIGH GARDEN SEASON

This is truly a fine vegetable soup as written. But for me, it is a particularly nostalgic one. It is the first great soup I ever made. And as with just about everything great I ever learned to make, I learned it from a Julia Child recipe while I was looking for ways to use seasonal ingredients. We lived on the side of a canyon in Laguna Beach, California. At the bottom of that canyon, my husband grew more green beans, tomatoes, and fresh basil than any young couple with one tiny child could ever hope to consume or give away. Directed by Julia's recipe, I made the original version of this soup and was awestruck by the flavors. They came only from the herbs and vegetables without a speck of meat juices.

Given the need to make this soup year-round and in large quantities, Pasta & Co. cooks have had to make numerous adjustments to the original recipe. However, to fully experience the beauty of this recipe, I urge you to make it as I once did. It must be on a pleasantly warm summer afternoon with a fresh breeze blowing. Skip the canned kidney beans, the canned tomatoes, and the frozen peas or corn, and use the fresh substitutes just picked from your garden. (Perhaps you will have grown the other vegetables as well — all the better.) Make a supper of the soup with nothing more than good wine, crusty bread, and sweet butter. I think you will understand what I mean about this soup.

RED LENTIL SOUP

•••

Judy Birkland, of our University Village store, first developed this soup in response to customer requests for vegetarian and low-fat soups. We make it on the spicy side. Adjust the red pepper flakes to your taste. And when you feel indulgent, know that a dollop of sour cream, yogurt, or Quark (see page 91) topping each bowl of soup makes the taste even more stellar. **PREPARE-AHEAD/SERVING NOTES:** The soup keeps well for days and freezes without a flaw.

¼ cup cooking oil

½ tablespoon whole cumin seeds

½ tablespoon ground coriander

½ teaspoon turmeric

2 medium onions, peeled and cut into ¼-inch pieces

2 cloves garlic, finely minced or put through a garlic press

¾ teaspoon red pepper flakes

2 quarts water

2 cups red lentils, washed

1 cup Paradiso brand crushed tomatoes in purée

¼ cup tomato paste

1½ teaspoons salt

½ teaspoon freshly cracked black pepper

7 sprigs cilantro, washed and tied together

¼ cup lemon juice

3 tablespoons cilantro (or more to taste), well-washed, dried, and finely chopped

Optional: Sour cream, yogurt, or Quark, to top

In a large saucepan, combine oil, cumin seeds, coriander, and turmeric. Over low heat, cook mixture until seeds darken. Remove from heat and add onions, garlic, and red pepper flakes. Sauté over medium heat until onions are translucent. Add water, lentils, tomatoes, tomato paste, salt, black pepper, and cilantro sprigs. Bring to a boil and simmer 20 to 30 minutes until lentils are very soft. Remove soup from heat, take out cilantro sprigs, and beat soup a few minutes with a large whisk just to break up any remaining pieces of lentil (do *not* purée this soup). Stir in lemon juice and chopped cilantro. Taste for seasoning (may need additional salt) and texture (may need to be thinned with a small amount of water).

MAKES 10 CUPS.

NOTE FROM NUTRITION WORKS*

Pasta & Co.'s Red Lentil Soup is low in fat and high in fiber. One cup contains: 200 calories, 12 grams protein, 28 grams carbohydrates, 6 grams dietary fiber, 6 grams total fat (less than 1 gram is saturated), no cholesterol, and 425 milligrams sodium. Percent of calories from fat: 26. And legumes such as lentils and black beans help stabilize blood sugar and lower blood cholesterol.

*NUTRITION WORKS is Evette M. Hackman, RD, PhD, a Seattle-based consulting nutritionist.

TOMATO BASIL SOUP

Since it freezes well, use this soup as a way to store summer's fresh basil for winter. If you have a crop of fresh tomatoes as well, substitute fresh for all or some of the canned tomatoes, being sure to use all the juices. If the soup is too thin, thicken with a small amount of tomato paste or purée to taste. **PREPARE-AHEAD/ SERVING NOTES:** The soup holds well for several days refrigerated. Be sure to freeze in convenient portions. **ESSENTIAL GEAR:** Electric food processor

¼ cup pure olive oil

2 large onions, coarsely chopped

1 large clove garlic, finely minced or put through a garlic press

1 (28-ounce) can crushed tomatoes — we use Paradiso brand Italian-style tomatoes, peeled and crushed in a heavy purée

2 (14.5-ounce) cans reduced-salt chicken broth

¼ cup water

2 ounces basil leaves

¾ teaspoon sugar

½ teaspoon pepper

½ teaspoon thyme

Heat olive oil in large kettle. Add onions and garlic and sauté until onions are soft. Do not burn garlic. Stir in tomatoes, broth, water, basil, sugar, pepper, and thyme and simmer for 20 minutes. Remove from heat and purée in two or three batches in food processor.

Serve hot or chilled.

MAKES 8 CUPS.

SIMPLE LUNCH

■ Tomato Basil Soup (page 139)
■ Baked Cheese Wafers (page 19)
■ Italian Shortbread (page 246)
■ Fresh Fruit

CARROT CILANTRO SOUP

•••

Make this one as fiery as you like; it all depends on how much red pepper you use to season it and how much chicken broth you use to thin it. It is a good first-course soup, since it is neither too rich nor too filling. And it can be served hot or cold. **PREPARE-AHEAD/SERVING NOTES:** Make the soup up to three days before serving. It also freezes well (this is a good recipe for using up a bumper crop of garden carrots). **ESSENTIAL GEAR:** Electric food processor

¼ cup butter (if you use unsalted, you may need to add salt at end of recipe)

6⅔ cups (approximately 2¾ pounds untrimmed) carrots, peeled and coarsely chopped

1 teaspoon red pepper flakes

2½ cups onions (or about 2 medium onions), coarsely chopped

6 cups homemade chicken stock or canned broth — you may need extra to thin the soup

3 tablespoons finely chopped cilantro

1 teaspoon finely chopped orange zest

3 tablespoons fresh orange juice

Optional: Dollops of sour cream, yogurt, or Quark (page 91), to top

In a saucepan, melt butter. Add carrots, red pepper flakes, and onions. Cover and let vegetables "sweat" over low heat for about 5 minutes. Add chicken stock and cook until vegetables are tender.

With a slotted spoon, remove vegetables to the bowl of a food processor equipped with a steel blade. Process until completely smooth. Stir puréed vegetables back into reserved liquid. Stir in cilantro, orange zest, and orange juice. Taste for seasoning and texture. If soup is too thick, thin with a small amount of additional chicken stock. Heat thoroughly over low heat, stirring to blend. Serve with the sour cream, yogurt, or Quark, if desired.

MAKES 10 CUPS.

FRESH FENNEL AND
CHICKEN SOUP

◆◆◆

. . . .

A fragrant broth chock-full of chicken meat and fresh fennel makes this an attractive soup — low in calories and fats, high in flavor and sophistication. The soup makes splendid light lunch or supper fare with the addition of nothing more than hot bread. **PREPARE-AHEAD/SERVING NOTES:** The soup keeps well for several days refrigerated. (Freezing will rob the crunchiness from the fennel.)

1 tablespoon olive oil

1¼ cups leeks, sliced ½ inch thick (use white parts only, and wash away any sand that may be in the leeks)

½ cup onion, chopped roughly into ¼-inch pieces

1 large clove garlic, put through a garlic press

1 cup dry white wine

1 teaspoon dried green peppercorns or green peppercorns in brine, rinsed well

¼ teaspoon salt

1¾ cups canned whole pear tomatoes, coarsely chopped, including all juices

2 tablespoons tomato paste (see page 158)

¾ teaspoon whole fennel seeds

1 strip orange zest, 2 inches by 1 inch, well trimmed of pith

¾ teaspoon harissa **OR** your favorite hot sauce, to taste

½ teaspoon dried thyme **OR** 2 teaspoons fresh thyme, finely minced

7½ cups homemade chicken stock or canned chicken broth

¾ pound skinless, boneless chicken thighs, cut into bite-size pieces

1 medium-size fennel bulb, trimmed of feathers, cut in half, cored, and thinly sliced

¼ cup capers, very thoroughly rinsed and drained of all brine

3 tablespoons finely chopped parsley

1½ teaspoons balsamic vinegar, or to taste

Juice of ¼ orange or to taste

Salt and freshly cracked black pepper, to taste

SOUPS

In a 4-quart saucepan, heat olive oil over medium heat. Add leeks, onion, and garlic and cook until tender. Add wine, green peppercorns, and salt, and boil hard — about 2 minutes. Lower heat and add tomatoes and juices, tomato paste, fennel seed, orange zest, harissa, and thyme. Simmer 15 minutes. Add chicken stock, chicken thighs, and fennel and bring mixture to a low simmer. Cook just until chicken is done. (Undercook just a bit at this point, since chicken will continue to cook in the hot soup.) Remove soup from heat and stir in capers, parsley, vinegar, and orange juice. Salt and pepper to taste.

MAKES ABOUT 11 CUPS.

GRAND LUNCH

■ Hot Olives (page 28)

■ Focaccia (page 120)

■ Big bowls of Fresh Fennel and Chicken Soup (page 141)

■ Alix's Chocolate Layer Cake (page 249)

HAMBURGER AND
BARLEY SOUP

◆◆◆

. . . .

Not only does this soup make sure-to-please family fare, but it is also appealing for casual entertaining. We cannot imagine a better choice for feeding a crowd after a football game or a day of skiing. This recipe yields a good-size batch, but should you want even more, it can be easily doubled or tripled. One caution: Even though we specify extra-lean ground beef, be certain to thoroughly drain the fat off of the meat once it is cooked. **PREPARE-AHEAD/SERVING NOTES:** Make lots! The soup freezes perfectly.

2 pounds extra-lean ground beef

2 cups celery, cut into ½-inch dice

2 cups carrots, cut into ½-inch dice

2 cups cabbage, cut into ½-inch dice

½ cup onion, cut into ½-inch dice

2 (50-ounce) cans beef broth or consommé (we like Sexton brand)

1 (28-ounce) can Paradiso brand whole tomatoes, coarsely chopped, including all juices

⅔ cup uncooked barley

2 teaspoons thyme

1 teaspoon basil

2 cloves garlic, finely chopped

1 tablespoon plus 2 teaspoons brown sugar, or to taste

1 tablespoon plus 2 teaspoons balsamic vinegar, or to taste

2 teaspoons Worcestershire sauce

Freshly cracked black pepper, to taste

In a large kettle, brown ground beef just until it is no longer pink, crumbling the meat into small pieces. Thoroughly drain off fat. (Most reliable method — especially when doing larger batches — is to pour meat and fat through a strainer set over a large mixing bowl and allow meat to drain for 5 to 10 minutes.)

Return drained meat to pan and add celery, carrots, cabbage, onion, consommé, tomatoes and juices, barley, thyme, basil, and garlic. Cover pan and bring mixture to a boil. Reduce heat and simmer 45 minutes to 1 hour or until vegetables and barley are tender. Remove from heat and stir in brown sugar, vinegar, Worcestershire sauce, and black pepper. Check seasoning and serve.

MAKES 18 CUPS.

UPDATE ON BALSAMIC VINEGAR

Over the past 10 years, this brown-colored Italian vinegar has become a valued ingredient in American kitchens. When the San Francisco-based retailer Williams-Sonoma first imported the vinegar in 1977, the U.S. market for balsamic vinegar was virtually nonexistent. Then, surrounded by extensive lore about a centuries-old process of aging the juice of Trebbiano grapes until it finally produced a rich, syrupy vinegar, balsamic vinegar began showing up on the finest menus and in the best cookbooks. Americans tasted it. Americans liked it. And today, importers estimate, the U.S. balsamic vinegar market has grown to several million bottles annually.

We now know that at the current volume of production, any balsamic vinegar most of us can afford for cooking has never seen the inside of a wooden barrel, and, in fact, has been produced in a giant stainless tank in a matter of days or weeks rather than years. Still, most of the product on the market is good enough to work flavor wonders on everything from chicken to pasta. Our stores now sell capers packed in balsamic vinegar that make quite blissful eating served over greens or grilled fish or meat. (Ask for Club du Faisan brand; others on the market are not nearly as good.)

In this book, we have used the balsamic vinegar of Monari Federzoni — Italy's biggest producer of mass-produced balsamics — to serve with olive oil and bread (page 17) and to flavor tofu (page 61), white beans (page 24), pasta (page 80), Fresh Fennel and Chicken Soup (page 141), and even Hamburger and Barley Soup (page 143). (The judicious addition of vinegar generally is a smart way to cut the taste of meat fat or chicken fat in a dish. We do this in our Veal Ragout, page 207, and in our Big-Chunk Beef Stew, page 227.)

Certainly, the truly mythical balsamics are around. They cost $12 to $30 for six to eight ounces and are made from vinegars aged 7 to 15 years. We currently sell three of these: Due Frati, Cavalli, and Lorenza de Medici (with the highest price, currently $18 for 8.45 fluid ounces). Though too precious for marinades, they are noticeable and sometimes worth the price for use in salad dressings, sauces, and condiments. And they are mellow and sweet enough to dress fresh strawberries (as Italians do).

CORNED BEEF SOUP

***

Ever wonder what to do with all the strongly flavored broth left when you cook corned beef? This soup is the answer. (Don't miss the sister recipe for corned beef hash, page 229.) If you are in a hurry and have no time to cook corned beef, try the "speedy" version. Either way, you will have a cold-weather soup guaranteed to please family and friends alike. **PREPARE-AHEAD/SERVING NOTES:** Refrigerated, the soup keeps well for up to five days. Freeze only as a last resort, since freezing will soften the potatoes.

2 cups liquid reserved from cooking the corned beef (page 229), strained, and fat removed

2 (14.5-ounce) cans reduced-salt chicken broth

1 (14.5-ounce) can beef broth

1 (14.5-ounce) can whole peeled tomatoes, coarsely chopped, including all juices

6 to 8 ounces cooked corned beef, shredded into bite-size pieces

½ large onion, cut into 1-inch dice

2 tablespoons barley

¼ large cabbage, chopped into 1-inch dice (about 3 to 4 cups)

½ pound red-skinned potatoes, unpeeled, cut into ½-inch dice

1 cup carrots, cut ½ inch thick

¼ cup finely chopped parsley

Place corned beef cooking liquid, chicken broth, beef broth, tomatoes, corned beef, onion, and barley in stockpot and bring to a boil. Reduce heat and simmer 15 minutes.

Add cabbage, potatoes, and carrots and simmer 20 to 30 minutes longer, until vegetables are to your liking. Add parsley and serve.

MAKES 11 CUPS.

SPEEDY CORNED BEEF SOUP

♦♦♦

1 (49.5-ounce) can beef broth or chicken broth

2 cups water

1 (14.5-ounce) can whole peeled tomatoes, coarsely chopped, including all juices

1 very thick slice (6 to 8 ounces) corned beef from a supermarket deli, shredded into bite-size pieces

½ large onion, cut into 1-inch dice

2 tablespoons barley

¼ large cabbage, chopped into 1-inch dice (about 3 to 4 cups)

½ pound red-skinned potatoes, unpeeled, cut into ½-inch dice

1 cup carrots, sliced ½ inch thick

¼ cup finely chopped parsley

Cook according to regular recipe. (Yield will be the same.)

NOTE FROM NUTRITION WORKS*

Surprise! Pasta & Co.'s Corned Beef Soup is low-fat and low-calorie. One cup contains: 115 calories, 9 grams protein, 12 grams carbohydrate, 2.4 grams dietary fiber, 3.5 grams total fat (1.4 grams saturated), 16 milligrams cholesterol, and 645 milligrams sodium. Percent of calories from fat: 28. Sodium content can be reduced by using homemade broth.

*NUTRITION WORKS is Evette M. Hackman, RD, PhD, a Seattle-based consulting nutritionist.

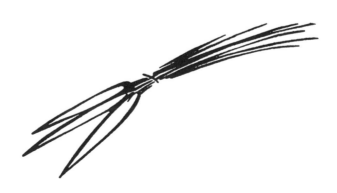

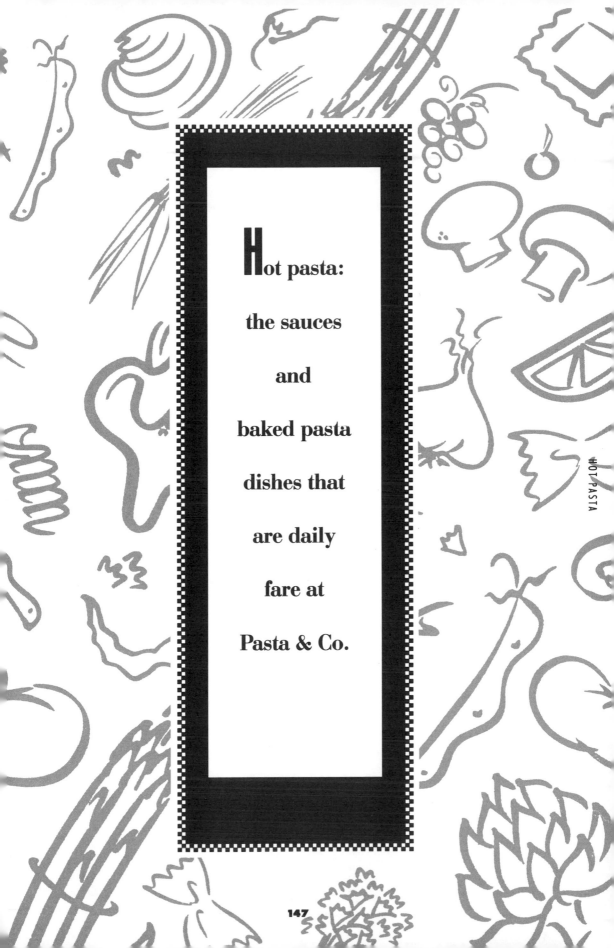

Hot pasta:
the sauces
and
baked pasta
dishes that
are daily
fare at
Pasta & Co.

We have made literally tens of thousands of pints and pans of these products. Along with our fresh pasta, they make up the basics of our business. They are Pasta & Co. standard products — those that enjoy such popularity that they are nearly always offered in our stores. ■ Some of these recipes are our versions of such classics as spaghetti sauce (Bolognese Sauce, page 151) and Macaroni and Cheese (page 181). Others are Pasta & Co. originals — sauces that were tailored for a particular pasta or developed to meet a specific market demand. Here they are, our biggest successes: the Pasta & Co. regulars.

PASTA RULES NEVER TO BE BROKEN

No matter how perfect a sauce or baked dish may be, its success depends on how you handle the basic pasta. These are tips we published in our first cookbook. They remain essential to the making of great pasta dishes.

■ SELECT A PASTA THAT COMPLEMENTS THE SAUCE. As a rule, smooth sauces go with smooth noodles, chunky sauces with chunky pastas. With filled pastas, consider the flavor of the filling when choosing the sauce. Often, you will repeat the dominant filling flavor in a topping. For example, sprinkle hazelnut-filled tortellini with chopped hazelnuts, or pesto-filled tortellini with toasted pine nuts. Or consider completing a classic combination — shrimp ravioli, whether tossed with a light tomato sauce or a creamy Alfredo, is superb topped with capers, a traditional accompaniment for shrimp.

■ COOK THE PASTA LAST. Have the sauce — and, in fact, any accompanying food — ready before cooking the pasta. Most hot pasta dishes do not wait well. For some that do, see pages 176–186.

■ COOK PASTA WITH CARE. Cook until tender but still firm, or — as the Italians say — "al dente." Do not trust the clock. Bite into the pasta. If there is a visible white line running through the thickest part of the pasta, it is not done.

Pasta needs to move while it cooks so that it will cook evenly and not stick together. Allow 4 quarts of water per pound of pasta and stir frequently, at least until the boil itself is vigorous enough to move the pasta.

■ TO SALT OR NOT TO SALT? One tablespoon of salt added to 4 quarts of water optimizes flavor. However, if you are watching sodium intake, this is a good place to drop salt. One important exception: Pasta being cooked for pasta salads needs to be cooked in salted water (page 79).

■ DRAIN VERY WELL. Any cooking liquid left on the pasta dilutes the sauce or dressing.

Do *not* rinse the pasta unless you fear that you have overcooked it (rinsing with cold water will halt the cooking) or if it is to be used in certain pasta salads (see page 79).

■ GO IMMEDIATELY FROM COLANDER INTO HOT SAUCE AND TOSS WELL. The pasta should be well-coated with the sauce or it will stick together, as one Seattle restaurant reviewer aptly put it, like "impassioned night crawlers."

If not using a sauce, toss pasta with butter or olive oil. If preparing for a salad, toss immediately with the dressing. For most dishes, the pasta should not be in a lake of sauce, but rather just amply coated. Toss with cheese only after the pasta is well-coated with sauce.

HOT PASTA

■ SPECIAL NOTE: For tossing long noodles, nothing works better than two Sporkits — long-handled plastic utensils that are a cross between a spoon and a fork. No avid pasta cooker should be without a pair. On the same note, be warned that Sporkits are *not* the tool for tossing filled pastas — rather, you need the largest rubber spatula you can find.

■ HOT PLATES HELP. However, there is no substitute for simply moving quickly through these steps.

■ WHEN COOKING PASTA FOR A CROWD: 1. Select, if possible, a short pasta, filled or not. You will find it easier to cook, sauce, and keep hot than a long noodle. 2. Recruit a helper. 3. Cook and serve no more than two pounds at a time. That way, every guest gets hot pasta. 4. Consider a baked pasta dish, such as lasagne, pasticcio, or macaroni and cheese (pages 176–186).

BOLOGNESE SAUCE

◆◆◆

We think of pasta sauce recipes in two categories: those you make in big pots to feed crowds or stock your freezer, and those you make in a sauté pan for a quick meal. As you might guess, this sauce, which is Pasta & Co.'s version of spaghetti sauce — a thick, richly flavored meat sauce — is a "big pot" sauce. Because the sauce is thick, allow up to 1 cup per ¼ pound of pasta. It makes enough to sauce 2½ pounds of fresh pasta (10 average adult servings). **PREPARE-AHEAD/ SERVING NOTES:** Store the sauce refrigerated for up to five days. Freeze it for months in convenient portions for dressing pastas and for topping pizza dough (page 156). **SUGGESTED PASTA AND CHEESE:** In theory, the rule goes that chunky sauces are best for chunky pastas. But meat sauce goes well on just about any shape pasta. Let your preference be your guide, but do not overlook some of the more novel cuts, such as *fusilli lunghi*, *chitarra*, and *creste gallo* (page 87). And, of course, top with a blizzard of freshly grated Parmesan or Romano cheese.

3 to 4 (a little over ½ pound) Italian sausages, hot or sweet — we use Isernio brand

1 pound lean ground beef

¾ cup chopped yellow onion

¼ cup chopped carrot

¼ cup chopped celery

Optional: ½ cup chopped mushrooms and/or ¼ cup chopped zucchini

8 cloves garlic, finely minced or put through a garlic press

2 teaspoons oregano

1 teaspoon basil

1 teaspoon salt, or to taste

½ teaspoon ground black pepper

½ teaspoon allspice

½ teaspoon fennel seeds

¼ teaspoon ground nutmeg

1 small bay leaf

⅓ cup dry white wine

¼ cup tomato paste, diluted with ¼ cup water

2 (28-ounce) cans crushed tomatoes — we use Paradiso brand Italian-style tomatoes, peeled and crushed in heavy purée

Remove sausage from casings and slowly brown with ground beef in a 3- to 4-quart saucepan. Be sure to break up sausage as it browns. Drain off fat.

As meat is browning, chop onion, carrot, celery, if desired, mushrooms and zucchini. This can be done by hand or in a food processor. If using a food processor, each vegetable must be chopped separately. As each is completed, put it into a large bowl.

Add garlic, oregano, basil, salt, black pepper, allspice, fennel seeds, nutmeg, and bay leaf to vegetables in bowl.

After draining fat from meat, add vegetables and spices to meat. Sauté meat and vegetables together until onions begin to cook. Do not burn garlic.

Add white wine and diluted tomato paste to meat mixture. Bring to a simmer. Add tomatoes and their juices. Return mixture to a simmer.

Simmer over low heat, partially covered, for 1 hour, stirring occasionally.

MAKES 9 TO 10 CUPS.

HOW MUCH SAUCE FOR HOW MUCH PASTA?

As a general rule, Pasta & Co. stores suggest 1 cup of our packaged sauces for every ½ pound of pasta. By warming the sauce with a tablespoon or two of butter, this formula usually lightly coats the pasta and makes 2 average adult main-course servings.

In this book, however, we have been more generous with sauce allotments and — for the most part — have eliminated the need to add butter. Usually, we allow ¾ cup sauce for every ¼ pound of fresh pasta, or 1 cup for every ¼ pound of dried pasta.

Remember, if you come up a little short of sauce, add butter, olive oil, or stock. But do make certain that there is enough sauce to evenly coat the pasta and keep it from sticking together.

FRESH VS. DRIED PASTA

As a general rule, dried pasta yields a higher volume of cooked pasta than does fresh. In some cases, it yields as much as twice the amount. Therefore, you will need more sauce (or, for a pasta salad, more dressing) per pound of uncooked dried pasta than for uncooked fresh.

MARINARA SAUCE

•••

H ere is another "big pot" sauce. This one is a fresh-flavored, light-textured classic tomato sauce. It is our biggest seller, not only because it is excellent, but also because it is versatile. It is as good over chicken or fish as it is over pasta. The recipe below makes enough to sauce 1½ pounds of fresh pasta (6 main-course servings). **PREPARE-AHEAD/SERVING NOTES:** As with almost all tomato sauces, this one keeps well for days in the refrigerator and freezes without a flaw for months. Since this recipe makes enough for 1¾ pounds of pasta (7 average adult servings), you may want to tuck half of it away in the freezer. Or, since the sauce doubles without any problems, you may want to make an even bigger batch and boost your frozen supply. **SUGGESTED PASTA AND CHEESE:** Fresh egg fettuccine (allow ¼ pound for every ⅔ cup sauce) and about ⅓ cup of freshly grated Parmesan or Romano cheese for every ½ pound of pasta.

3 tablespoons pure olive oil	**2 cups dry white wine**
¾ teaspoon basil	**1 (28-ounce) can crushed tomatoes — we use Paradiso brand Italian-style tomatoes, peeled and crushed in heavy purée**
¾ teaspoon oregano	
¼ teaspoon red pepper flakes	**½ teaspoon salt or to taste**
2 cloves garlic, finely minced or put through a garlic press	**Optional: ½ teaspoon sugar**

In a heavy 2-quart saucepan, over medium heat, sauté basil, oregano, red pepper flakes, and garlic in olive oil for 1 to 2 minutes. Be careful not to brown the garlic.

Add wine and simmer for 10 to 12 minutes, or until all the alcohol has evaporated.

Add tomatoes. Cover partially. Simmer over low heat for about 20 minutes, stirring occasionally.

Taste the sauce. Add salt to taste. We use a scant ½ teaspoon.

Stir sauce and taste again. Now you must make a decision about the sugar. The amount needed will depend upon the residual sugars in the wine you have used. With a very dry California chablis, we use ½ teaspoon sugar to mellow the acidity of the tomatoes and round out the flavor of the sauce. Stir and simmer 1 or 2 minutes longer.

MAKES 4 CUPS.

NOTE FROM NUTRITION WORKS*

¼ pound pasta, ⅔ cup Pasta & Co. Marinara Sauce, and 1 tablespoon Parmesan cheese gives you a low-fat, low-cholesterol, high-complex-carbohydrate meal: 365 calories, 11 grams protein, 44 grams carbo-hydrates, 5 grams dietary fiber, 11 grams total fat (only 2 of which are saturated), 51 milligrams cholesterol, and 500 milligrams sodium (see reduced-salt version below). Percent calories from fat: 27.

*NUTRITION WORKS is Evette M. Hackman, RD, PhD, a Seattle-based consulting nutritionist.

REDUCED-SALT MARINARA

Most canned tomatoes are packed with salt. Therefore, it is impossible to make a salt-free marinara without using fresh tomatoes or specially canned no-salt tomatoes. You can (and we do), however, make a "no-salt-added" marinara sauce that has 40% less sodium than the regular version. Simply eliminate the ½ teaspoon salt in the recipe.

THE PASTA & CO. BIG SAUTÉ PAN METHOD
OF SAUCING PASTA

Get yourself a 12-inch or 14-inch SilverStone sauté pan. It is by far the best pan for heating pasta sauces, because you can add the cooked and drained pasta directly into the hot sauce. The pan gives you a great wide-open space for tossing pasta with sauce until the pasta is well-coated. (For long pasta, the serving tool of choice is one or two "Spork-its," a clever hybrid of spoon and fork; for short or filled pasta, use a large rubber spatula.) If the situation requires it, you can slide the pasta onto a heated serving dish. Or, as Judy Birkland says, "If you've got your guests trained right, they can just line up to be served out of the pan."

MATRICCINA SAUCE

◆◆◆

$\mathbf{P}$asta & Co. insiders generally agree that this is the best red sauce the company makes. It is a masterpiece of flavor and texture. The recipe makes enough to generously sauce 2 pounds of fresh pasta (8 main-course servings). **PREPARE-AHEAD/ SERVING NOTES:** You can double or triple this recipe for a "big pot" sauce (just adjust the time for boiling the wine mixture). The recipe as written makes a medium-size batch — probably enough for one meal and enough to freeze for a second. The sauce keeps for days in the refrigerator and freezes well. **SUGGESTED PASTA AND CHEESE:** Fresh egg fettuccine or pescine (allow ¼ pound for every ⅔ cup sauce) and about ⅓ cup of freshly grated Parmesan or Romano cheese for every ½ pound of pasta.

½ cup pure olive oil

1¼ teaspoons basil

¾ teaspoon red pepper flakes

4 to 5 cloves garlic, minced or put through a garlic press

⅓ to ½ pound prosciutto, sliced thin and julienned

1½ cups dry white wine

1 (28-ounce) can crushed tomatoes — we use Paradiso brand Italian-style tomatoes, peeled and crushed in heavy purée

¼ to ½ teaspoon salt (will depend on saltiness of prosciutto)

¼ to ½ teaspoon sugar (will depend on sweetness of wine)

Combine in large, heavy saucepan the olive oil, basil, red pepper flakes, and garlic. Add juliénned prosciutto.

Carefully sauté the mixture until oil turns golden and garlic is cooked. Stir frequently. The garlic must not burn.

Add wine and simmer uncovered for 10 to 12 minutes, or until alcohol has evaporated.

Add tomatoes, bring to a simmer, and cook, partially covered, for about 20 minutes.

Add salt and sugar to taste. Stir and simmer 1 or 2 minutes longer.

MAKES 5 CUPS.

IF YOU WANT TO MAKE PIZZA

1½ cups of Matriccina Sauce (page 155), Marinara Sauce (page 153), or Bolognese Sauce (page 151) spread over a 13-inch round of pizza dough and topped with cheeses and other condiments makes a splendid red-sauce pizza. (See the chapter on pizza, page 111). If you find Matriccina or Marinara too thin for pizza, simmer 2 cups of the sauce over medium heat for about 10 minutes or until the sauce is the thickness and volume you desire.

A FAVORITE PASTA DINNER

- Hot Focaccia (page 120), served with Olive Oil and Vinegar (page 17)
- Matriccina Sauce (page 155), served with fresh egg fettuccine and grated Parmesan cheese
- Mixed salad greens tossed with The Greens Dressing (page 105) and Pasta & Co. Croutons (page 110)
- Italian Shortbread with Almonds, Brandy, and Lemon (page 246)

GIARDINIERA SAUCE

◆◆◆

T his is the vegetarian red sauce that has been a daily favorite in our stores since shortly after Pasta & Co. opened for business. It is zesty. The vegetables are cut tiny and cooked crunchy. The sauce is best served over egg rotini and topped with freshly grated Parmesan or Romano cheese. The recipe makes enough to sauce 3 pounds of fresh pasta (12 main-course servings). **PREPARE-AHEAD/SERVING NOTES:** Same as for Bolognese Sauce (page 151). You could make a smaller batch, but what would you do with all the leftover vegetables? Instead, stock your freezer or throw a dinner party when you make this sauce. **SUGGESTED PASTA AND CHEESE:** Fresh egg rotini or pescine (allow ¼ pound for every ⅔ cup sauce) and about ⅓ cup of freshly grated Parmesan or Romano cheese for every ½ pound of pasta.

HOT PASTA

1¼ cups cauliflower, cut into approximately ¼-inch dice	½ bay leaf
1¼ cups zucchini, cut into ¼-inch dice	½ to ¾ teaspoon red pepper flakes
1 cup celery, cut into ½-inch dice	6 cloves garlic, finely minced or put through a garlic press
1 green bell pepper, cut into ½-inch dice	1½ cups dry white wine
1 cup carrots, in large chunks	1 (28-ounce) can crushed tomatoes — we use Paradiso brand Italian-style tomatoes, peeled and crushed in heavy purée
1 cup onion, cut into ½-inch dice	
⅓ cup pure olive oil	¼ cup tomato paste
1 teaspoon basil	½ teaspoon salt
1 teaspoon oregano	½ teaspoon sugar, or to taste

Wash and dice cauliflower and zucchini and set aside in a large bowl.

Carefully chop celery, bell pepper, and carrots separately in work bowl of a food processor equipped with a steel blade (the vegetables should be roughly the same size as the zucchini and cauliflower you have chopped by hand). Add these to the bowl with the cauliflower and zucchini.

Chop the onion coarsely, then process lightly in food processor. Set aside separately.

Combine in a 4-quart saucepan olive oil, basil, oregano, bay leaf, red pepper flakes, garlic, and onions.

Cook mixture over medium heat until onion is translucent. It should not brown.

Stir to prevent garlic from burning.

Add wine. Bring to a simmer. Simmer 10 to 12 minutes, uncovered, until alcohol evaporates.

Add reserved vegetables, tomatoes, tomato paste, salt, and sugar. Simmer, partially covered, about 5 minutes. The vegetables should be crunchy.

MAKES 8 CUPS.

NOTE FROM NUTRITION WORKS

¼ pound pasta, ⅔ cup Giardiniera Sauce, and 1 tablespoon Parmesan gives you a low-fat, low-cholesterol, high-complex-carbohydrate meal: 340 calories, 11 grams protein, 48 grams carbohydrate, 6 grams dietary fiber, 10 grams fat (only 2 are saturated), 51 milligrams cholesterol, and 325 milligrams sodium. Percent calories from fat: 28.

*NUTRITION WORKS is Evette M. Hackman, RD, PhD, a Seattle-based consulting nutritionist.

TOMATO PASTE IN TUBES

How many times have you opened a 6-ounce can of tomato paste, used a tablespoon of it, and stored the remainder in the refrigerator, where it molded beyond use in less than a month?

The solution to the problem is imported Italian tomato paste that comes packed in a toothpaste-type tube. It is truly a remarkable product that every cook should know about and use. You use however much paste you need, and store the tube in the refrigerator. Because there is so much less surface exposed to the air, the paste is likely to remain good for up to a year. There are several brands. We prefer Pagani.

SLIM ALFREDO SAUCE

••••

lfredo Sauce — the Italian cream-and-cheese classic — is such a standard recipe that we have it printed on all our bags. Some years back, however, we discovered that by reducing the cream, butter, and cheese by 25% and substituting defatted chicken stock, we had an Alfredo that was more in keeping with our current preference for lighter, lower-fat foods. Once you have had this version, you may never go back to Alfredo's original. Makes enough to sauce up to 1½ pounds of filled pasta (5 to 6 main-course servings) or 1 pound of unfilled pasta (4 main-course servings). **PREPARE-AHEAD/SERVING NOTES:** The sauce reheats well and freezes with almost no loss in quality. **SUGGESTED PASTA AND CHEESE:** The traditional pasta for this sauce is fettuccine — either egg, spinach, or a mixture of both. It is also a good choice for pescine or filled pastas. For cheese lovers, allow ⅓ cup additional freshly grated Parmesan cheese for topping each ½ pound of pasta.

1 cup heavy cream

¾ cup chicken stock, regular or reduced-sodium

3 tablespoons butter

3 grinds black pepper

Pinch nutmeg

¾ cup freshly grated Parmesan cheese

Place cream, stock, butter, black pepper, and nutmeg in a heavy 12-inch sauté pan (a pan with a nonstick finish is most desirable).

Bring mixture to a simmer. Let simmer 8 minutes.

Remove pan from heat and whisk in Parmesan cheese.

MAKES 2 CUPS.

ALTER THIS SAUCE TO FIT THE PASTA

For instance, when we use Slim Alfredo Sauce over shrimp ravioli, we substitute clam juice for some or all of the chicken stock and add a good dose of finely minced fresh garlic.

CALORIE- AND CLOCK-WATCHERS TAKE NOTE

What better low-calorie and quick way to sauce pasta than with defatted chicken or beef broth?

Homemade broths are most desirable, but some canned broths do nicely also. (Pasta & Co., for instance, sells large cans of Swanson's brand chicken broth for this purpose.) Here is our suggestion.

8 cups defatted meat stock — homemade or canned

¾ to 1 pound fresh pasta

Optional: 2 cups any vegetables, such as frozen peas (thawed), carrots (julienned and blanched), broccoli flowerets (blanched), asparagus tips (blanched), spinach (washed well and cut into a chiffonade — page 37)

Optional: ⅓ cup freshly grated Parmesan cheese (highly recommended, if you can afford the calories)

Bring stock to a boil while you cook pasta in boiling water. When pasta is almost tender (it will continue to cook in the hot broth), drain and rinse quickly in cold water. When well-drained, add to the hot broth along with vegetables (if desired). Serve immediately in large soup bowls and, if you wish, top with Parmesan cheese.

SERVES 4 AS AN ENTRÉE.

GORGONZOLA SAUCE

❖❖❖

Unless you like a very heavy blue-cheese flavor, domestic Gorgonzola is fine for this sauce. For years it has been a Pasta & Co. favorite for saucing spinach fettuccine or veal-filled tortellini. The recipe makes enough to sauce 1 pound of fresh fettuccine (4 main-course servings) or 2 pounds of fresh tortellini (6 main-course servings). **PREPARE-AHEAD/SERVING NOTES:** The sauce is easily made just before you cook the pasta. However, if you want to make it ahead, it rewarms well. **SUGGESTED PASTA AND CHEESE:** 1 pound fresh egg or spinach fettuccine or 1½ pounds fresh tortellini and a generous topping of freshly grated Parmesan cheese.

¾ cup plus 2 tablespoons dry white wine

1⅓ cups cream

¼ pound domestic Gorgonzola cheese, crumbled

1 tablespoon freshly grated Parmesan cheese

⅛ teaspoon freshly grated nutmeg

Freshly cracked black pepper, to taste

Additional freshly grated Parmesan cheese, to top

In a large sauté pan, heat wine to a boil and reduce by one-half. (This will happen quite quickly, so watch closely.) Lower heat, add cream, and simmer about 10 minutes or until mixture is reduced by about one-third. Add Gorgonzola, Parmesan, nutmeg, and black pepper. Continue to simmer until Gorgonzola is melted and sauce is quite smooth. Taste for seasoning. Then toss with pasta and top with additional freshly grated Parmesan. (Here is a case where hand-grating a wedge of Parmigiano Reggiano (page 35) over the pasta is definitely an elevating finish.)

MAKES 1½ CUPS.

HOT PASTA

SPINACH WALNUT SAUCE

◆◆◆

This has been a perennial customer favorite since we first made it 10 years ago. It is a rich, chunky sauce that we have always liked best on a short pasta, such as rotini or pescine. And if you are a meat eater, the sauce and pasta should definitely be served with a side of the best Italian sausage you can obtain. It is a combination that has proven memorable time and time again. The recipe makes enough to sauce up to 2 pounds of fresh pasta (8 main-course servings). **PREPARE-AHEAD/ SERVING NOTES:** The problem with this sauce is that if you use an entire box of frozen spinach, you get enough sauce for 8 servings. And, we warn you, the sauce keeps well for only a couple of days and suffers noticeably from freezing. If you want the sauce in small quantities, you can special-order it from Pasta & Co. **SUGGESTED PASTA AND CHEESE:** We recommend serving this sauce over a short, curly pasta such as egg rotini or pescine and topping with ⅓ cup freshly grated Romano cheese for every ½ pound of pasta.

1 (10-ounce) package chopped frozen spinach	**½ teaspoon basil**
¾ cup ricotta cheese	**¼ cup pure olive oil**
½ cup freshly grated Romano cheese	**1 to 2 medium cloves garlic, finely minced or put through a garlic press**
½ cup half-and-half	**½ cup chicken broth**
⅓ cup coarsely chopped walnuts	**¼ cup butter, at room temperature**
¼ cup finely chopped parsley	

Place unwrapped block of spinach on cutting board to partially thaw while preparing other ingredients.

In a medium bowl, combine ricotta, Romano, half-and-half, walnuts, parsley, and basil.

Heat olive oil and garlic in a large, heavy sauté pan over low heat. Do not brown garlic. Add chicken broth to sauté pan and remove from heat.

By now, the block of frozen spinach will have thawed enough to chop. With a chef's knife, chop spinach into ½-inch slices, then turn the board a quarter turn and chop spinach into ½-inch slices again. (NOTE: Even though you are using chopped spinach, this additional chopping is necessary.)

Add chopped spinach to sauté pan. Return to low heat. Heat only enough to thaw the spinach (you do not want the spinach to discolor from too much heat).

When the spinach has thawed, add cheese mixture to saucepan. Stir over low heat until sauce is smooth and thoroughly heated. Remove from heat and add butter.

MAKES 4 CUPS.

BABY CLAM SAUCE

♦♦♦

This is a light, brothy clam sauce fragrant with garlic, red pepper, and olive oil. It was developed from a recipe in Marcella Hazan's bible of Italian cooking, *The Classic Italian Cookbook*. Hazan tells how the Italians love their clam sauce, complete with fresh, thumbnail-size Adriatic clams still in their shells. To sell a packaged version of the sauce, we needed a convenient source of tender, tiny clam meat. What we discovered was "boiled baby clams." Most are imported from Thailand. They come canned. They are generally a consistent product. However, you do need to watch for bits of shell and occasionally more sand than you wish (just rinse the clams well and run the juice through a paper coffee filter). We like them so much we also use them in our Clam Chowder (page 130). The recipe makes enough to sauce 1½ pounds of fresh linguine (6 main-course servings). **PREPARE-AHEAD/SERVING NOTES:** Though the sauce keeps well for several days refrigerated and also freezes well, it is certainly not a "big pot" sauce. You will usually want to make it just as you need it. **SUGGESTED PASTA AND CHEESE:** Fresh egg linguine or a mixture of egg and spinach linguine (allow ¼ pound for every ⅓ cup sauce) and about ⅓ cup freshly grated Parmesan cheese for every ½ pound of pasta.

1 (10-ounce) can boiled baby clams, including all juices

¼ cup pure olive oil

2 heaping tablespoons onion, cut into ¼-inch dice

1 scant tablespoon finely minced garlic

¼ teaspoon red pepper flakes

½ cup dry white wine

1 (8-ounce) bottle clam juice

¼ cup butter

2 tablespoons finely minced parsley

Place a strainer over a 1-quart measuring pitcher and drain clams into it. Pick through drained clams and discard any pieces of shell. Add bottled clam juice to the juice in the measuring pitcher. You should have about 1½ cups clam juice in the pitcher (the measurement can be off by a couple of tablespoons without any harm to the finished sauce). Set clams and broth aside.

In a heavy, flat-bottomed 1- or 2-quart saucepan over medium heat, sauté onion in olive oil until it begins to soften. Add garlic and red pepper flakes and sauté 2 to 3 more minutes. Stir constantly to keep garlic from burning.

Raise heat to high and add wine. Boil until liquid is reduced by one-half. The time will be determined by the diameter of the saucepan, but 5 minutes should be enough. If you are uncomfortable judging the level by eye, stick a ruler in the pan and measure liquid before it starts boiling. Then measure every 2 minutes until you have reduced liquid by half. It does not have to be exact — close is good enough.

Add reserved clam juice and boil down again until reduced by one-half. This should take 10 to 15 minutes. Use ruler method, if necessary.

Remove finished sauce from heat and add reserved clams, butter, and parsley. To serve immediately, pour sauce into a large sauté pan and use "The Pasta & Co. Big Sauté Pan Method of Saucing Pasta" (page 154).

MAKES 2 CUPS.

DOUBLING UP

This sauce can easily be doubled to serve 12. The only adjustment will be in the reduction times. It will take not quite twice as long to boil down the liquid, but close to it. Watch carefully.

RED BABY CLAM SAUCE

•••

This is a "red," or tomato, version of the preceding clam sauce. All the same notes apply. **SUGGESTED PASTA AND CHEESE:** Fresh egg linguine or a mixture of egg and spinach linguine (since this sauce is chunkier than the preceding Baby Clam Sauce, allow ¼ pound for every ½ cup of sauce) and about ⅓ cup freshly grated Parmesan cheese for every ½ pound pasta.

The recipe makes enough to sauce up to 1¾ pounds of fresh linguine (6 to 7 main-course servings).

1 (10-ounce) can whole baby clams, including all juices

1 (8-ounce) bottle clam juice

¼ cup pure olive oil

¼ cup onion, cut into ¼-inch dice

1 tablespoon finely minced garlic

½ teaspoon red pepper flakes

½ cup dry white wine

1 (14.5-ounce) can diced tomatoes in purée

1 tablespoon tomato paste

¼ cup butter

2 tablespoons minced parsley

Place a strainer over a 1-quart measuring pitcher and drain clams into it. Pick through drained clams and discard any shell fragments. Add bottled clam juice to the juice in the pitcher. You will have about 1½ cups of juice: a little more, a little less — no harm. Set clams and juice aside.

In a heavy, flat-bottomed 1- or 2-quart saucepan, sauté onion in olive oil until it begins to soften. Add garlic and red pepper flakes and sauté 1 or 2 minutes longer. Do not let garlic brown. Add wine and boil until contents are reduced by one-half. Add reserved clam juice and reduce contents by one-third. As with the Baby Clam Sauce (page 163), the exact measurement is not crucial, but if you are uncomfortable guessing, use a ruler.

After second reduction, add canned tomatoes and tomato paste. Cover, and simmer for 15 minutes. Add reserved clams, butter, and parsley.

MAKES APPROXIMATELY 3½ CUPS.

TORTELLINI SAUCE

◆◆◆

. . . .

Originally conceived to accompany our fresh veal-filled tortellini, this sauce is also excellent over fresh fettuccine noodles, topped with capers and a dusting of freshly grated Parmesan cheese. This is the "full-strength" recipe that is a customer favorite: thick, creamy, rich. If you prefer a lighter sauce — both in calories and in texture — thin with additional chicken stock. Want it with shellfish? Use clam juice or fish stock in place of the chicken stock. The recipe makes enough to sauce 1 pound of fresh fettuccine (4 main-course servings) or 2 pounds of fresh tortellini (6 to 8 main-course servings). **PREPARE-AHEAD/SERVING NOTES:** The sauce can be doubled, stored refrigerated for several days, or frozen. **SUGGESTED PASTA AND CHEESE:** Fresh egg fettuccine or a mixture of egg and spinach (allow ¼ pound for every ½ cup sauce) or fresh veal-, chicken-, or cheese-filled tortellini. Allow ⅓ cup freshly grated Parmesan cheese for every ½ pound of pasta.

¼ cup plus 2 tablespoons dry white wine

¼ cup homemade chicken stock or canned broth (regular or reduced-sodium)

1 tablespoon tomato paste (page 158)

⅓ cup pure olive oil

3 medium cloves garlic, put through a garlic press

1 cup whipping cream

½ cup half-and-half

⅛ teaspoon salt

2 grinds black pepper

3 tablespoons finely minced parsley

TO TOP:

Freshly grated Parmesan cheese

Capers, rinsed (if using fettuccine)

Whisk together wine, stock, and tomato paste until well-blended. Set aside.

Place olive oil and garlic in a large sauté pan over medium heat. When oil begins to bubble (but *before* garlic begins to brown), pour in tomato paste mixture all at once. (If you dribble it in, you may be spattered with hot oil.) Bring to a steady simmer and cook 10 minutes or until alcohol evaporates.

In a measuring cup, combine whipping cream, half-and-half, salt, and black pepper. Gradually whisk cream into tomato paste mixture. Simmer the sauce for a few minutes to let cream slightly thicken. Remove from heat and fold in parsley. Toss with pasta and top with the Parmesan and/or capers, if desired.

MAKES 2¼ CUPS.

SMOKED-SALMON SAUCE

This is a truly lovely sauce on fresh fettuccine topped with capers. It is an extravagant pasta entrée that warrants such accompaniments as good Champagne and fresh asparagus or sugar snap peas. Unless you cold-smoke your own salmon, you will face the expensive prospect of buying premium-priced sliced Nova-cured smoked salmon or lox. The smoked salmon for this recipe will probably cost you over $8. The recipe is also very good made with slightly less expensive boneless smoked trout fillets, hot-smoked salmon, or (far less expensive) leftover poached or barbecued salmon.

6 ounces Nova-cured smoked salmon
or lox

1½ cups crème fraîche (made or
purchased)

2 teaspoons Scotch

2 tablespoons butter

Freshly ground black pepper, to taste

1 pound fresh egg fettuccine (or
a mixture of egg and spinach)
or pescine

Optional: 2 tablespoons capers,
rinsed, to top

Roughly tear smoked salmon into bite-size pieces and put them into a 12-inch sauté pan. Add crème fraîche, Scotch, butter, and black pepper. Heat on lowest setting just until butter melts. Remove from heat.

Cook pasta until tender. Return sauté pan with sauce to low heat and add the drained pasta, tossing to coat with sauce. Heat very gently for 1 or 2 minutes and add capers, if desired.

SERVES 4 AS A MAIN COURSE OR 6 AS A FIRST COURSE.

BOUILLABAISSE SAUCE

❖❖❖

Inspired by the glorious fish stews of Provence, Bouillabaisse Sauce is the kind of pasta sauce everyone wants in 1991: low-fat, low-calorie, high flavor. We originally conceived the sauce to go over shrimp-filled ravioli. We like it just as well over fresh linguine or *chitarra*, a square-cut spaghetti. Grilled white fish and fresh asparagus are good complements to the sophisticated flavors of this pasta sauce. Pasta & Co. stores sell a pint — 2 cups — of this sauce for 1 pound of fresh pasta. But when you make the sauce at home, we suggest being generous with it. This way, you will have some sauce to nap over any vegetables or grilled seafood that may accompany the pasta. The recipe makes enough to sauce ¾ pound fresh pasta or ⅔ pound dried pasta (3 main-course or 4 side servings). **PREPARE-AHEAD/SERVING NOTES:** If you want to make the sauce in a larger batch, by all means do. It keeps up to a week refrigerated and freezes fine.

2 tablespoons pure olive oil

⅔ cup coarsely chopped onion

⅔ cup leeks, sliced into ¼-inch pieces and well rinsed of all grit (use white parts only)

⅛ teaspoon red pepper flakes, or to taste

3 cloves garlic, peeled and finely minced or put through a garlic press

¾ cup dry white wine

Pinch salt, to taste

1¼ cups canned or fresh pear tomatoes, coarsely cut or torn into ¼-inch dice, including all juices (if using canned tomatoes, just hold each tomato over measuring cup and tear into small pieces)

1 tablespoon tomato paste

½ teaspoon dried thyme **OR** 2 teaspoons finely chopped fresh thyme, if you have it

⅛ teaspoon fennel seed

1 strip orange zest (3-inch by 1-inch), well-trimmed of white pith

1⅓ cups canned clam juice

1 teaspoon arrowroot

2 teaspoons lemon juice

1 teaspoon white wine vinegar

2 tablespoons finely chopped parsley

1 tablespoon capers, rinsed and well-drained

Optional: ½ teaspoon Pernod

⅔ pound dried *chitarra* (square spaghetti) **OR** ¾ pound fresh egg linguine **OR** 1 pound fresh shrimp ravioli

Heat olive oil in a medium-size sauté pan. Add onions, leeks, and red pepper flakes. Cook over medium-low heat until onions are translucent. Add garlic and cook a minute longer. Add wine and salt. Boil until alcohol has evaporated, about 3 minutes. Add tomatoes, tomato paste, thyme, fennel seed, orange zest, and clam juice. Simmer over medium heat for 5 minutes. Remove orange zest.

Dissolve arrowroot in lemon juice and vinegar. Stir into sauce. Simmer 2 minutes, remove from heat, and stir in parsley, capers, and Pernod (if desired). Taste for salt.

Cook pasta in boiling water until tender. Drain well and toss immediately with sauce. Top with Parmesan and serve.

MAKES ABOUT 3¼ CUPS.

NOTE FROM NUTRITION WORKS

¼ pound pasta, 1 cup Bouillabaisse Sauce, and 1 tablespoon Parmesan cheese gives you a low-fat, low-cholesterol meal: 388 calories, 10 grams protein, 53 grams carbohydrate, 6 grams dietary fiber, 12 grams fat (less than 2 grams are saturated), 50 milligrams cholesterol, and 660 milligrams sodium. Percent calories from fat: 27.

*NUTRITION WORKS is Evette M. Hackman, RD, PhD, a Seattle-based consulting nutritionist.

CHÈVRE SAUCE

◆◆◆

The unique tanginess and slightly grainy texture of goat cheese make for a luscious and popular sauce. **PREPARE-AHEAD/SERVING NOTES:** The sauce can be made up to five days ahead and reheated. By serving the sauced pasta over the raw spinach, you have a one-dish meal. Cook the pasta, of course, at the last minute.

2 tablespoons pure olive oil

5 ounces prosciutto, thinly sliced and julienned

4 cloves garlic, peeled and put through a garlic press

½ cup Pasta & Co. Marinated Black Olives (purchased or made according to recipe on page 26), cut in halves and well drained of all marinade

1 cup chicken stock

½ cup half-and-half

1¼ teaspoons dried basil OR 1 heaping tablespoon finely chopped basil leaves

1¼ teaspoons dried oregano OR 1 heaping tablespoon finely chopped fresh oregano

6 Roma tomatoes, coarsely chopped

7 ounces chèvre (goat cheese, such as Montrachet), crumbled

1 pound fresh egg rotini, pescine, or fettuccine

3 cups spinach leaves, washed, dried, and cut into a chiffonade (page 37)

½ cup freshly grated Parmesan cheese

In a large sauté pan, heat olive oil over medium heat. Add prosciutto and sauté for about 3 minutes. Add garlic and continue to cook until garlic is golden but not browned. Add drained olives, chicken stock, half-and-half, dried basil, dried oregano, and tomatoes. (If you are using fresh herbs, do *not* add them here — fold them in at the end, just before you toss the pasta with the sauce.) Cook over medium heat another 5 minutes. Add chèvre and let melt over low heat. Remove sauce from heat and fold in fresh herbs now if you are using them.

Right before serving, make a bed of the spinach on four serving plates or on a large platter. Cook pasta until tender, drain, and toss with sauce over low heat. Pour over spinach and top with Parmesan.

SERVES 4 AS A MAIN COURSE.

GOAT CHEESE

To be sure, goat cheese, or chèvre, is one of those ingredients — along with sun-dried tomatoes and balsamic vinegar — that became a cliche in America's fine cooking of the last decade. Now moderation seems to have taken hold, and these truly wonderful ingredients have assumed a more reasonable role.

Pasta & Co. certainly has used its share of goat cheese. The cheese's pungent creaminess suits it to many uses. We combine it with peppers, onions, and walnut oil in the salsa that goes over lentils (page 68). Make the same mixture to serve with blue corn chips the next time you need a quick and stunning snack. There is also the Chèvre Sauce (page 170) and another best-loved daily dish — Marinated Chèvre (page 63 of our first cookbook).

Another customer favorite at Pasta & Co. is a goat cheese that comes from a tiny processor in Pie Town, New Mexico. Ten years ago, there were hardly any domestic goat-cheese makers. Now nearly every region of the country has a handful of small-scale farmers who pride themselves on their goat cheeses. Our New Mexican cheesemaker seasons her cheese with herbs and peppers and packs it in olive oil, which gives the cheese a long shelf life even unrefrigerated. Eaten straight from the jar with bread and wine, this Coon Ridge Goat Cheese is exuberantly good. Thinned with additional olive oil or some chicken stock, the product makes a quick pasta sauce.

The mere thought of the taste and popularity of all of these products makes us wonder what we would do without our ubiquitous goat cheese. (If you want to know more about chèvre and pick up some of the best goat cheese recipes of the past decade, read *Chèvre! The Goat Cheese Cookbook*, by pioneering cheesemaker Laura Chenel.)

ANCHO CHILE BUTTER

◆◆◆

The great thing about composed butters is that they keep so well and have so many uses. Let this butter, for example, hang around your refrigerator for a couple of months. Toss pasta with it. Make your next omelet with it. Sauté boneless chicken in it. Dollop some on a piece of grilled fish. Cook shrimp in it. Spread it on slices of an old baguette, run them under the broiler, and serve as an appetizer that will bring guests back for more. See what we mean? And do not forget to melt some of the butter over a baked potato.

This particular butter uses the mild dried ancho chile pepper to give it a Southwest flavor and a rich, rusty color. Allow 2 tablespoons of butter for every ¼ pound of pasta — a little more if you are adding other ingredients, such as vegetables or chicken, to the pasta. **PREPARE-AHEAD/SERVING NOTES:** The butter will keep refrigerated for at least three months. **ESSENTIAL GEAR:** Electric food processor

2 teaspoons pure olive oil

2 dried ancho chiles

5 cloves garlic, skins on

1 teaspoon ground coriander

⅓ teaspoon salt

⅓ teaspoon chili powder

Zest of ½ lemon

1 pound salted butter at room temperature

2 tablespoons finely chopped parsley

Fill a small bowl with very hot tap water. Place olive oil in small sauté pan and set over medium-high heat. When oil barely begins to smoke, add chiles and roast, turning until skins are soft and slightly puffed. Remove chiles to the hot water and let soak for 30 minutes.

In the same skillet and again over high heat, roast garlic cloves, shaking the pan until skins are golden brown and shriveling. Remove from heat. When cloves are cool to the touch, squeeze garlic out of the skins and reserve.

When chiles have finished soaking, drain, seed, and stem them. Place them and the garlic in the bowl of a food processor equipped with a steel blade. Add coriander, salt, chili powder, lemon zest, and one-fourth of the butter. Process until all ingredients are well-puréed. Gradually add the rest of the butter and process until it is incorporated. Add parsley and process a second more just to fold in.

Remove to a storage container and refrigerate to store. To use, melt the butter over low heat.

MAKES 2½ CUPS.

A SIMPLE, NOT-TO-BE-MISSED PASTA COMBO

At the height of asparagus season, blanch asparagus spears (we especially like California purple asparagus for its plump, tender stalks that require no peeling). Allow 4 to 6 meaty spears per serving. Drain and rinse with cold water. Set aside. In a large sauté pan, melt Ancho Chile Butter (page 172) — allow 3 to 4 tablespoons per serving. Add asparagus spears and quickly warm in the hot butter. With tongs, remove asparagus to hot plates. Leave any extra butter in the sauté pan. While asparagus warms, cook fresh egg fettuccine until tender. Drain and immediately toss with the remaining butter in sauté pan. Serve the pasta over the asparagus spears and top with a light grating of Parmigiano Reggiano (page 35).

SHERRIED CURRANT BUTTER

◆◆◆

This is a winter pasta sauce you will want to make in October and use through February. We make it especially to sell with pumpkin-filled ravioli, but it is just as well-suited to hazelnut-filled tortellini or fettuccine noodles served as a side or as a first course to a holiday meal. Do *not* skip the pomegranate seeds. They are a festive touch that adds both color and exquisite flavor. **PREPARE-AHEAD/SERVING NOTES:** Allow 8 hours for the currants to marinate before making the butter. The butter will keep for six months refrigerated. **ESSENTIAL GEAR:** Electric food processor

½ cup currants

2 tablespoons dry sherry

2 tablespoons freshly squeezed orange juice

¼ pound plus 3 tablespoons butter (salted or unsalted) at room temperature

¼ teaspoon ground allspice

¼ teaspoon ground or very finely crumbled sage

Pinch salt (adjust depending on butter)

8 grinds black pepper

TO TOP:

Freshly grated Parmesan cheese

Fresh pomegranate seeds

Soak currants in sherry and orange juice for at least 8 hours. Add them, undrained, to the work bowl of a food processor equipped with a steel blade, along with butter, allspice, sage, salt, and black pepper. Process until well-blended and currants are coarsely chopped. Refrigerate to store.

Allow 2 to 3 tablespoons of the butter per ¼-pound serving of pasta. Top buttered pasta with the Parmesan and pomegranate seeds.

MAKES 2 CUPS.

HAZELNUT AND FRESH
SAGE PESTO

◆◆◆

. . . .

Marcella grows a profusion of herbs each summer, and most of them end up in Pasta & Co. products. This sauce is similar to the traditional pesto made with fresh basil, pine nuts, cheese, garlic, and olive oil, but this version takes advantage of the end-of-summer sage crop. It is yet another way to salvage a fresh herb for winter use. Over and over, customers request this pesto for tossing with egg fettuccine, cheese- or hazelnut-filled tortellini, or pumpkin-filled ravioli. **PREPARE-AHEAD/SERVING NOTES:** The recipe halves fine, but we like to make a lot since it keeps for months refrigerated, and it also freezes well. **ESSENTIAL GEAR:** Electric food processor

⅔ cup sage leaves, washed, dried, and coarsely chopped

1¼ cups vegetable oil

¾ cup walnut oil, preferably French

½ cup peanut oil, preferably Leriva brand

2 cups hazelnuts, toasted

1 cup walnuts, toasted

1 tablespoon plus 1 teaspoon garlic, peeled and coarsely chopped

1 teaspoon allspice

2 cups freshly grated Parmesan cheese

TO TOP:

Additional freshly grated Parmesan cheese

Optional: fresh pomegranate seeds

Place in the bowl of a food processor bowl equipped with a steel blade the sage leaves, oils, hazelnuts, walnuts, garlic, and allspice. Process until nuts are finely chopped but *not* puréed. Remove to a bowl and fold in Parmesan.

Allow ¼ cup pesto for each ¼ pound pasta. Top all with a light grating of Parmesan and/or pomegranate seeds.

MAKES 6½ CUPS.

BEEF LASAGNE

◆◆◆

. . . .

This is the lasagne we have made and sold for a decade. Several things set this version apart from the dozens of other lasagne recipes. Its sauce is strongly seasoned with oregano. It calls for a thick filling of béchamel instead of ricotta cheese. It uses feta cheese to step up the flavor of the dish. And it takes advantage of fresh lasagne noodles, which can go into the dish with no precooking. Our sales of this product are the best proof that the formula works. **PREPARE-AHEAD/SERVING NOTES:** Make a day ahead and bake when needed, or do as we do and freeze. Take the lasagne straight from the freezer to the oven and adjust the cooking time accordingly. Caution: Be sure to let the lasagne sit 20 minutes before serving. **ESSENTIAL GEAR:** Shallow baking pan (9 by 13 inches)

SAUCE:

1¼ pounds lean ground beef

¼ cup pure olive oil

1⅓ cups coarsely chopped onions

1 heaping tablespoon oregano

1½ teaspoons finely minced garlic

1½ teaspoons basil

1 teaspoon salt

¼ teaspoon black pepper

¼ teaspoon red pepper flakes

1 cup plus 3 tablespoons dry white wine

3¼ cups Paradiso brand crushed tomatoes in purée. (There will be a couple of ounces left in the 28-ounce can. Save it. You will use it in assembling the lasagne.)

5 ounces frozen spinach (half of a 10-ounce box; keep the other half frozen for another use), thawed and squeezed dry of all liquid

CHEESE:

3 cups mozzarella cheese, grated

½ cup feta cheese, crumbled

BÉCHAMEL:

1½ cups milk

1 cup cream

Big pinch white pepper

Big pinch thyme

Big pinch nutmeg

Big pinch basil

3 tablespoons butter

⅓ cup plus 1 tablespoon flour

⅓ cup plus 1 tablespoon grated Parmesan cheese

3 tablespoons grated Romano cheese

NOODLES:

Uncooked fresh lasagne noodles, enough for three layers in a 9-inch by 13-inch pan

TOPPING:

¼ cup unseasoned bread crumbs

2 tablespoons freshly grated Parmesan cheese

1 teaspoon very finely chopped parsley

To make sauce, cook ground beef in a sauté pan over medium heat until pink is gone and meat is crumbly. Remove from heat and pour meat through a colander to drain off all fat. Reserve meat. (Be certain it is well-crumbled. If it is not, break it up using a potato masher or large wooden spoon.) In the same sauté pan, heat olive oil and add onions, oregano, garlic, basil, salt, black pepper, and red pepper flakes. Cook over medium heat until onions are translucent. Add wine, bring to a boil, and cook until alcohol has evaporated — about 10 minutes. Stir in tomatoes. Add spinach and reserved meat. Continue simmering for a few minutes. Remove from heat and reserve.

Mix together mozzarella and feta cheeses and set aside.

To make béchamel, heat milk, cream, white pepper, thyme, nutmeg, and basil in a small saucepan until it nears a boil. Turn off heat. Melt butter in a medium-size sauté pan. When foam from butter recedes, remove from heat, add flour, and mix well. Return to medium-low heat and, stirring frequently, simmer for 2 to 3 minutes to cook, but not brown, the flour. Gradually stir in hot milk and cream mixture. Raise heat to medium-high and continue stirring until mixture is smooth and thick — about 5 minutes. Add Parmesan and Romano cheeses and whisk until smooth. This should be the texture of wallpaper paste, not of the white sauce more often associated with béchamel.

To make topping, mix together bread crumbs, Parmesan, and parsley. Reserve.

TO ASSEMBLE AND BAKE:

Preheat oven to 400°F.

Spread 2 tablespoons of the tomato juices left in the can of tomatoes on the bottom of a shallow baking dish (9 by 13 inches). Lay in one layer of the uncooked lasagne noodles. Spoon on 3 cups of the meat sauce. Spread 1 cup of béchamel across the sauce in two diagonals (no need to spread evenly at this point). Top with 2 cups of cheese mixture. Lay on another layer of lasagne noodles and repeat, using the same amounts of sauce (be sure to get every dab of the meat sauce — there is no extra to spare), béchamel, and cheese. Top with last layer of noodles, and with fingertips, press lightly to distribute béchamel smoothly in the layers. Using a long metal spatula, "frost" top layer of noodles with remaining béchamel. Be sure to completely cover noodles so that they do not dry out in baking. Sprinkle evenly with reserved bread crumb mixture.

Bake lasagne at 400°F for about 60 minutes or until sauce bubbles around the edge and top is nicely browned. If top browns too quickly, cover with aluminum foil during last 10 minutes of cooking. If baking the lasagne straight from the freezer, add about 20 minutes to cooking time.

Once out of the oven, let lasagne set up for about 20 minutes before serving. (This is critical for ease of serving.)

SERVES 8 TO 10.

LASAGNE FEED

- Hot Bread with Olive Oil and Vinegar (page 17)
- Beef Lasagne (page 176)
- A trio of room-temperature vegetables:
  Carrots Marinated with Garlic and Oregano (page 35, *Pasta & Co —The Cookbook*)
  Green Beans or Sugar Snap Peas in Walnut Oil (page 55)
  Napa Cabbage and Olive Slaw (page 50, *Pasta & Co.—The Cookbook*)
- Italian Shortbread with Almonds, Brandy, and Lemon (page 246), fresh fruit, and an assortment of favorite after-dinner drinks

GIARDINIERA LASAGNE

◆◆◆

H ere is our very tasty, ever-popular vegetarian lasagne — just slightly spicy, very saucy, and chock-a-block with tiny pieces of tender but crunchy vegetables. Like the Beef Lasagne recipe that precedes it, Giardiniera Lasagne uses fresh lasagne noodles that require no precooking. **PREPARE-AHEAD/SERVING NOTES:** Same as for Beef Lasagne (page 176). **ESSENTIAL GEAR:** Shallow baking pan (9 by 13-inches)

SAUCE:

6 cups Pasta & Co. Giardiniera Sauce, purchased or made using recipe on page — (if making the sauce, we suggest doubling the amount of tomato paste called for in the recipe; if using purchased Giardiniera Sauce, add 3 tablespoons tomato paste)

CHEESE:

⅔ cup (2.5 ounces) feta cheese, well drained of brine and crumbled

3⅓ cups (12 ounces) mozzarella cheese, grated

BECHAMEL:

1½ cups milk

1 cup cream

Big pinch white pepper

Big pinch thyme

Big pinch nutmeg

Big pinch basil

3 tablespoons butter

⅓ cup plus 1 tablespoon flour

⅓ cup plus 1 tablespoon grated Parmesan cheese

3 tablespoons grated Romano cheese

NOODLES:

Uncooked fresh lasagne noodles — enough for three layers in a 9-inch by 13-inch pan

TOPPING:

¼ cup unseasoned bread crumbs

2 tablespoons freshly grated Parmesan cheese

1 teaspoon very finely chopped parsley

Mix together mozzarella and feta cheeses and set aside.

To make béchamel, heat milk, cream, white pepper, thyme, nutmeg, and basil in a small saucepan until near the boil. Turn off heat. Melt butter in a medium-size sauté pan. When foam from butter recedes, remove from heat, add flour, and mix well. Return to medium-low heat and, stirring frequently, simmer for 2 to 3 minutes to cook, but not brown, the flour. Gradually stir in hot milk and cream mixture.

Raise heat to medium-high and continue stirring until mixture is smooth and thick — about 5 minutes. Add Parmesan and Romano cheeses and whisk until smooth.

To make topping, mix together bread crumbs, Parmesan, and parsley. Reserve.

TO ASSEMBLE AND BAKE:

Preheat oven to 400°F.

Spread 2 tablespoons of the Giardiniera Sauce in bottom of a shallow baking dish (9 by 13 inches). Lay in one layer of uncooked lasagne noodles. Spoon on 3 cups of sauce. Spread a scant cup of the béchamel across the sauce in two diagonals (no need to spread evenly at this point). Top with 2 cups of cheese mixture. Lay on another layer of lasagne noodles and repeat, using same amounts of sauce, béchamel, and cheese. Top with last layer of noodles, and with fingertips, press lightly to distribute béchamel smoothly in the layers. Using a long, narrow metal spatula, "frost" top layer of noodles with remaining béchamel. Be sure to completely cover noodles so that they do not dry out in baking. (There will be no béchamel to spare, so, using a rubber spatula, salvage every speck.) Sprinkle evenly with bread crumb mixture.

Bake lasagne at 400°F for about 60 minutes or until sauce bubbles around the edge and top is nicely browned. If top browns too quickly, cover with aluminum foil during last 10 minutes of cooking. If baking the lasagne straight from the freezer, add about 20 minutes to cooking time. Once out of the oven, let lasagne set up for about 20 minutes before serving. (This is critical for ease of serving.)

SERVES 8 TO 10.

THE GREAT AMERICAN
MACARONI AND CHEESE
◆◆◆

This is the classic: precisely cooked pasta bathed in a creamy béchamel and encrusted in browned cheeses. Mom *should* have made this kind of macaroni and cheese, but probably did not.

Pasta & Co. makes hundreds of these a week in small foil pans, but the dish is worthy of much more. It is a quintessential baked pasta dish that makes for splendid party fare. We filled one customer's vintage copper au gratin pan with this recipe for a Christmas Eve celebration, where it was accompanied by roasted ham, Brussels sprouts, and well-chosen wines. Be assured: This dish will impress from the minute it is pulled all rusty-brown from the oven until the last spoonful is tugged with cheese stringing behind from the serving dish.

As with all deceptively humble dishes, there are ingredients here so critical and techniques so basic that you will want to apply them to other cooking as well. For example, even though the recipe calls for a hefty amount of Tabasco as well as chili powder, it is by no means a fiery dish. What the pepper sauce and powder do here is enhance the Cheddar flavor without noticeably stepping up the heat of the dish. Notice, too, that the choice of pasta is very specific: rigatoni. We use our own fresh rigatoni, a ribbed tube roughly 1 inch long and ¼ inch in diameter that is by our definition just the right size and texture for a baked pasta dish. You may substitute a good-quality dried rigatoni, but do not substitute a smooth tube, such as penne, ziti, or elbow macaroni. None of these will give you comparable results. **PREPARE-AHEAD/SERVING NOTES:** The dish can be prepared a day or two ahead of baking. Or it can be frozen, and baked immediately before serving.

1 pound sharp Cheddar cheese, grated	**2 teaspoons Tabasco or Jardine's brand Texas Champagne**
1 pound mozzarella cheese, grated	**⅓ teaspoon white pepper**
3 cups milk (whole, 2%, or 1%)	**1½ pounds fresh rigatoni (if you need to substitute dried, use just under a pound)**
7 tablespoons unsalted butter	
½ cup flour	**¾ teaspoon chili powder or hot paprika, to top**
½ cup freshly grated Parmesan cheese	**¾ cup milk (whole, 2%, or 1%)**
¼ cup freshly grated Romano cheese	

Combine grated Cheddar and mozzarella and set aside.

In a small saucepan, heat milk until near boiling. Turn off heat. Melt butter in a heavy pan large enough to hold the pasta after it is cooked. (It will take at least a 14-inch sauté pan or a large casserole that can take direct heat.) When foam from butter recedes, remove from heat, add flour, and mix well. Return to medium-low heat, and, stirring occasionally, simmer for 2 to 3 minutes to cook, but not brown, the flour. Gradually stir in hot milk. Raise heat to medium-high and continue stirring until mixture is smooth and thick — about 5 minutes. Add Parmesan and Romano cheeses. Whisk until smooth. Add Tabasco and white pepper and blend.

Cook rigatoni in boiling salted water about 4 minutes. (It will be underdone, but will finish cooking later.) Thoroughly drain rigatoni and fold it into the béchamel.

If cooking immediately, preheat oven to 375°F.

Layer one-half of the rigatoni mixture into a 9-inch by 13-inch pan. Top with one-half of the cheese mixture. Repeat layers. Top with chili powder, sprinkled evenly over top.

If not baking immediately, cover tightly with plastic wrap and refrigerate or freeze. When ready to bake, drizzle the ¾ cup milk over the dish. Bake for approximately 1 hour. If frozen, add at least 20 minutes to baking time. The dish should be rusty brown on top. Should it appear to be browning too fast, cover with foil for part of cooking time. Be sure to check for doneness in the very center of the dish.

SERVES 8 TO 10.

EARLY FALL DINNER AMERICANA

- ■ Hot Olives (page 28) served with a favorite bread
- ■ Great American Macaroni and Cheese (page 181)
- ■ Brown-Bottom Meat Loaf (page 225)
- ■ Roasted Tomato Sauce (page 194)
- ■ Chocolate Layer Cake (page 249)

LOW-FAT GREAT MAC*

•••

. . . .

Commendable work has been done on low-fat cheeses in recent years. And while there is a definite loss in flavor and texture, the fact that their butterfat content ranges from 20% to 30% compared with that of regular cheese at 40% to 50% makes them credible products to be seriously considered by those with diet concerns.

We especially like Olympia brand low-fat cheeses, made in Olympia, Washington. The Tabasco and chili powder in this recipe help to enhance the flavor of the low-fat cheeses. The biggest drawback is the texture of the cheeses when melted, which you will find more rubbery than with regular cheeses. While we are not nutritionists, our best guess is that by substituting with low-fat cheeses and using margarine for butter, and skim milk for whole, you will be cutting the fat content of this dish by approximately 50%.

Make the following substitutions:

For 1 pound sharp Cheddar cheese, grated, use ½ pound Olympia brand low-fat mild Cheddar *and* ½ pound Olympia brand low-fat sharp Cheddar. (We have not found a satisfactory low-fat sharp yellow Cheddar. Olympia's sharp Cheddar is white. To maintain the yellow Cheddar color of the dish, we use low-fat mild Cheddar for half the normal sharp Cheddar.)

For 1 pound mozzarella cheese, grated, use 1 pound Stella brand low-fat mozzarella or Lorraine "Lite" mozzarella.

For 7 tablespoons butter, use 7 tablespoons solid (not whipped) margarine (we like Imperial).

For the 3¾ cups milk, use 3¾ cups 1% milk.

For the ¾ teaspoon chili powder, use 1 teaspoon chili powder or hot paprika (this will further enhance the Cheddar flavor and step up the dish's color, which is diluted somewhat by the use of white Cheddar).

*Not recommended for party fare — celebrations are cause for indulgence.

PASTICCIO

◆◆◆

Next time you need a baked pasta dish for a buffet but do not want lasagne, try this. It is a zesty pasta topped with a custard cap that puffs and browns to a memorable taste and texture. All you need serve with this hearty dish is a green salad — one dressed with The Greens Dressing (page 105) gives just the right balance of flavors. **PREPARE-AHEAD/SERVING NOTES:** Prepare a day ahead and bake just before serving, allowing at least 20 minutes for the pasticcio to set up before cutting. Since the dish is as good at room temperature as it is steaming from the oven, you need not cut the timing uncomfortably close. And the unbaked dish freezes without a flaw. Place in the oven straight from the freezer and adjust cooking time accordingly. **ESSENTIAL GEAR:** Electric food processor, ovenproof baking dish (9 by 13 inches)

MEAT SAUCE:

1 pound ground beef

1 pound ground lamb

1 cup onion, peeled and coarsely minced

3 tablespoons finely minced garlic (or puréed in food processor, page 17)

2 teaspoons oregano

2 teaspoons pepper

½ tablespoon salt

½ teaspoon cinnamon

⅓ teaspoon nutmeg

⅛ teaspoon cloves

3½ cups Paradiso brand tomatoes crushed in purée

1⅓ cups chicken stock

⅓ cup dry white wine

¼ cup tomato paste

BÉCHAMEL:

1¼ cups milk

½ cup cream

⅛ heaping teaspoon basil

⅛ heaping teaspoon thyme

⅛ heaping teaspoon nutmeg

⅛ heaping teaspoon white pepper

7 tablespoons butter

¾ cup flour

PASTA:

14 ounces fresh rigatoni

CUSTARD:

2 eggs

⅓ cup freshly grated Parmesan
cheese

¼ **pound feta cheese, well drained of
brine and crumbled**

Cooled béchamel

¼ **teaspoon cinnamon**

To make meat sauce, cook ground beef and lamb together in a large sauté pan until meat is no longer pink. Drain off fat, return meat to pan, crumble well with a potato masher or large wooden spoon. Add onions, garlic, oregano, pepper, salt, cinnamon, nutmeg, and cloves. Cook over medium heat about 5 minutes. Add tomatoes, chicken stock, wine, and tomato paste. Cook another 15 minutes. Remove from heat and reserve.

To make béchamel, heat milk and cream in a 1-quart saucepan with basil, thyme, nutmeg, and white pepper just until a skin starts to form. In another pan of equal size, melt butter over medium-low heat. Add flour, blend well, and cook for 2 minutes. Add warm milk mixture to the roux, blending with a whisk and cooking over medium heat until thick and smooth — it should be the texture of wet mashed potatoes. Remove from heat and let cool.

Cook rigatoni barely 2 minutes in boiling water (it will continue cooking in the baked dish). Immediately rinse rigatoni with cold water and drain very well. Then fold into meat sauce. Spoon pasta and sauce mixture into an ovenproof dish (9 by 13 inches). Reserve.

To make custard, place eggs, Parmesan, and feta in the work bowl of a food processor equipped with a steel blade. Process until eggs are foamy. Add cooled béchamel and blend until well-incorporated.

Spoon custard mixture over the pasta and meat. Smooth as if frosting a cake, being sure to cover all the pasta. Sprinkle evenly with cinnamon (best method is to rub the cinnamon through your fingers to control coverage).

When ready to bake, preheat oven to 400°F. Bake uncovered for about 60 minutes or until sauce bubbles around edge and top is nicely browned. If top browns too quickly, cover with aluminum foil. If baking the pasticcio straight from the freezer, add about 20 minutes to cooking time. Once out of the oven, let dish set up for 20 minutes before serving. (This is critical for ease of serving.)

SERVES 8 TO 10.

CANNELLONI FILLED WITH
VEAL, SPINACH, AND
WILD MUSHROOMS

◆◆◆

W e tried dozens of cannelloni recipes before settling on this one to make for sale in our stores. We suggest saucing either with Marinara Sauce (page 153), Gorgonzola Sauce (page 161), or Alfredo Sauce (the "slim" version on page 159) works well), and topping with freshly grated Parmesan cheese. This is a big recipe, making enough cannelloni to feed 11 adults. Freeze in convenient portions for your family, or count on this as a sure-to-please dish for a party. **PREPARE-AHEAD/SERVING NOTES:** The cannelloni can be made hours ahead of baking and serving. Better yet, freeze them, with or without the sauce and cheese. Note, too, that while the recipe appears to be a time-consuming task, the process can be spread over a couple of days by making the filling one day and assembling the next. The recipe doubles easily.

½ cup water

¼ cup chopped dried wild mushrooms, Woodland Pantry brand

3 tablespoons butter

½ cup finely minced onion

4 medium cloves garlic, put through a garlic press

2 ounces prosciutto, coarsely chopped

1½ pounds ground veal

½ cup dry white wine

⅔ cup heavy cream

⅓ teaspoon salt

10 grinds black pepper

¼ teaspoon nutmeg

⅔ cup béchamel (see recipe page 188)

⅓ cup finely minced parsley

¾ cup freshly grated Parmesan cheese

1 cup frozen chopped spinach, thawed and well-drained

8 fresh lasagne sheets, each measuring 4½ inches by 13 inches

TO SAUCE:

Approximately 5½ cups Marinara Sauce (page 153) *OR* approximately 4 cups Gorgonzola Sauce (page 161), Alfredo Sauce, or Slim Alfredo Sauce (page 159)

About ½ cup freshly grated Parmesan cheese

Toasted walnuts (if using Gorgonzola sauce)

    In a small saucepan, bring water to a boil and add mushrooms. Remove from heat and let stand 1 hour.

In a large skillet, melt butter over low heat. Add onion, garlic, and prosciutto. Cook over medium-low heat, stirring occasionally, until onion is translucent — about 10 minutes.

Add veal and increase heat to medium. Cook, stirring to break up veal, until meat is crumbly and has just lost its pink color — about 10 minutes.

Place a colander over a large bowl. Strain meat mixture through colander, reserving drippings. Place meat mixture in a large bowl, and if meat is still lumpy, break it apart with a potato masher. Add ½ cup of the drippings back into meat.

Place wine in a 2-quart saucepan and boil down to ¼ cup. Add mushrooms and their steeping water, cream, salt, black pepper, and nutmeg, and cook down until sauce coats a wooden spoon (10 to 15 minutes). Remove from heat. Fold in béchamel, parsley, and Parmesan and mix well. Set aside.

Squeeze excess water out of spinach and break apart. Mix with veal, making sure spinach is well-distributed through the meat. Fold in cream mixture and combine well.

(Filling can be made a day ahead, covered, and refrigerated. Let return to room temperature before proceeding.)

Cut each lasagne sheet into thirds. In a large pot of boiling salted water, blanch the pasta, about 3 to 4 pieces at a time, for 40 seconds. (A pasta cooker works best for this.) Drain the pieces of pasta and plunge them immediately into a bowl of cold water. Remove from water and lay on damp cloth tea towels to drain.

Put ¼ cup filling in the middle of each piece of pasta. Roll pasta over filling to form a tube, then gently press on the middle of the tube to evenly distribute filling. Place in a lightly buttered ovenproof dish. A 9-inch by 13-inch pan will hold two rows of six each. (When completed, you will probably have a little extra filling. If you do, you can just tuck a bit into the end of each cannelloni. You will also have two extra sheets — this should make up for any torn ones.) Dish can be held refrigerated for 8 to 10 hours or can be frozen at this point.

Preheat oven to 375°F. For every cannelloni, allow ¼ cup marinara or 3 tablespoons of cream sauce. Pour sauce evenly over cannelloni. Sprinkle with Parmesan, allowing 1 teaspoon for each cannelloni.

Bake in the upper third of the oven until sauce is bubbling and cannelloni are lightly browned — about 15 to 20 minutes. (If frozen, adjust baking time.) Remove from oven and serve immediately. If using Gorgonzola sauce, top the baked cannelloni with toasted walnuts.

MAKES APPROXIMATELY 22 CANNELLONI.

TO MAKE ⅔ CUP BÉCHAMEL:

1 tablespoon butter
2 tablespoons flour
⅔ cup half-and-half
Tiny pinch each: white pepper, thyme, nutmeg, and basil
2 tablespoons freshly grated Parmesan cheese
1 tablespoon freshly grated Romano cheese

In a small saucepan, melt butter over medium heat, add flour, and cook 2 minutes without browning. Add half-and-half and white pepper, thyme, nutmeg, and basil and cook until thickened to the consistency of pancake batter. Stir in Parmesan and Romano cheeses. Remove from heat and reserve.

Other hot pasta dishes: recipes from a more private collection.

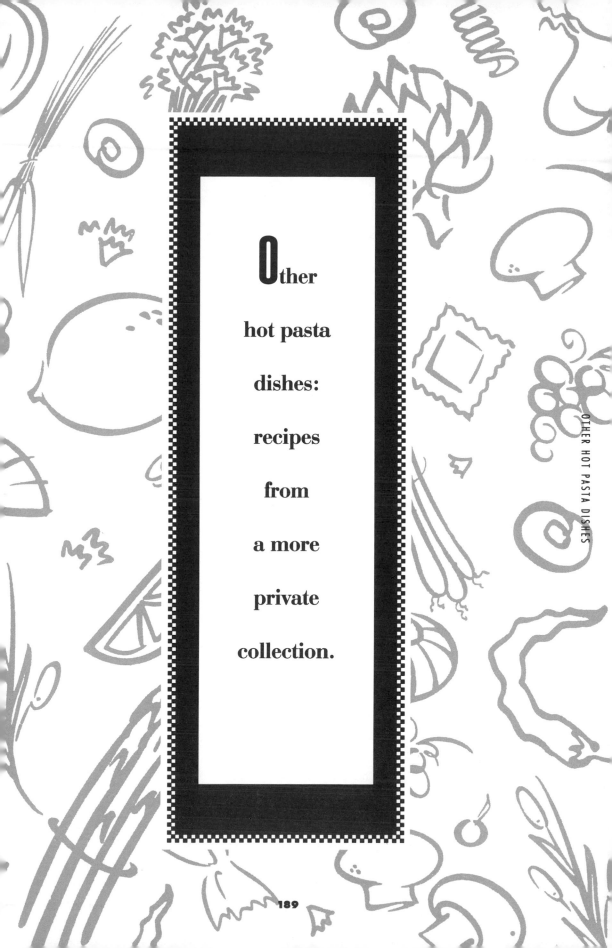

. . . .

These are the pasta recipes we like to make at home when we do *not* want dinner out of a Pasta & Co. container. Generally, we do not sell these dishes, though in some cases, even some of these — such as Roasted Tomato Sauce (page 194) — get packaged for sale when their ingredients are in season. They are standout pasta dishes. In fact, to Marcella, these recipes are the true gems of this book.

PASTA HDR

◆◆◆

. . . .

This is a celebration pasta — one of the best and most generally appealing pasta dishes we have created. In fact, it was developed especially to mark the 50th birthday of one of the company's owners, Harvey Rosene (who secretly loves steak more than pasta).

Do *not* skip the Olive and Tomato Salsa (see Insert, page 193) that tops the dish, nor the bed of raw spinach that goes under it, creating a one-dish meal. A simple appetizer and dessert is all you need to turn this into a princely menu. **PREPARE-AHEAD/SERVING NOTES:** Do not be put off by what looks like an involved preparation. This one is superb for entertaining because it can be prepared weeks ahead. The meat can and should be cooked days before serving (see Marinated Beef Tenderloin, page 34). The sauce can be prepared up to the point of the addition of the cream and cheese days ahead and refrigerated — or weeks ahead and frozen. (If necessary, you can add the deglazing liquid from roasting the meat when you reheat the sauce.) Just finish it all off with the cream and cheese right before serving.

For more than 6 servings, the recipe doubles, triples, and quadruples perfectly. When it comes to the final cooking of the pasta, cook 1 pound (6 servings) of pasta at a time and use fresh water after every two batches. **ESSENTIAL GEAR:** Electric food processor

2 ounces pancetta, cut into ⅛-inch dice (to dice, buy pancetta thinly sliced and freeze until you are ready to use it — without thawing, it cuts easily)

½ cup red onion, peeled and coarsely chopped

¼ cup leek, well-washed and sliced (use white part only)

¼ cup carrot, peeled and coarsely chopped

¼ cup coarsely chopped celery

2 tablespoons coarsely chopped parsley

3 cloves garlic, coarsely chopped

1 teaspoon Pasta & Co. House Herbs

½ teaspoon coarsely ground pepper mélange or black pepper

½ cup dry red wine

1/16 teaspoon ground cloves

2 cups homemade beef stock or canned beef consommé

1 cup deglazing liquid from roasting the tenderloin (page 34)

1 teaspoon green peppercorns in brine (you may use the brine, or drain and rinse the peppercorns)

1 bay leaf

3 Roma tomatoes, cut into ¼-inch dice (including seeds and juices — about 1¼ cups)

1 tablespoon sherry wine vinegar, or to taste

½ cup heavy cream

⅓ cup freshly grated Parmesan cheese

Approximately 10 ounces (weight, not volume) of the Marinated Beef Tenderloin (page 34), cut into ½-inch strips (a 1½ pound tenderloin should yield at least 10 ounces of meat after trimming and roasting)

1 pound fresh pappardelle, pescine, or other wide egg pasta of your choice

6 cups raw spinach leaves, well-washed and cut into a chiffonade (page 37)

Tomato and Olive Salsa (see Insert, page 193)

Parmesan cheese, freshly grated

Sauté pancetta in a large, heavy-bottomed saucepan and cook until golden but not browned. While pancetta cooks, place onion, leek, carrot, celery, parsley, garlic, House Herbs, and pepper mélange in a food processor bowl equipped with a steel blade. Process until vegetables are cut into tiny pieces (be careful not to overprocess — vegetables should be a very fine dice but not liquefied). Add vegetable and herb mixture to pancetta and sauté over medium heat for about 3 minutes or until the vegetables begin to give off juices.

Add wine and cloves, raise heat, and boil about 10 minutes or until alcohol has evaporated. Add beef broth, reserved meat drippings, green peppercorns, bay leaf, and tomatoes. Lower heat and let simmer. Add vinegar to taste after about 15 minutes. Partly cover and simmer about 45 minutes. The sauce can be completed to this point hours or days before serving.

When ready to serve, bring cream to a boil in a separate pan and stir in Parmesan until it is melted. Stir cream and cheese mixture into the sauce and heat gently until well-blended. Fold in strips of marinated tenderloin with all of its juices and continue to heat just until meat is warmed through (you want to minimize any further cooking of the meat).

Cook pasta until tender. Drain well and toss with sauce. Serve over the spinach and top with the Olive and Tomato Salsa and a dusting of Parmesan.

SERVES 6 AS A MAIN COURSE.

OLIVE AND TOMATO SALSA

This is a flavor and texture combo you will want to use again and again. If nothing else, make up a big bowl of it and serve with corn chips. Use it to garnish other pasta dishes, soups, salads. Just use it. You will be glad you did.

If at all possible, use the Santa Barbara brand olive oil specified in the recipe. The unique and pungent flavor of this California oil is particularly suited to this recipe.

2 Roma tomatoes, cut into ⅛-inch to ¼-inch dice (including seeds and juices)

32 Moroccan or kalamata olives, pitted and coarsely chopped (Pasta & Co. stores sell a pitted kalamata, but other good imports require pitting — see page 27)

½ cup red onion, cut into ⅛-inch to ¼-inch dice

¼ cup Santa Barbara Olive Co. brand extra virgin olive oil

Toss ingredients together until well coated with the oil. Serve at room temperature. This salsa is best if served within a few hours of preparation.

MAKES 2 CUPS.

ROASTED TOMATO SAUCE

♦♦♦

Make this recipe *only* when you have summer's best tomatoes and fresh basil or rosemary. And then make *lots*. The sauce freezes well (if you can keep people from eating it). Use the sauce not only for pasta, but as a side to grilled meats, combined with such vegetables as green beans or zucchini, or over potatoes and eggs. Do not miss it served warm with our favorite meat loaf (page 225). To serve on pasta, we suggest a sturdy cut, such as penne or rigatoni, topped with lots of freshly grated Parmesan or Romano cheese. Better yet, try using "shards" (page 35). **PREPARE-AHEAD/SERVING NOTES:** This is easy, easy, but allow plenty of oven time. The tomatoes *must* cook so long that they begin to brown. Any less and you will not develop the full flavor of this sauce. It may happen in two hours, but often it will take at least three. **ESSENTIAL GEAR:** Electric food processor

3 pounds tomatoes — as ripe as you can get them before they mold

½ cup pure olive oil

8 medium to large cloves garlic, peeled

1 cup fresh basil leaves OR 3 table-spoons fresh rosemary, coarsely chopped

½ teaspoon salt

½ teaspoon freshly cracked black pepper

Preheat oven to 325°F.

Remove stems from tomatoes. Halve the tomatoes horizontally and place in a shallow baking pan with cut sides up.

Place olive oil, garlic, basil or rosemary, salt, and black pepper in a food processor bowl equipped with a steel blade. Process until garlic is finely chopped.

Pour mixture over tomatoes and bake 2 to 3 hours or until tomatoes collapse, become saucy, and actually begin to caramelize. Stir the tomatoes now and then, breaking them up as you do.

When tomatoes have been reduced to a chunky sauce, remove from oven. If the amount of tomato skin is objectionable, run all or part of the sauce through the food processor.

MAKES 4½ CUPS.

PESCINE WITH RED BEANS

❖❖❖

A sign of things old and new, this recipe builds on the traditional combination of beans, pasta, and braising juices to make a dish fit for today's needs: no butter, no cream, little cholesterol, and only the fat given off in the browning of the pancetta.

If you do not mind the extra fat, make the more substantial "sausage version." Either way, the dish must have the kicker topping of chopped kalamata and jalapeño-stuffed olives mixed with your best olive oil. The "shine" from the olive oil will keep the dish looking tops on a platter if you choose to serve family-style. **PREPARE-AHEAD/SERVING NOTES:** Everything except the pasta can be prepared a day or two ahead and reheated. Cook the pasta and assemble right before serving. **ESSENTIAL GEAR:** Electric food processor

Optional: ⅔ pound Isernio brand bulk hot Italian sausage

4 ounces pancetta, cut into ¼-inch dice

1 cup red onion, peeled and coarsely chopped

½ cup leek, well-washed and sliced (use white part only — usually 1 leek)

½ cup carrot, peeled and coarsely chopped

4 large cloves garlic, peeled and coarsely chopped

2 tablespoons coarsely chopped parsley

½ cup coarsely chopped celery

2 teaspoons Pasta & Co. House Herbs or your choice of dried herbs

1 cup dry red wine

1 cup homemade beef stock or canned beef consommé (may need additional stock, especially if using sausage)

1 Roma tomato, chopped, including all juices

1 tablespoon balsamic vinegar

2 cups cooked small red beans (approximately ⅓ pound uncooked; first choice is Tongues of Fire beans — page 64)

TO ASSEMBLE:

20 pitted kalamata olives, well-rinsed and drained

10 jalapeño-stuffed green olives, well-rinsed and drained

¼ tablespoons extra virgin olive oil

½ pound fresh pescine

About 2 cups raw spinach leaves, washed, stemmed, and cut into a ¼-inch chiffonade (page 37)

Freshly grated Parmesan cheese (Parmigiano Reggiano cut into "shards" — page 35 — is worth the extra effort for this dish)

If using sausage, cook in a large sauté pan until no longer red. Drain off fat and remove sausage, crumbling into ½-inch pieces, and reserve. Place pancetta in the same sauté pan in which you cooked the sausage and cook until golden but not browned. While pancetta cooks, place red onion, leek, carrot, garlic, parsley, celery, and House Herbs in a food processor bowl equipped with a steel blade. Process until vegetables are cut into tiny pieces (be careful not to overprocess). Add vegetables and herbs to pancetta and sauté over medium heat for about 3 minutes. Add wine, raise heat, and boil about 10 minutes or until alcohol has evaporated. Add beef stock, tomato, and vinegar. Simmer about 5 minutes.

Stir in beans and reserved sausage, if used. Taste for seasoning and sauciness. If mixture seems dry, add a small amount of broth. Remove from heat and reserve.

Chop olives together and combine with olive oil. Reserve.

When ready to serve, cook pescine in boiling water until tender. While pasta cooks, heat sauce. When pasta is done, drain well and immediately toss with the sauce.

To serve, make a bed of the raw spinach. Spoon pasta and sauce over it and top with the olive mixture and Parmesan.

SERVES 4 AS A MAIN COURSE.

RIGATONI IN LAMB SAUCE

•••

Try it this way first. Next time you can adjust it to your taste (maybe you will want to reduce the feta cheese, or even eliminate the kopanisti). But Marcella loves the delicious excess of this dish: lots of sauce and pungent, pungent flavors over a sturdy pasta and raw greens. **PREPARE-AHEAD/SERVING NOTES:** The sauce can be made several days before serving and reheated. If you are making your own kopanisti, remember that it can be made weeks ahead and frozen.

1 pound ground lamb

2 tablespoons pure olive oil

5 cloves garlic, put through a garlic press

1 tablespoon cumin

1 tablespoon tomato paste

1 teaspoon oregano

½ teaspoon basil

⅛ teaspoon ground allspice

1 (28-ounce) can Paradiso brand pear tomatoes in juice, coarsely chopped, including all juices

1½ cups chicken stock

⅔ cup grapeleaf kopanisti (see page 45)

2 tablespoons freshly squeezed lemon juice

1 pound fresh rigatoni OR ¾ pound dried penne

3 to 4 cups fresh spinach leaves or Napa cabbage, cut into a chiffonade (page 37)

Olive and Feta Salsa (recipe below, page 198)

Parmesan cheese, freshly grated

In a large sauté pan, cook lamb over medium heat until no longer pink and meat is well-crumbled. Drain meat through a colander to remove grease and reserve.

To the same sauté pan, add olive oil, garlic, cumin, tomato paste, oregano, basil, and allspice. Cook over medium heat until well-blended. Add tomatoes, chicken stock, kopanisti, lemon juice, and reserved cooked lamb. Simmer until heated through and flavors are blended — about 10 minutes.

Cook pasta until tender. Drain and toss with the sauce. Place spinach or cabbage chiffonade on a serving platter or on individual plates to form a bed. Top with pasta and sauce, then with a couple of spoonfuls of salsa and a light sprinkling of Parmesan cheese over all.

SERVES 4 TO 6 AS A MAIN COURSE.

OLIVE AND FETA SALSA

We know. These toppings are becoming a habit for us, but they are so good.

1 Roma tomato, cut into ⅛-inch dice, including all juices

16 imported black olives, pitted (page 27) and finely chopped

¼ cup red onion, cut into ⅛-inch dice

1 to 2 tablespoons Santa Barbara Olive Co. brand extra virgin olive oil

2 ounces feta cheese

Freshly cracked black pepper

Combine tomato, olives, onion, and olive oil. Crumble feta over the top and season to taste with black pepper.

SHRIMP SAUCE

◆◆◆

This is our favorite "brew" for quickly poaching shrimp. It is garlicky, spicy, and herby all at once. Sometimes we skip the pasta, use large prawns in their shells, and serve the quickly cooked prawns and sauce in big bowls with hot bread and piles and piles of napkins. Messy, but there's hardly a better way to eat prawns. (Of course, if so inclined, you can shell the prawns before cooking, but definitely leave the tails on for visual effect.)

Only one caution: Choose your shrimp carefully. Ordinary salad shrimp will not do. If you cannot get rock shrimp (a plump, firm-textured variety from Florida that is available from late summer through winter), use small prawns and shell them before cooking. **PREPARE-AHEAD/SERVING NOTES:** The garlic-and-herb purée can be prepared days ahead of serving the dish. (In fact, if you have a bumper crop of fresh herbs, freeze several batches of the purée.) Just proceed with the remainder of the recipe right before cooking the pasta. **ESSENTIAL GEAR:** Electric food processor

¼ **cup extra virgin olive oil**

2 **tablespoons freshly squeezed lemon juice**

½ **teaspoon dried rosemary OR** 2 **teaspoons fresh rosemary**

½ **teaspoon dried oregano OR** 4 **teaspoons fresh oregano**

1 **teaspoon sweet or hot paprika (depending on how fiery you want this)**

½ **teaspoon salt**

¼ **teaspoon cayenne or African bird pepper**

8 **medium cloves garlic, coarsely chopped**

¼ **pound butter**

2 **bay leaves**

½ **pound rock shrimp or small prawns, shelled but uncooked**

¾ **pound fresh linguine OR** 9 **ounces dried** *chitarra* **(square spaghetti)**

2 **cups raw fresh spinach leaves, cut into chiffonade (page 37)**

2 **Roma tomatoes, cut into ¼-inch dice**

Parmesan cheese, freshly grated, to top

In a food processor bowl equipped with steel blade, purée to a paste the olive oil, lemon juice, rosemary, oregano, paprika, salt, cayenne, and garlic. Stop the motor a couple of times, and scrape down the sides of the work bowl with a spatula to make sure garlic is getting finely minced.

In a large sauté pan, melt butter. Add olive oil mixture and bay leaves. Sauté briefly over medium heat. Do not burn garlic. Add shrimp to the pan. Roll shrimp around in pan so each shrimp is coated with the hot sauce and cooks quickly. As soon as shrimp are barely cooked (be careful not to overcook — it may take only 1 or 2 minutes), remove pan from heat while you cook the pasta. When pasta is cooked and well-drained, return sauté pan to low heat, add pasta, and toss with the shrimp sauce to coat. Fold in spinach and tomatoes. Serve immediately, topped with Parmesan.

SERVES 3 AS A MAIN COURSE.

A PASTA DINNER

- Pita Chips (page 18) with Highly Seasoned Tofu (page 20)
- Shrimp Sauce (page 199) (no need for a green vegetable or salad)
- Fresh Lemon Tarts (page 233) — or quicker, purchase lemon sorbet and drizzle with The Berry Sauce (available at Pasta & Co.) or Boysenberry Purée (page 186 of *Pasta & Co. — The Cookbook*)

TINY PENNE WITH GRILLED
WHITE FISH

◆◆◆

This is a meal all by itself, wanting nothing more than a heady and crisp white wine to accompany it. The dish is bold with the taste of garlic, olives, and white fish fresh off the grill. It can be served immediately or allowed to cool to room temperature. Especially critical is the choice of olive — the Moroccan oil-cured black olive — and the pasta, a tiny dried penne called *penne mezzane* that measures 1½ inches long by about ⅛ inch in diameter. **PREPARE-AHEAD/SERVING NOTES:** Prepare the ingredients — even grill the fish — hours ahead of assembly. Once put together, the dish holds well for at least a day.

⅔ cup extra virgin olive oil

½ cup pine nuts, coarsely chopped

½ teaspoon red pepper flakes

2 teaspoons dried basil OR ½ cup fresh basil, cut in juliénne

4 teaspoons garlic, finely minced or put through a garlic press, OR 4 teaspoons garlic purée (page 17)

44 Moroccan olives, pitted (page 27) and chopped

2 tablespoons fresh lemon juice

10 ounces *penne mezzane* pasta

1 pound cooked white fish, such as ling cod, grilled rare (preferably seasoned with lovage — see Insert,

page 202) and flaked into bite-size pieces — beware of bones

½ cup of some combination chopped parsley, snipped fresh chives, or other fresh herbs

½ cup spinach leaves, cut into a chiffonade (page 37)

4 Roma tomatoes, cut into ¼-inch dice and seasoned lightly with salt and sweet paprika

⅓ cup freshly grated Parmesan cheese

2 tablespoons extra virgin olive oil

Freshly cracked black pepper to taste

Freshly grated Parmesan to top

In a large sauté pan, warm the ⅔ cup olive oil over medium heat and add pine nuts and red pepper flakes. Cook slowly until pine nuts are golden. Stir in basil (if using fresh basil, do not add here but at the end of the recipe, with other fresh herbs and spinach), garlic, and olives and cook a couple minutes longer until garlic is translucent. Do not brown the garlic. Stir in lemon juice and remove from heat.

Cook pasta until very tender (be sure to stir frequently, as it tends to stick together). Drain well.

Return sauce to low heat and toss pasta, fish, fresh herbs and spinach, tomatoes, Parmesan, and the 2 tablespoons olive oil together. Season with black pepper. Remove from heat. Spoon onto serving dish or plates.

Top with a light grating of Parmesan. Serve immediately or let cool and serve at room temperature.

MAKES 4 MAIN-COURSE SERVINGS.

LOVAGE

This little-known hardy herb that weathers every wicked winter and squeezes even the lavender bush out of the herb garden is the perfect seasoning for grilled fish. Use branches of lovage to stuff inside a whole fish or to layer around fillets in a grilling rack. Drizzle the fish and the lovage with olive oil and season well with salt and pepper and you will have a memorable grilling experience. These lovage leaves were somehow meant to be charred against fish flesh. Such is the wonder of cooking.

A PASTA SUPPER

■ Focaccia (page 120), served with White Bean Hummus (page 24)

■ Tiny Penne with Grilled White Fish (page 201)

■ Fresh Lemon Tarts (page 233) if you dare, or settle for the season's best fresh fruit

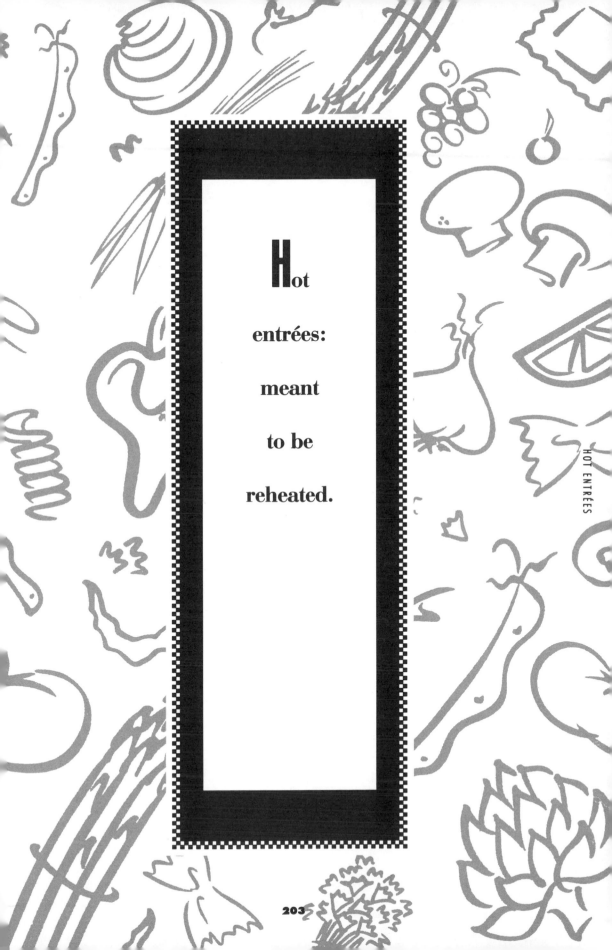

Hot

entrées:

meant

to be

reheated.

HOT ENTRÉES

From the beginning, Pasta & Co. never was envisioned as just a "pasta shop." We wanted to be part of something much bigger. It had to do with the way we were beginning to eat in the early eighties. It had to do with an unprecedented enthusiasm and curiosity about food. And it had to do with lifestyle trends that were fueling a growing demand for high-quality take-home foods. ■ Our fresh pasta and sauces filled the bill for busy customers who liked to eat well. So did our bevy of room-temperature dishes. But the market also wanted prepared entrées that were designed to be reheated without tasting like leftovers. The following dishes are these very foods.

SAUTÉED CHICKEN IN RED WINE VINEGAR SAUCE

♦♦♦

. . . .

This was our very first ready-to-reheat entrée. By coincidence, it is tailor-made for today's tastes: a full-flavored, low-fat dish. Keep it that way by serving the chicken over the best raw salad greens you can find. The hot vinegar sauce will wilt the greens and the result is one of the best-tasting low-calorie dinners you can imagine. **PREPARE-AHEAD/SERVING NOTES:** Although the dish reheats very well, it is better served as soon as it is made. Prep all the ingredients up to a day ahead, however, and the dish will be no bother to make at the last minute. **ESSENTIAL GEAR:** Electric food processor, nonstick sauté pan

4 cloves garlic, peeled	**Cooking oil**
1½ teaspoons rosemary — if fresh, use a heaping tablespoon of the needles	**2½ pounds split, bone-in chicken breasts**
½ teaspoon beef bouillon cube (about ⅔ of a cube), crumbled	**15 mushrooms, wiped clean and trimmed — halved if large**
1⅓ cups homemade chicken stock or canned chicken broth	**12 pit-in black olives — or a mixture of green and black**
⅔ cup red wine vinegar	**3 tablespoons finely chopped parsley, to top**
3 tablespoons dry white wine or vermouth	

Place garlic, rosemary, bouillon cube, chicken stock, vinegar, and wine in a food processor bowl equipped with a steel blade. Process approximately 5 minutes or until garlic and rosemary are finely minced.

Thoroughly rinse chicken in cold water and drain well. Trim off excess fat. Heat a small amount of oil in a large nonstick sauté pan over high heat. When oil is hot, add chicken breasts, skin-side-down, and sauté over medium-high heat until skin is a very golden brown (or use Judy's no-oil SilverStone method, page 206). Turn breasts to brown edges and bottoms until pink is gone. With breasts skin-side-up, add vinegar mixture, which should come about halfway up the sides of the breasts but not cover them. Bring sauce to a boil, then reduce to a simmer and cook for approximately 15 to 20 minutes. Breasts are done when an instant-read thermometer inserted into thickest portion registers 165°F.

Cover serving platter or individual plates with a bed of salad greens. Top with chicken. Add mushrooms and olives to the sauce and simmer for only a minute.

Spoon mushrooms and olives over chicken. Taste sauce — it may need pepper or it may be too sharp in flavor (in which case, add a small amount of additional stock or water). Pour finished sauce over chicken and top with chopped parsley. Serve immediately.

MAKES 4 TO 6 CHICKEN BREASTS.

JUDY BIRKLAND'S SYSTEM FOR BROWNING CHICKEN WITH NO OIL

A new, commercial-weight SilverStone 12-inch or 14-inch sauté pan can be used to brown chicken without adding any oil to the pan. Rinse chicken breasts under cold water and put them directly into the pan, SKIN-SIDE-UP. At this point, pull off the biggest, most obvious gobs of fat. Place pan over medium heat and allow the chicken to render its own fat. By the time all the water that was on the chicken has evaporated, there will be enough chicken fat in the pan to brown the top of the breasts successfully.

A nutritionist, of course, would point out here that chicken fat has cholesterol and olive oil does not. Judy's answer is that this method is for chicken being sautéed with its skin and bones anyway, so you save the 125 calories that are in each tablespoon of olive oil. Also, at the point that the chicken begins to brown well, you can pull off the skin to save a few additional calories.

Now, the only catch is that this method does not work with a pan that has lost its nonstick surface — a virtual inevitability for any pan that is around the average household for more than a year or two. The pans, however, are inexpensive enough to replace without mortgaging the farm. After a couple of years, your chicken pan becomes your red meat pan (since red meat does not brown properly on a good nonstick surface anyway), your old red meat pan goes in with the camping gear, and you buy a new chicken pan. This is Judy's SilverStone system. And it works. (What is more, you can use the old sauté pan for the Pasta & Co. "Big Sauté Pan Method of Saucing Pasta" — see Insert, page 154.)

VEAL RAGOUT

◆◆◆

This dish has been a perennial customer favorite ever since we perfected it nearly nine years ago. As with all dishes, the quality of the ingredients is critical, and this is especially so with the choice of meat for this dish. Good stew meat is not easy to find. For this ragout, specify to your butcher that you want stew meat from the shoulder. Accept nothing less or more. (Veal round or rump will be leaner and freer of gristle, but both cuts stew with all the distinction of sand.) **PREPARE-AHEAD/SERVING NOTES:** The ragout is perfect for reheating. Make it up to 3 days ahead of serving.

3 pounds veal stew meat, cut from the shoulder

Cooking oil

2 cups onions, cut into 1-inch dice

¼ cup flour

1 (8-ounce) can tomatoes, coarsely chopped, including all juices

1 teaspoon basil

1 teaspoon oregano

2 bay leaves

1 teaspoon salt

½ teaspoon black pepper

1 teaspoon garlic, finely minced or put through a garlic press

2 cups homemade chicken stock OR 1 (14.5-ounce) can chicken broth

1⅓ cups dry white wine

2 tablespoons sherry vinegar

2 cups carrots, peeled and cut into 3-inch by ½-inch strips

3 cups mushrooms, trimmed, wiped clean, and halved if very large

½ cup finely chopped parsley

Trim veal of the most obvious fat and gristle and cut any large pieces into about 1-inch to 1½-inch cubes. If meat seems very moist, pat it dry with a paper towel so that it will brown well.

Set an ovenproof roasting pan next to the stove. Film a large sauté pan with oil and heat to medium-high. Brown meat in three or four batches. As each piece becomes suitably brown, remove it to roasting pan. Regulate heat between high and medium-high. You don't want the meat to burn, but it should be well-browned. Veal is very gelatinous meat. Should the pan become too sticky for meat to brown nicely, simply deglaze with some of the chicken stock. (Pour some of the chicken stock into the sauté pan, bring to a boil, and pour broth and drippings into roasting pan.) Add some more vegetable oil to the sauté pan, and begin browning anew.

When meat is all browned, preheat oven to 325°F. Add another thin film of oil to sauté pan and sauté onions over medium-high heat. When they are translucent, add flour and cook until mixture is golden, but not browned. Add tomatoes, basil, oregano, bay leaves, salt, black pepper, and garlic. Simmer briefly. Add mixture to browned meat, using a rubber spatula to get all of the drippings into the roaster. (Hang on to that sauté pan. You are not ready to wash it yet!) Add chicken stock, wine, and vinegar to the roasting pan and bring stew to a simmer on top of the stove.

Cover roasting pan with a tight-fitting lid and place in preheated oven. Braise at 325°F for approximately 1¼ hours or until meat is tender.

While the ragout is braising, cook carrots in boiling salted water just until they are tender. Drain and rinse under cold water. Reserve. Using the same sauté pan as above, sauté mushrooms in a very small amount of hot oil, just until they begin to brown. Reserve.

When ragout is done, stir in carrots and mushrooms. Mix well; taste for salt and pepper. When ready to serve, toss with parsley. Serve with tiny boiled red potatoes or over a bed of pasta (we like fresh pescine, dried penne, or creste gallo — see page 87).

SERVES 6 TO 8.

A NOTE ABOUT "THROWING TOGETHER" DINNER

When customers ask us (and they frequently and quite desperately do), "What can we just throw together for a quick great dinner?" we often find ourselves at a loss for suggestions. Obviously, dinner from your local take-out food shop is one answer. But sometimes that is not what you want. You really do want to cook a meal — in person, complete with all the smells and feelings cooking invokes. Yet it has to be done with the last 30 minutes of energy you have left in your day.

We empathize, but we are not 10-minute chefs. And other than with very obvious quick meals, such as omelets and pasta with butter and cheese, we are not notably sage. The following recipes, however, were conceived specifically to be made ahead and rewarmed with impeccable results. If you like to cook and plan ahead, they could be the answer to many menu-planning dilemmas.

TURKEY PICCATA

◆◆◆

....

Another popular Pasta & Co. entrée, Turkey Piccata makes a sure-to-please hot buffet dish for a party. Do not be wary of the numerous cloves of garlic called for. The dish is sprightly, but smooth and balanced as well. While it is usually served over pasta or rice, a bed of freshly steamed, coarsely chopped broccoli provides a color and taste that could not be a better match. Only one caution: Do not overcook the turkey. If you do, you will have tasteless, stringy meat instead of the succulent morsels that are intended. **PREPARE-AHEAD/SERVING NOTES:** This is a strong candidate for entertaining. The recipe doubles and triples perfectly, holds for several days, and rewarms without a flaw. Because of the mushrooms, freeze only as a last resort. **ESSENTIAL GEAR:** Electric food processor

½ cup plus 1 tablespoon flour

1 teaspoon salt

⅓ teaspoon freshly cracked black pepper

2¼ pounds boneless turkey breast, cut into 1-inch cubes

Vegetable oil

1½ cups onions, chopped into ½-inch by 1-inch pieces

1⅓ cups homemade chicken stock or canned chicken broth

⅓ cup dry sherry

¼ cup freshly squeezed lemon juice

9 medium cloves garlic, peeled

½ lemon, washed, seeded, and cut into large pieces

2 tablespoons plus 1 teaspoon olive oil

Pinch nutmeg

Pinch allspice

Pinch ground cloves

⅔ pound mushrooms, wiped clean, trimmed, and halved

¾ cup cream

⅓ cup capers, well-drained

⅓ cup finely chopped parsley

TO TOP:

Thinly sliced lemon

Additional finely chopped parsley

On a baking sheet, mix together flour, salt, and black pepper. Toss turkey pieces in flour mixture to coat evenly. Set them aside. Be careful that the pieces do not stick together. Save remaining flour for later use in the recipe.

Put a thin film of the oil in a large sauté pan and place over medium-high heat. The oil is hot enough if it sizzles when a piece of turkey meat is dropped in. Brown meat in three or four batches, taking care not to crowd the pieces. Remove browned pieces and let drain on paper towels. Continue browning the rest of the meat. Keep heat adjusted so that flour particles left on the bottom of the pan do not burn. If they do, scrape out pan and add fresh oil.

When all the turkey has been cooked, add another light film of oil to the pan. Add onions and cook until they are soft. While the onions are cooking, mix together chicken stock, sherry, and lemon juice. Add the reserved flour mixture to cooked onions and stir until flour has cooked, but not browned. Add half the chicken stock mixture and simmer about 3 minutes to make a smooth sauce. Pour sauce into a flameproof casserole large enough to hold all the turkey. Add turkey and set aside.

In the work bowl of a food processor equipped with a steel blade, place garlic cloves, lemon, olive oil, nutmeg, allspice, and ground cloves. Process until ingredients form a paste. Fold mixture into the casserole and set aside.

Add remaining stock mixture to the sauté pan and boil to loosen all the drippings from cooking the meat and onions. Add mushrooms and simmer a minute or so. Pour mixture into the casserole and stir to blend.

Simmer mixture over low heat on top of the stove until sauce begins to thicken and the turkey barely loses its pink color — about 5 to 7 minutes. Stir in cream, capers, and parsley. Simmer a couple minutes more.

When ready to serve, remove to serving dish and garnish with thinly sliced lemon and additional chopped parsley.

SERVES 6 TO 8.

CHICKEN EN CROÛTE

◆◆◆

. . . .

Here is another good candidate for a hot buffet or a luncheon. It is a dressy "pan product." (We make and sell dozens of them a week in 6-inch by 8-inch foil pans for baking at home.) An herby rice mixture chock-full of poached chicken and artichoke hearts is topped with a crust of papery phyllo dough. This recipe is written for a 9-inch by 13-inch rectangular baking dish, but you can also use a 13-inch porcelain oval for a more impressive presentation. Just cut your phyllo dough to fit. **PREPARE-AHEAD/SERVING NOTES:** The dish freezes so well that you may want to double the recipe and freeze half. For each pan you plan to make, you will need 8 sheets of thawed phyllo dough. When ready to bake, the dish can go straight from the freezer to the oven. Add about 20 minutes to your baking time if frozen. **ESSENTIAL GEAR:** Shallow ovenproof baking dish (9 by 13 inches)

2 cups water

1 cup dry white wine

1 tablespoon thyme

1¼ teaspoons rosemary

1 scant teaspoon salt

1 bay leaf

2½ pounds boneless, skinless chicken thighs

1 (9-ounce) box frozen artichoke hearts, thawed and drained

5 tablespoons butter

2½ cups onions, peeled and cut into ¼-inch dice

3 tablespoons garlic, peeled and finely minced *OR* 3 tablespoons garlic purée (page 17)

1¼ pounds fresh mushrooms, wiped clean, trimmed, and coarsely chopped

1½ cups homemade chicken stock or canned broth

1 tablespoon summer savory

½ teaspoon salt

1 tablespoon plus 1 teaspoon freshly squeezed lemon juice

1 cup long-grain white rice

2 tablespoons butter

¼ cup flour

1 teaspoon white pepper

½ teaspoon Tabasco or Jardine's brand Texas Champagne

½ cup cream

8 sheets frozen phyllo dough, thawed

3 tablespoons butter (salted preferred)

In a large sauté pan, combine water, wine, thyme, rosemary, the scant teaspoon salt, and bay leaf. Place over medium heat and add chicken. Poach approximately 15 minutes (see page 39). As chicken loses its pink color, remove to a large bowl and let cool. When all the chicken has been poached, reduce poaching liquid to 2 cups. Remove from heat and reserve. Tear chicken meat into bite-size pieces. Add artichokes to bowl. Reserve.

In a 3-quart kettle, melt the 5 tablespoons butter and add onions, garlic, and mushrooms. Cook over medium heat 2 minutes. Add stock, summer savory, the ½ teaspoon salt, and lemon juice. Bring mixture to a boil. Stir in rice, reduce heat, and simmer 20 minutes or until rice is tender but not overcooked. Stir occasionally to keep rice from sticking. If there is extra liquid left on the rice once it is tender, drain it off. Toss rice with reserved artichokes and chicken meat.

In a small sauté pan, melt the 2 tablespoons butter over medium-low heat. Add flour, white pepper, and Tabasco and cook about 2 minutes. Add the reserved poaching liquid and cream. Boil, whisking continuously for 2 minutes. Fold sauce into the chicken and rice, making sure all ingredients are evenly distributed.

Lightly oil a shallow ovenproof pan (9 by 13 inches). Spoon the mixture into pan. Cut all 8 phyllo sheets to correct size. Melt the 3 tablespoons salted butter in a small saucepan (be careful not to boil the butter). Lay first sheet of phyllo on top of rice mixture. With a pastry brush, spread about 1 teaspoon of the butter over phyllo. Lay on the next phyllo sheet and repeat process until all the phyllo and butter is used. (You will have approximately 2 teaspoons of butter left for the top layer of phyllo.)

Preheat oven to 400°F. Bake for about 50 minutes, or until phyllo is very well browned (do not settle for less than a browned crust). Cool on a rack for 10 to 15 minutes before cutting and serving.

A COUPLE OF HINTS FOR WORKING WITH PHYLLO: If you are not ready to use the thawed phyllo sheets immediately, cover them with a damp cloth to prevent them from drying out. On the other hand, if your phyllo dough is so moist it is sticking together, leave out to air-dry a bit before working with it. And it does not hurt to allow yourself a couple extra sheets, in case some of them tear badly.

SERVES 8 TO 10.

GORGEOUS DIRTY RICE

◆◆◆

. . . .

A Deep South specialty, dirty rice is typically a fiery slurry of overcooked rices, pork, and chicken livers. We take away the chicken livers and call for a combination of firm-textured rices. Then, using some of the dish's traditional ingredients, we give it a brightly colored topping to make it look "gorgeous."

Season the Dirty Rice as spicy as you dare, knowing that a generous garnish of either sour cream (or Quark — page 91) or crabmeat will somewhat offset the heat. Accompanied by a simple tossed green salad or steamed vegetable, Dirty Rice makes fine family fare. It is also stellar party food (see menu on page 214). **PREPARE-AHEAD/SERVING NOTES:** The entire dish up to the point of garnishing can be prepared two to three days before serving. Just reheat either covered in the oven or in a sauté pan on top of the stove. Place on serving platter and top with garnish.

8 ounces ground pork (*not* sausage meat)

¾ cup onion, cut into ¼-inch dice

½ cup celery, cut into ¼-inch dice

½ cup green bell pepper, cut into ¼-inch dice

½ cup red bell pepper, cut into ¼-inch dice

1 tablespoon finely minced garlic

1 teaspoon salt

1 teaspoon freshly ground black pepper

1 teaspoon ground cumin

½ teaspoon dried oregano

¼ to ¾ teaspoon cayenne (depending on its strength, even ¼ teaspoon can make this a very fiery dish)

2 cups homemade chicken stock or canned broth — may need additional stock, depending on how quickly rice cooks

1 cup California Calmati rice

1 cup Indian basmati rice or long-grain white rice

TO TOP:

½ cup green bell pepper, cored, seeded, and cut into ⅛-inch dice

½ cup red bell pepper, cored, seeded, and cut into ⅛-inch dice

6 green onions, sliced thinly on the diagonal

1 cup sour cream or Quark (page 91)

Optional: ½ pound cooked crabmeat

In a large, heavy saucepan, sauté pork until pink color is gone and meat is crumbly. Remove pork. Pour off all but 2 tablespoons of the fat and add onion, celery, and ½ cup each of the bell peppers. Sauté over low heat for 5 minutes. Then add garlic, salt, black pepper, cumin, oregano, and cayenne. Stir, and cook an additional 3 minutes. Meanwhile, bring stock to a boil in another saucepan.

Add Calmati rice to vegetable mixture and sauté for a couple of minutes. Add hot stock and reserved pork. Bring to a boil; reduce heat, cover, and simmer for 50 to 60 minutes, or until rice is cooked. (Most of the broth will have cooked away; if necessary, add more. NOTE: Even when the Calmati rice is cooked, it maintains a slightly crunchy texture.)

While Calmati rice is cooking, boil basmati rice in another pan according to the directions on box. When tender, drain well and reserve. When Calmati rice is done, fold in cooked basmati rice. If necessary, add more broth. The dish should be moist, but not saucy.

Top with the bell peppers, green onions, sour cream or Quark, and crabmeat. If using crabmeat, you may want to offer the sour cream in a separate bowl on the side.

SERVES 6 AS AN ENTRÉE.

DAZZLING WINTER BUFFET

■ Spiced Almonds (page 15)

■ Mixed imported olives

■ Great American Macaroni and Cheese (page 181)

■ Gorgeous Dirty Rice (page 213)

■ A green salad

■ Seasonal fresh fruit

■ Italian Shortbread with Almonds, Brandy, and Lemon (page 246)

CHICKEN HASH

✦✦✦

. . . .

Here is yet another company dish for a crowd. Our Chicken Hash is especially good for an early spring entrée to serve alongside the season's first fresh asparagus. **PREPARE-AHEAD/SERVING NOTES:** The dish can be prepared in its entirety, then rewarmed and browned under the broiler right before taking it to the table. The recipe easily feeds 8, but remember — this dish was designed to make great leftovers. **ESSENTIAL GEAR:** 12-inch sauté pan

3 cups homemade chicken stock or canned chicken broth

2½ pounds boneless, skinless chicken thighs

4 teaspoons salt

4 medium-size white-skinned potatoes, cut into ½-inch dice

3 medium-size carrots, peeled and cut into ½-inch dice

2 medium-size turnips, peeled and cut into ½-inch dice

¼ pound butter

3 medium-size onions, cut into ½-inch dice

1½ tablespoons summer savory

½ teaspoon salt

¾ teaspoon black pepper

½ cup cream

⅔ pound mozzarella cheese, thinly sliced or shredded

Heat chicken stock to a simmer in a 12-inch sauté pan. Add half of the chicken thighs and poach until just barely cooked through (see page 39 — be careful not to overcook, since the chicken will be cooked again later in the recipe). Remove cooked thighs from the simmering broth and poach remaining pieces of chicken. When chicken is all cooked, remove it from heat and reserve. Raise heat and reduce stock to 2 cups.

While stock is reducing, bring a large saucepan of water to a boil. Add 2 of the 4 teaspoons salt and the diced potatoes and boil until tender. Drain and reserve. Fill saucepan with fresh water, bring to a boil, and add remaining 2 of the 4 teaspoons salt. Add carrots and boil until tender. Lift carrots out with a slotted spoon and add them to potatoes. Add the turnips to the boiling water and cook until tender. Drain well and add to potatoes and carrots.

By now the chicken stock should be reduced. Strain it into a 1-quart measuring pitcher. Tear cooled chicken along its natural tissue separations. Discard any fat.

In the sauté pan, melt the butter. Add onions, summer savory, the ½ teaspoon salt, and black pepper. Cook slowly until onions are translucent and the flavors have blended — about 10 minutes. Add reserved chicken, vegetables, stock, and cream.

Simmer, uncovered, for about 15 minutes. At the end of this period, you should see signs of browning and the sauce should be thick enough to coat the meat and vegetables. Taste for salt and pepper.

Place hash in a broilerproof dish and top with the mozzarella. To serve immediately: Turn on broiler; place the dish under the broiler until cheese is bubbling and lightly browned.

To serve later: 30 minutes before serving, place in a 350°F oven and warm about 20 minutes. When sauce begins to bubble and cheese has melted, run the dish under the broiler until the cheese has browned lightly.

SERVES 6 TO 8.

COWBOY BEANS
AND RICE
◆◆◆

We do this dish as a vegetarian entrée in our stores, but it is also a candidate to serve with grilled burgers or chicken. While you can make it with grocery-store pinto beans, the dish has more interest if made with any one or two of the smaller Potage U.S.A. beans (see page 64). **PREPARE-AHEAD/SERVING NOTES:** The dish keeps well for three or four days and reheats perfectly. Freeze if you must.

(see page 64)

1 tablespoon cooking oil

1 cup onion, cut into ¼-inch dice

1 cup celery, cut into ¼-inch dice

1 cup green bell pepper, cut into ¼-inch dice

2 teaspoons garlic, minced or put through a garlic press

1¼ cups tomato sauce OR ⅔ cup chili sauce and ½ cup catsup

1 cup Pasta & Co. Great American Barbecue Sauce (purchased or made according to recipe on page 222)

1 tablespoon red wine vinegar

1 to 3 teaspoons brown sugar, according to taste

½ tablespoon cumin

4 cups cooked beans (2 cups — approximately 14 ounces — uncooked) (Choose a "pinto-size" bean, such as Tongues of Fire, or do half one variety and half another, cooking the varieties separately since each requires a different length of time; we like using Appaloosa and Jackson Wonder.)

2 cups cooked long-grain rice (approximately ⅔ cup uncooked)

In a large sauté pan, heat oil over medium heat. Add onion, celery, bell pepper, and garlic, and cook until soft. Add tomato sauce, barbecue sauce, vinegar, brown sugar, cumin, beans, and rice and heat through to blend flavors.

MAKES 7 CUPS.

HOT ENTRÉES

TWO SAUCES YOU WILL WANT FOR SMOKED OR ROASTED CHICKEN, TURKEY, OR PORK

◆◆◆

. . . .

WINTER FRUIT SAUCE FOR ROASTED OR SMOKED MEATS

This is a way of putting the bumper crop of fall apples, pears, and prunes to use all winter long. The recipe makes a sauce that is just the right balance of sweet, hot, and tart tastes. We spoon it over smoked game birds before heating them. Serve the birds with boiled rice and garnish with a couple of spoonfuls of the Kumquat and Sour-Cherry Sauce, page 240, and the Thyme-Flavored Onions, page 226. Or just pass the sauce in a bowl the next time you serve ham or pork roast. Allow about ½ cup of sauce for each serving of meat and freeze in convenient portions. **PREPARE-AHEAD/SERVING NOTES:** You can either freeze the fruit and make up the sauce as needed throughout the winter, or make up a batch or two as soon as you harvest, then freeze it in convenient portions. The batch is big, because we could not imagine wanting to make less. **ESSENTIAL GEAR:** Electric food processor

6 cups apple cider vinegar

4½ cups sugar

9 pounds pitted prunes, cored apples, or cored pears, cut into approximately 1-inch pieces (you may use one fruit or a combination of any two or three; if you have frozen the fruit, add it frozen to the sauce)

1 cup water

⅔ cup additional cider vinegar

¼ cup Pasta & Co. Red Currant Jelly (page 219)

2 jalapeño peppers, seeded and finely minced

1 tablespoon garlic, peeled and finely minced

1½ teaspoons salt

1 teaspoon green peppercorns in brine, drained

½ tablespoon hot curry powder

¼ teaspoon cayenne

½ cup homemade chicken stock or canned broth (*omit* chicken stock if you use all prunes)

In a large saucepan, boil the 6 cups vinegar and sugar together for about 15 minutes or until it becomes slightly syrupy. Add fruit, water, the ⅔ cup vinegar, jelly, jalapeño peppers, garlic, salt, peppercorns, curry, and cayenne. Simmer gently until fruit is soft — about 15 minutes. Remove from heat and let cool 15 minutes. Decant in batches into the work bowl of a food processor equipped with a steel blade. Process until sauce is smooth. Continue to process until all the sauce is puréed. If using chicken stock, stir in and adjust seasoning.

MAKES 20 CUPS.

RED CURRANT JELLY SAUCE

You can make this sauce as fiery as your palate and your menu allow. It is not to be missed with baked ham, fresh spinach, and boiled new potatoes in the spring, or with roast pork, acorn squash, and braised kale in winter. **PREPARE-AHEAD/ SERVING NOTES:** The sauce will keep for up to a month refrigerated. Reheat without boiling.

⅔ cup Pasta & Co. Red Currant Jelly

1 tablespoon extra virgin olive oil

2 teaspoons red wine vinegar

¾ teaspoon oregano, thyme, or a mixture, very well crumbled

½ teaspoon Tabasco or Jardine's brand Texas Champagne OR your favorite hot sauce, to taste

¼ teaspoon red pepper flakes

¼ teaspoon coarsely ground black pepper

In a small saucepan, combine jelly, olive oil, vinegar, oregano, Tabasco, red pepper flakes, and black pepper. Place over medium heat and cook just until jelly is melted. Do not boil. Remove from heat.

MAKES ¾ CUP.

PASTA & CO. RED CURRANT JELLY

Tart little red currants make a crystal-clear jelly with a sweet-tart flavor is very desirable for glazes, sauces, pastries, and even the morning toast. Red currants grow particularly well on Vashon Island, one of the Puget Sound islands within easy ferry reach of downtown Seattle. It is on Vashon Island that Maury Island Farming Co. grows currants and makes the best red currant jelly on the market. We like this simple jelly so much that we convinced Maury Island to make it under our label as well as theirs.

We regularly serve the red currant jelly with inch-thick slices of Seattle's best toast at our downtown food bar. We use it in the Winter Fruit Sauce (page 218) and in Pasta & Co. Cranberry Sauce (page 48). In the Red Current Jelly Sauce recipe above, we turn the jelly into a savory sauce for smoked meats, roasted pork, or chicken.

WHITE CHILI

•••

O ur White Chili is a variation on a chili recipe that we first saw in *Beyond Parsley*, a book published by the Junior League of Kansas City, Missouri. Serve the dish over beds of shredded iceberg lettuce and accompany it with Mexican or Southwest condiments, such as warm tortillas, corn chips, salsa, and guacamole. Step up the seasoning to 5-alarm status, if you wish. Or just follow the recipe. **PREPARE-AHEAD/SERVING NOTES:** The dish benefits from sitting for a day before serving.

1 pound dried white beans

1 (49.5-ounce) can chicken broth OR 6 cups homemade chicken stock

4 onions, peeled and cut into ½-inch dice

1 tablespoon finely minced garlic OR 1 tablespoon garlic purée (page 17)

2½ pounds skinless, boneless chicken thighs

2 tablespoons vegetable oil

6 Anaheim chiles, seeded and cut into ¼-inch dice

2 tablespoons cumin

1 tablespoon oregano

Scant 1 teaspoon cayenne

Scant ½ teaspoon ground cloves

12 ounces Monterey jack cheese, grated

Pick through beans and discard any stones or debris. Rinse well and put them into a heavy 4-quart kettle along with broth, half the onions, and garlic. Bring to a boil. Reduce heat, cover, and simmer until beans are very tender — approximately 1½ to 3 hours, depending on beans.

While beans cook, poach the chicken thighs according to the directions on page 39. Remove chicken from poaching liquid and separate the meat along its own tissue. Discard any fat. Set aside.

In a 12-inch sauté pan, heat oil and sauté remaining 2 onions until they begin to soften. Add chiles, cumin, oregano, cayenne, and ground cloves, and sauté until vegetables are cooked and the flavors have blended. Fold in reserved cooked chicken and set aside.

When beans are cooked, add onion/chicken mixture. If mixture seems dry, fold in additional broth. To serve immediately: Heat broiler; place chili in a broilerproof serving dish, top generously with the grated cheese, and place under the broiler until well-browned.

HOT ENTRÉES

To serve later: Place chili in an ovenproof casserole, top with the cheese, cover, and refrigerate. When ready to serve, bake in a preheated 350°F oven until cheese begins to bubble and brown — about 20 to 30 minutes.

SERVES 6 TO 8.

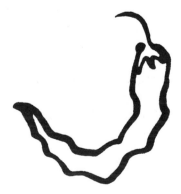

THE GREAT AMERICAN
BARBECUE SAUCE
♦♦♦

. . . .

his is the snappy, sweet-sour-type barbecue sauce we sell in our stores. For grilling chicken and burgers "American-style," we have not found one better. Tailor the hotness and sweetness to your own taste. **PREPARE-AHEAD/SERVING NOTES:** The sauce will keep refrigerated for up to three months. No need to freeze. **ESSENTIAL GEAR:** Electric food processor

Vegetable oil

2⅔ cups coarsely chopped onions

4 cloves garlic, coarsely chopped

2 (10¾-ounce) cans tomato purée

2⅔ cups apple cider vinegar

2 tablespoons Pasta & Co. Spaghetti Western Barbecue Spice

2 tablespoons grainy mustard

2 tablespoons Worcestershire sauce

2 tablespoons soy sauce

2 tablespoons water

1 tablespoon Tabasco (more, if you want more fire)

1 tablespoon salt

1 tablespoon white pepper

5 bay leaves

4 to 5 cups granulated sugar (depending on desired sweetness)

Heat a thin layer of oil in a 4-quart saucepan over medium heat. Add onions and cook slowly, stirring occasionally, until golden brown — about 20 to 30 minutes. (You may want to lower the heat. Browning should be gradual.)

Add garlic and sauté briefly (do not brown the garlic). Add tomato purée, vinegar, barbecue spice, mustard, Worcestershire sauce, soy sauce, water, Tabasco, salt, white pepper, and bay leaves. Bring to a simmer over medium heat. When simmering, slowly add sugar, stirring constantly, and continue cooking until sugar is entirely dissolved — about 10 minutes. Stir frequently.

Let sauce cool slightly. Then, using a food processor equipped with a steel blade, purée mixture until smooth. Do this in four batches. (If you attempt bigger batches, the food processor bowl will overflow.) Refrigerate to store.

MAKES 7 TO 8 CUPS.

FOR BARBECUED CHICKEN OR BURGERS

We suggest using 2 cups of the sauce to marinate 5 pounds of chicken pieces or hamburger patties. Let the meat have several hours in the sauce before cooking on a hot grill. Be sure to scoop up any leftover marinade. You can bring it to a boil in a small saucepan and serve hot alongside the grilled meat as a dipping sauce.

BACK TO BASICS, BUT ONLY THE BEST OF THEM

The final four entrée recipes are direct responses to the demand for homey, unpretentious food made to today's standards of taste. They are all big sellers.

HERB-ROASTED CHICKEN
◆◆◆

. . . .

What could be better than splendidly roasted and seasoned chicken? Jerry Malmevik perfected the technique by tucking extravagant amounts of herbs and garlic under the bird's skin. **PREPARE-AHEAD/SERVING NOTES:** The chicken keeps well refrigerated for three or four days. Return to room temperature or gently reheat to serve. The recipe doubles and triples well.

2 heaping teaspoons Pasta & Co. House Herbs

¼ teaspoon salt

½ tablespoon garlic, put through a press or finely minced

1 whole chicken, halved and cleaned

Pure olive oil

Sweet paprika

Mix together House Herbs, salt, and garlic.

Preheat oven to 350°F.

Loosen skin of chicken by running hand underneath skin, including the meaty part of the leg. Line with foil a shallow, ovenproof dish just large enough to hold chicken comfortably without crowding. Brush foil lightly with olive oil. Place chicken skin-side-up on prepared dish. With fingertips, spread three-fourths of the herb mixture generously under the skin. Brush the outside of chicken with olive oil and dab remaining herb mixture on top side of chicken. Sprinkle lightly with paprika. Bake for 50 to 60 minutes or until temperature reading on an instant-read thermometer inserted into meatiest part is 165°F.

Serve chicken hot over a bed of greens along with any pan drippings, or let cool in its juices and serve at room temperature.

SERVES 2 TO 4.

BROWN-BOTTOM
MEAT LOAF
◆◆◆

. . . .

We tried dozens of meat loaf recipes before settling on one that originated in a Venice, California, restaurant called 72 Market Street. The recipe had been published in *Vogue* magazine in the early 1980s. And when Julee Rosso and Sheila Lukins brought out their latest volume — *The New Basics* — they printed the recipe as "Market Street Meat Loaf."

Running the recipe through our kitchens a couple of dozen times altered it in lots of little ways. For example, some of us craved the crusty, browned undersides of the meat loaves our moms used to make. So we eliminated baking with a water bath (ergo, "Brown-Bottom"). And once the meat loaf was baked, we topped it with paprika- and cumin-spiced onions to make it look spiffier. **PREPARE-AHEAD/SERVING NOTES:** At Pasta & Co., we increase this recipe four times and form the meat mixture into 10 mini-loaves sized to feed two apiece. If you like to keep handy meals in your freezer, you might make a double batch and freeze five little loaves. Just form them and bake on a rimmed cookie sheet. They freeze well, but they also keep in the refrigerator for up to five days and rewarm just fine. You can also successfully freeze the meat loaves unbaked.

2 teaspoons butter

⅓ cup onion, cut into ⅛-inch dice ice

⅓ cup green onion, sliced ¼-inch wide (use white parts only)

¼ cup carrot, peeled and cut into ⅛-inch dice

3 tablespoons green bell pepper, cut into ⅛-inch dice

2 tablespoons celery, cut into ⅛-inch dice

2 medium cloves garlic, put through a garlic press

2 eggs, well-beaten

¼ cup catsup

¼ cup half-and-half

¾ teaspoon ground cumin

¾ teaspoon salt

¾ teaspoon black pepper

⅛ teaspoon cayenne

⅛ teaspoon ground nutmeg

1¼ pounds ground beef

⅔ pound pork sausage (*not* Italian sausage)

⅓ cup bread crumbs

TO TOP:

¼ teaspoon cumin

1 tablespoon cooking oil

¼ teaspoon sweet paprika

½ onion, cut into ½-inch slices and
separated into rings

In a medium-size sauté pan, melt butter and add onions, green onions, carrot, bell pepper, celery, and garlic. Cook until vegetables are soft. Remove from heat and cool.

Preheat oven to 375°F.

In a large bowl, beat together eggs, catsup, half-and-half, the ¾ teaspoon cumin, salt, black pepper, cayenne, and nutmeg. Add beef, pork sausage, and bread crumbs. Knead together by hand till smooth. Add cooled vegetable mixture and blend thoroughly.

You can pack the meat mixture into a standard loaf pan (8½ by 4½ by 2⅝ inches), but we prefer to form the meat into a flatter loaf shape and place in an oven-proof shallow baking dish for maximum browned surface in baking. Use a dish that is at least 1 inch larger around than the meat loaf. That way you can easily lift the loaf out of the drippings to serve.

Either way, bake at 375°F for 50 to 55 minutes or until done through. While meat loaf bakes, place cooking oil in a small sauté pan. Add onion rings, the ¼ teaspoon cumin, and paprika and let cook until golden. Remove from heat.

When meat loaf is done, remove from oven and drain off grease. Top with warm onion rings and serve.

SERVES 4.

A MENU NOTE

If it's tomato season, make up a batch of the Roasted Tomato Sauce (page 194). Serve it with the Brown-Bottom Meat Loaf and mashed potatoes (or our Great American Macaroni and Cheese — page 181) and you will see the real meaning of the "food revolution" that hit this country during the 1980s. Meat-loaf dinner is now truly better than ever.

ESPECIALLY WHEN WALLA WALLA
SWEET ONIONS ARE IN SEASON

The idea of flavoring onions the way we do to top the meat loaf is one you can use for many dishes. For instance, substitute 1½ tablespoons dried thyme or ¼ cup fresh for the cumin and paprika, and the onion is just right for topping smoked or roasted meats. (See page 218).

BIG-CHUNK BEEF STEW

♦♦♦

. . . .

The simple things in cooking do not seem to come easily. What we wanted here was just plain great beef stew — fork-tender meat and vegetables in a rich, satiny-brown sauce. We have tried many formulas. This straightforward recipe is the one we settled on. **PREPARE-AHEAD/SERVING NOTES:** Like all stews, make it two or three days ahead of serving, confident that the dish only improves with a reasonable amount of age.

3 pounds stew meat or boneless beef chuck

Vegetable oil

½ cup flour

1 teaspoon salt

1 teaspoon freshly ground black pepper

2 large onions, cut into 1-inch dice

2 (14.5-ounce) cans beef broth

1 (28-ounce) can tomatoes, coarsely torn, including all juices (we use Paradiso Italian-style peeled tomatoes)

½ teaspoon thyme

1 bay leaf

1½ pounds russet potatoes, peeled and cut into 1-inch dice

1 pound carrots, peeled and cut into 1-inch pieces

2 cups celery, cut into 1-inch pieces

1 large turnip, peeled and cut into 1-inch dice

⅓ cup chopped parsley

Trim away any obvious fat and gristle on meat. Make sure all pieces are roughly 1½-inch cubes. As you trim the beef, lay the pieces on paper towels. The meat will not brown if it is damp.

Preheat oven to 475°F.

In a large sauté pan, over fairly high heat, brown beef in just enough oil to keep the meat from sticking. This should be done in several batches to avoid crowding the meat. Regulate heat so that it browns evenly without burning meat. Do not cook until hard and crusty — just nicely browned. Add more oil, if necessary. As each piece is browned, remove to a 4-quart ovenproof casserole.

When all the meat has been added to the casserole, toss it with flour, salt, and black pepper. Set casserole, uncovered, in 475°F oven for 5 minutes. Toss meat again and return to oven for 5 more minutes. This will result in a nice brown crust on the meat.

While meat is cooking, sauté onions in the same skillet in which you browned the meat. Add a small amount of oil, if necessary.

After meat has browned in the oven, remove casserole. Reduce oven heat to 325°F. Add the browned onions to the meat. Then pour one of the cans of beef broth into the sauté pan and scrape up any bits of beef and onion that remain. Pour it all into meat mixture. Add second can of beef broth along with tomatoes and their liquid, thyme, and bay leaf. Place casserole back into oven and cook at 325°F for 2 hours. Regulate heat so that the liquid simmers slowly during the cooking time.

After 2 hours, add potatoes, carrots, and celery. Continue cooking 30 minutes. Add turnip and cook an additional 30 minutes. Test for doneness. The vegetables should be tender, not mushy. The carrots will be the last to cook.

Remove from oven and stir in parsley.

MAKES 16 CUPS.

ATTENTION, POTATO LOVERS

Judy Birkland suggests the following variation: Follow the directions above but omit the potatoes. During last half-hour of cooking time, cook up a big batch of mashed potatoes. Serve the finished stew over the mashed potatoes. Garnish with more chopped parsley. It's Dinty Moore gone to heaven!

CORNED BEEF HASH

♦♦♦

As with so many of the recipes we have developed, we know there are scads of corned beef hash recipes. But how many of them are perfectly seasoned with browned onion, cayenne, nutmeg, and red wine vinegar? (We know that some of the most venerated hash makers mix heavy cream into the mixture, but as good as it sounds, we refrained.) And how many recipes make an absolutely ravishing soup out of the leftover meat and cooking juices (page 145)? We are proud of the refinements we have made to this old American standby. **PREPARE-AHEAD/SERVING NOTES:** Make up a big batch and freeze in convenient portions. You will be glad some cold winter morning or evening when you can quickly brown off your hash, add your eggs and condiments, and feast. **A TIP FOR BUYING AND COOKING YOUR MEAT:** To yield 1 pound of cooked corned beef, you will need a 2½-pound corned beef brisket. Cook it in ¼ inch of water in a covered pan in a 300-degree oven for about 2½ to 3 hours. However, if you want to also make the Corned Beef Soup on page 145 (and you should), roast enough corned beef for dinner, the hash, and the soup. That probably means a 6-pound piece of meat to start. **ESSENTIAL GEAR:** Electric food processor

1 pound cooked corned beef, trimmed of most fat

2 teaspoons salt

1 pound red-skinned potatoes, unpeeled, cut into ½-inch dice

2 to 3 tablespoons butter

3½ cups onions, peeled, cut into ½-inch dice

1 teaspoon sugar

1 green bell pepper, cut into ¼-inch dice

3 cloves garlic, finely minced

½ teaspoon salt

¼ teaspoon coarsely ground black pepper

¼ teaspoon cayenne

¼ teaspoon nutmeg

1 tablespoon red wine vinegar

Finely chopped parsley, to top

SUGGESTED CONDIMENTS:

Fried or poached eggs, sour cream, catsups, or hot sauces

In a food processor equipped with a steel blade, coarsely chop corned beef. Process in short spurts; do not turn the meat to mush. Bring a saucepan of water to a boil. Add salt and potatoes. Cook just until tender. Drain well and set aside.

In a large sauté pan cook onions in half the butter until translucent. Add sugar and continue cooking over medium-low heat until onions are golden brown. Remove onions to a large container. In the same skillet, sauté bell pepper and garlic just until pepper is slightly tender, taking care not to burn the garlic. Add to onions. Melt remaining butter in the skillet, add potatoes, and cook until browned.

Toss potatoes and chopped corned beef with onion mixture. Fold in salt, black pepper, cayenne, nutmeg, and vinegar.

Before serving, warm hash in a sauté pan and top generously with parsley.

SERVES 6.

CORNED BEEF BRUNCH

- Baked Cheese Wafers (page 19), warm from the oven and served with fresh fruit
- Corned Beef Hash (page 229)
- Eggs to your liking
- A bevy of condiments: sour cream or Quark (page 91), ketchups, or hot sauces
- Apricot and Sour Cherry Bread Pudding (page 247) served with a side of barely sweetened whipped cream

---

Desserts and baking: from fresh lemon tarts to grown-up granola.

The few sweets and baked goods that we make have been made so many times that the recipes are now sure-fire successes. The results — we guarantee — will please.

PASTA & CO. FRESH
LEMON TARTS

•••

. . . .

This is it. The most important dessert ever to come out of Pasta & Co. kitchens. *Bon Appétit* magazine described Pasta & Co. Lemon Tarts as "not to be missed." We have made thousands of these tarts over the past decade. We cannot think of a more classic way to end a meal than with the palate-cleansing taste of tartest lemon in a shortbread crust. Also consider using the shells for other fillings, such as the mousses on pages 237 and 238. **PREPARE-AHEAD/SERVING NOTES:** Be warned. These tarts are tedious and time-consuming to make. But by spreading the chore over at least several days, the recipe has a lot of prepare-ahead ease. But you must plan in advance. The tart dough is durable. It can be made and refrigerated for days before pressing into shells. The shells themselves can be made and frozen or baked days before finishing off with the filling. The lemon filling, too, can be made days before cooking and being put it into the shells. Fill the shells, however, on the day you plan to use them; a few hours before serving is fine. **ESSENTIAL GEAR:** Electric food processor and eight 3-inch tart tins with removable bottoms (available at Pasta & Co. stores) *OR* two 8-inch tart tins with removable bottoms

THE TART SHELLS:

½ cup powdered sugar

½ cup plus 2 tablespoons salted
butter at room temperature

1½ cups flour

Pam (nonstick spray coating)

Place sugar in the bowl of a food processor equipped with a steel blade or in an electric mixer bowl with a dough hook. Process just long enough to remove any lumps. Add butter in small pieces and process until mixture is almost fluffy. Gradually add flour and continue processing until mixture forms a firm dough. Remove dough from bowl and place on a large piece of plastic wrap. Gather dough into a ball and wrap well. Chill at least until dough is no longer warm from processing. You can chill the dough for days, but it needs to be at room temperature to be pliable enough for making the shells.

To make tart shells, spray tart tins with Pam. Separate dough into 8 equal pieces. Place a ball of dough in center of each tin. Press dough across bottom of tin and up the sides until it reaches the top edge. The dough should be spread thin enough that the tin just barely shadows through. Be sure dough is not too thick where the bottom turns up into the side of the tin. It is not necessary to use all the dough (see page 235). Refrigerate tart shells at least 20 minutes before baking, or freeze them. Before baking, prick bottom of each tart several times with a fork.

To bake, preheat oven to 325°F. Bake approximately 15 minutes. Rotate shells and bake approximately 15 minutes more. Check for color. Shells should be golden brown.

Cool on a baking rack for at least 45 minutes (shells should be at room temperature before removing from pans and filling).

When cool, examine edges of tarts. If they are stuck to the sides of the tins at any spot, loosen gently with the point of a small knife. Then, holding tart tin with one hand, gently push up on the removable bottom with other hand. With point of knife, carefully separate tart from tin bottom.

Unfilled shells will hold at room temperature in an airtight tin for up to two weeks.

MAKES EIGHT 3-INCH TART SHELLS OR TWO 8-INCH TART SHELLS.

THE LEMON FILLING AND FINAL BAKING OF THE TARTS:

3 whole eggs

3 egg yolks

¾ cup freshly squeezed lemon juice

¾ cup granulated sugar

1 tablespoon arrowroot

1½ teaspoons finely minced lemon zest

4 ounces cream cheese at room temperature

Preheat oven to 350°F.

In a food processor bowl equipped with a steel blade, place whole eggs, yolks, and lemon juice. Process until eggs are well-beaten. Then, with machine running, gradually add sugar, arrowroot, and lemon zest. When well-mixed, add cream cheese — a chunk at a time — and purée until specks of cream cheese are no longer visible.

Pour lemon mixture into a medium-size saucepan. Place over medium heat, and, stirring constantly with a wooden spoon, cook until filling is steaming and coats the spoon, but is still thin enough to pour. When filling has begun to thicken, pour into a large measuring cup or pitcher. If filling has thickened so that it is no longer pourable, stir in a teaspoon or two of warm water.

Place prepared pastry shells on a cookie sheet. Carefully pour hot filling into pastry shells. (When pouring, hold the measuring cup close to the shell to avoid making bubbles as filling hits shell.)

Place tarts in the oven and bake at 350°F for 4 to 6 minutes or until the filling does not jiggle when tart is moved. Remove from oven and let cool on a rack for at least an hour before refrigerating. Refrigerate at least a couple hours before serving. Refrigerate tarts to store.

MAKES EIGHT 3-INCH TARTS OR TWO 8-INCH TARTS.

GREAT COOKIES

If you have any tart dough left after making your shells, it makes great shortbread cookies. Preheat oven to 350°F. Roll out dough on a lightly floured board to any desired thickness (from ⅛ inch to ¾ inch) and cut into desired shapes. Place cookies on an ungreased baking sheet. Bake 8 to 25 minutes, depending on the thickness of the cookie and how brown you want them.

IF YOU HAVE ANY LEMON FILLING LEFT OVER

Refrigerate it and use it as what the British call "lemon jam" or "lemon curd." It is marvelous spread on toast or English muffins, not to mention as a filling for cake or crepes, or over ice cream. Refrigerated, it will keep at least a couple of weeks.

CRANBERRY TARTS

◆◆◆

. . . .

Need a jewel-like fresh fruit tart for a Christmas celebration? Frost the tart shells from the previous recipe with a thin layer of bittersweet chocolate. Then fill the shells with cranberries that have been glazed with Pasta & Co. Red Currant Jelly and rum. **PREPARE-AHEAD/SERVING NOTES:** Spoon in the chocolate layer the day before you fill the tarts so that the chocolate has time to set. The tarts should be served the same day they are filled with the glazed cranberries.

¼ **pound bittersweet chocolate**	**1 (12-ounce) bag cranberries**
½ **cup whipping cream**	¾ **cup sugar**
Twelve 3-inch OR two 8-inch tart shells, made and baked according to recipe on page 233 (for ease of serving, we suggest the 3-inch tarts)	½ **cup Pasta & Co. Red Currant Jelly (page 219)**
	2 tablespoons rum

Over very low heat, carefully melt chocolate. Remove from heat and stir in cream. Coat just the bottom of each 3-inch tart shell with 1 tablespoon of the chocolate mixture. (If using two 8-inch shells, split the chocolate mixture between the two, again just coating the bottom — not the sides — of the shells.) Let shells sit until chocolate hardens, preferably for several hours.

Wash and pick over cranberries. Allow to drain well. Place sugar and jelly in a large sauté pan over low heat. Cook, stirring occasionally, for about 10 minutes, or until jelly and sugar are melted. Fold in cranberries and continue cooking over low heat until you notice that one or two of the berries are beginning to pop. Remove from heat immediately (you want the berries whole for the tarts). Cool berries to room temperature. Stir in rum.

If using 3-inch tart shells, spoon 3 tablespoons of the berries and glaze into each, gently rolling berries into a single layer. If using 8-inch shells, split the berries and glaze between the two shells. Drizzle any remaining glaze over the berries, but be careful not to get glaze on top edge of shell. If you have extra cranberries or glaze (there will not be more than a couple of tablespoons), use them on your morning toast, over ice cream, or just fold into a batch of cranberry sauce (page 48).

Allow tarts to set a few hours before serving.

MAKES TWELVE 3-INCH TARTS OR TWO 8-INCH TARTS.

DARK CHOCOLATE MOUSSE

♦♦♦

Here is our no-fuss way to make the quintessential chocolate mousse — light, airy, and dense all at once. Serve the mousse in all the standard ways. Or spoon it into our tart shells (page 233). (If you want to keep this dessert "fast and easy," order the empty shells from Pasta & Co.) You take it from there. Top each tart with barely sweetened whipped cream or shaved chocolate; serve in a pool of Pasta & Co. Berry Sauce (available at Pasta & Co.) or Fresh Caramel Sauce (page 242). Or make this mousse *and* the White Chocolate Mousse (page 238) and fill the tart shells with half dark and half white. **PREPARE-AHEAD/SERVING NOTES:** Using the "Whip it" stabilizes the mousse so that it will hold for three or four days refrigerated. If you are serving it in the tart shell, however, spoon in shortly before eating, since the shell will pick up moisture from the mousse and lose its great crispness.

6 ounces semisweet chocolate, chopped coarsely

2 cups heavy cream, well-chilled

2 (⅓ -ounce) packets "Whip it" (page 239)

2 large egg yolks

¼ cup confectioners' sugar, sifted

1 teaspoon espresso powder, dissolved in 1 tablespoon warm water

Place a 2-quart mixing bowl and the beaters you plan to use for whipping the cream in the freezer to chill.

In a double boiler, melt chocolate. Remove from heat and let cool to the touch. (If chocolate is too hot, it will "curdle" the mousse; if too cold, it will begin to solidify into chunks. So be sure the chocolate is just cool to the touch.)

Place cream and "Whip it" in the chilled bowl and beat with an electric mixer until cream forms very stiff peaks. Remove whipped cream to another bowl and refrigerate.

Using the unwashed bowl in which you whipped the cream, add egg yolks and beat until light yellow. Gradually add confectioners' sugar and beat until light and fluffy and the sugar is incorporated into the eggs. Stir in the dissolved espresso and the cooled chocolate.

Stir one-third of the whipped cream into chocolate mixture. Then add remaining cream, stirring until mixture is smooth and creamy. (Do not be timid in folding the cream into the chocolate mixture. It is not like egg whites; it is only whipped cream. *Keep stirring* until mixture is velvety.) When thoroughly mixed, refrigerate until ready to serve. If holding the mousse more than a few hours, you may need to briskly stir it again before serving to restore its texture.

MAKES 4 CUPS.

WHITE CHOCOLATE MOUSSE

♦♦♦

This recipe is made almost identically to the Dark Chocolate Mousse on page 237. Both recipes come from Cory Vicens, our University Village store manager, who suggests using the mousses side by side in the same dessert or for filling layer cakes. **PREPARE-AHEAD/SERVING NOTES:** Same as for Dark Chocolate Mousse.

6 ounces Lindt White Chocolate Confectionery Bar, coarsely chopped and melted according to the directions below

2 cups heavy cream, well-chilled

2 (⅓-ounce) packets of "Whip it" (page 239)

2 large egg yolks

¼ cup confectioners' sugar, sifted

2 teaspoons vanilla

Follow directions for Dark Chocolate Mousse (page 237), substituting vanilla for espresso. In this recipe, however, incorporating chocolate mixture into whipped cream requires even more aggressive stirring.

MAKES 3½ CUPS.

MELTING WHITE CHOCOLATE

Chop white chocolate into pieces.

Never attempt to melt more than 8 ounces at a time.

Use the top of a double boiler set over hot — not quite simmering — water. Do not let the hot water touch the bottom of the chocolate pan or the chocolate will "stiffen" instead of melt.

Be sure to stir white chocolate frequently while melting it, scraping down the sides of the pan to ensure that it melts evenly.

■ THE MICROWAVE ALTERNATIVE: Microwave the chopped white chocolate at 50% power, stirring every 30 seconds. It will not appear melted until you stir it, distributing the heat. It should take no more than a couple of minutes. Before using the chocolate, let it cool to lukewarm.

DESSERTS AND BAKING

ALL WHITE CHOCOLATE IS NOT CREATED EQUAL

In fact, some white chocolate tastes downright nasty.

The best white chocolate for cooking that we have found is the Lindt White Chocolate Confectionery Bar. Pasta & Co. stores carry 3-ounce and 14-ounce bars.

WHAT IS THIS STUFF CALLED "WHIP IT"?

According to its label, "Whip it" is a mixture of dextrose, precooked starch, and tricalcium phosphate, which, when added to heavy cream before whipping, causes the whipped cream to remain firm. The maker of "Whip it" recommends it for cake decorating and dessert toppings, but we have found that it helps to hold the texture of whipped cream in anything from fruit-salad dressing to eggnog (see page 243).

KUMQUAT AND
SOUR-CHERRY SAUCE
◆◆◆

This makes a dazzling winter fruit sauce for topping chocolate mousse, plum pudding, cheesecake, or ice cream. It is also tart enough to be an excellent condiment for roasted or smoked meats, as we suggest on page 218. And besides, hardly anyone knows what to do with those absolutely gorgeous little firecrackers of flavor called kumquats. This is something sure to please. **PREPARE-AHEAD/SERVING NOTES:** The sauce keeps well refrigerated for a month or two.

¾ cup dried sour cherries

½ cup water

3 tablespoons sugar

1 cup fresh kumquats, halved, seeded, and cut into thin strips

Optional: Cognac or Grand Marnier to taste

Soak cherries in enough warm water to cover them for 1 hour. Drain and reserve cherries.

In a small saucepan, heat water and sugar and simmer until sugar dissolves. Add kumquats and reserved cherries. Simmer over low heat for 5 minutes. Remove from heat and add Cognac or Grand Marnier to taste, if desired.

CAVEAT: Should you prefer the sauce without sour cherries (as we do when serving with gingerbread), increase the kumquats to 2 cups, cut the water to ¼ cup and the sugar to 2 tablespoons, and add ¼ cup raisins, 2 tablespoons Grand Marnier, 1 teaspoon vanilla extract, and a pinch of nutmeg.

Or, if you just want to make a kumquat sauce, increase the kumquats to 2 cups, cut the water to ¼ cup, use 3 tablespoons sugar, and season as you like with Grand Marnier (or another brandy), vanilla extract, or nutmeg.

MAKES 2 CUPS.

ABOUT DRIED SOUR CHERRIES

When we first discovered these in 1986, we immediately recognized them as a "food find." In our first cookbook, we tossed them with pork and pasta and used them in Cherries Jubilee and in an almond cake. Now they are in our scones (page 253), our muffins (page 251), our Christmas cakes (page 244), our bread pudding (page 247), our cranberry sauce (page 48), and this fruit sauce. We should be embarrassed by such redundancy, except that dried sour cherries are so irresistibly good.

Do not substitute dried bing cherries. They are far too sweet.

PASTA & CO.'S
CHOCOLATE SAUCE
♦♦♦

We have sampled dozens of chocolate sauces — from jars and from scratch — and are convinced that this recipe makes the best one. Hot or cold, it is a satiny sauce that rewarms without a flaw. Use it over ice cream, fresh fruit, cakes, crepes, pastries — you'll never need another chocolate sauce recipe. **PREPARE-AHEAD/SERVING NOTES:** Definitely do. It keeps refrigerated for a couple of months.

5 ounces unsalted butter

½ cup unsweetened cocoa powder — we like Bensdorp brand Royal Dutch

4 ounces bittersweet or semisweet chocolate, finely chopped — we use the bulk Valrhona that we sell (NOTE: if you use unsweetened chocolate, increase the amount of sugar to 1½ cups)

1½ cups evaporated milk

1 cup sugar

2 teaspoons espresso powder

2 pinches salt

1 tablespoon plus 1 teaspoon vanilla extract — we use either Pasta & Co. House Vanilla, which is Madagascar, or Tahitian vanilla

In a small saucepan, melt butter over low heat, being careful not to brown. Remove from heat and whisk in cocoa powder until smooth. Stir in chopped chocolate, evaporated milk, sugar, and espresso powder. Return to heat and cook over medium, whisking, just until sugar is fully incorporated into the sauce. Avoid boiling, but make certain sauce is not grainy. Remove from heat. Stir in salt. Let cool, then stir in vanilla.

MAKES 3 CUPS.

FRESH CARAMEL SAUCE

◆◆◆

. . . .

This is not the sticky caramel we all love on ice cream sundaes. Rather, it is a creamy sauce you will want to use as a pool for a fresh fruit tart or a favorite mousse. Drizzle it over seasonal fruits and pound cake. And, of course, try it over ice cream for a change from the traditional sticky variety. **PREPARE-AHEAD/SERVING NOTES:** Use warm or store refrigerated. If a skin forms on top of the sauce, pour it through a fine strainer or stir well to blend. The sauce keeps well refrigerated for at least a month.

½ **cup plus 2 tablespoons sugar**

2 cups whipping cream

½ **tablespoon arrowroot**

½ **teaspoon your best vanilla extract (we like Tahitian)**

Optional: 2 tablespoons Cognac

DESSERTS AND BAKING

Place sugar in a medium-size nonstick sauté pan. Place 1 cup of the cream in a 1-quart saucepan and stir in arrowroot until it is well-mixed. Add remaining cream, place over medium-high heat, and, stirring constantly, bring to a simmer. When there is ½ inch of bubbles around the circumference of the pan, remove from heat and reserve.

Immediately after removing cream from heat, place the pan of sugar on the burner and raise heat to high. Stir constantly with a wooden spoon for 4 to 6 minutes, lifting pan off heat now and then to prevent burning, until the sugar melts, turns a dark amber, and is a smooth syrup.

Remove sugar mixture from heat and carefully stir a small amount of the warm cream into the sugar. Do not be alarmed that the cream hitting the sugar seems somewhat explosive. Just keep adding cream gradually until it is all blended into the sugar. Return pan to heat and bring mixture to a boil. Let simmer until cream coats spoon. Be careful that cream does not boil over. When thickened sufficiently, remove from heat and stir in vanilla.

Add Cognac, if desired. The Cognac adds a depth of flavor that is a nice contrast to the sweetness of the sauce. It also enables you to adjust the texture of the sauce to your liking.

Pour sauce through a strainer into a clean storage container. Use a rubber spatula to get all the sauce out of the pan.

Use warm or store refrigerated.

MAKES ABOUT 2 CUPS.

PASTA & CO. CHRISTMAS EVE EGGNOG

◆◆◆

. . . .

We do not sell this product, but it is a Pasta & Co. tradition. Every Christmas Eve, we dispense the frothy brew, careful that everyone only gets a hint of the celebration our eggnog implies. In an eggnog competition, we think this one might win for ease of preparation and festive flavors. **PREPARE-AHEAD/SERVING NOTES:** The eggnog holds well for about six hours before it loses its frothiness. Using "Whip it" extends the eggnog's body for up to 12 hours. **ESSENTIAL GEAR:** Electric mixer

14 eggs, separated

1¼ cups super-fine sugar

1 quart whole milk

1 cup Cognac

1 cup brandy

½ cup dark rum

1 tablespoon plus 1 teaspoon vanilla, Tahitian if possible

1 teaspoon nutmeg, freshly grated if possible

1 cup whipping cream

Optional: ⅓-ounce packet "Whip it"

Place egg yolks in the bowl of an electric mixer and beat at high speed until blended. Continue beating, adding sugar gradually, until eggs are very thick and sugar has dissolved. Remove to a serving bowl and whisk in milk, Cognac, brandy, rum, vanilla, and nutmeg.

In same electric mixer bowl, whip the cream and "Whip it" (if desired) until soft peaks barely form. Fold into the other ingredients.

Thoroughly wash and dry beaters. In a large, clean, dry bowl, beat half the egg whites until they are firm. (Use the other half of the egg whites for another purpose, such as scrambled eggs or meringue Christmas cookies.) Fold into cream mixture. Refrigerate 15 to 30 minutes before serving.

Note: As you serve the eggnog, you will notice that the egg whites form a foam on top. We think the eggnog tastes better if that foam is gently folded through the drink as it is served, rather than left on top.

MAKES 10 SERVINGS.

CHRISTMAS CAKES
◆◆◆

Marvelously boozy cakes packed with dried sour cherries, dried apricots, raisins, and nuts — these are what holiday baked goods should be all about. The cakes make impressive gifts. They store well. They ship well. They lend an air of anticipation and celebration. And, maybe best of all (at least for some of us), they taste *nothing* like fruitcake. Although they are good warm out of the oven, their festiveness comes from bathing them in the liquor and letting them season for at least two weeks before serving. **PREPARE-AHEAD/SERVING NOTES:** These are easy enough to make. They just require planning. Note that the fruit must soak a week before baking the cakes. **ESSENTIAL GEAR:** Electric food processor, six mini-loaf pans (6 by 3 by 2 inches deep), parchment paper

THE FRUIT:

1¾ cups plus 1 tablespoon dried sour cherries

1¾ cups plus 1 tablespoon dried apricots, cut into ½-inch dice

1 cup plus 1 tablespoon currants

1 cup golden raisins

1 cup raisins

½ cup whole walnuts

1 cup plus 1 tablespoon cream sherry

¼ cup plus 1 tablespoon freshly squeezed orange juice

THE BATTER:

2½ cups flour

1¼ teaspoons baking powder

½ teaspoon salt

1 cup butter, softened

1 cup sugar

½ cup light brown sugar

6 eggs at room temperature

¼ cup freshly squeezed orange juice

THE NUTS:

3 cups raw macadamia nuts

CURING SOLUTION:

¾ cup Grand Marnier

¾ cup bourbon

One week before you want to bake the cakes, toss cherries, apricots, currants, all raisins, and walnuts with sherry and orange juice. Let stand at room temperature for a week. Stir mixture daily.

On baking day, toss fruit, including all the juices, with 2 tablespoons of the flour and set aside.

Preheat oven to 250°F. Line just the bottoms of pans with sheets of parchment cut to fit.

Sift together flour, baking powder, and salt. Set aside.

Place the butter in the work bowl of a food processor equipped with a steel blade, and process until it is light in color. Add sugars. Process briefly. Add eggs, one at a time, processing briefly after each egg. Add orange juice and process to blend. Add flour mixture gradually, and process until mixture is well-blended. Turn batter into a large bowl and fold in soaked fruits and nuts along with all the liquid.

Place 1½ cups (not level, but not too heaping) of batter into each loaf pan. Smooth batter to level. Then press ½ cup of the macadamia nuts into each cake.

Place 3 cakes on each of two baking sheets.

Depending on the size of your oven, you will probably want to bake one tray of cakes at a time. Bake at 250°F for 15 minutes. Rotate tray and bake another 15 minutes. Raise heat to 300°F and bake another 15 to 30 minutes or until golden and crusty on top. Test with a bamboo skewer to make sure you do not overbake and dry out the cakes.

Remove cake pans to a rack and brush each cake well with 1 tablespoon of the curing solution. Cool for 30 minutes and remove from pan by running a knife around the sides of the pan, inverting pan over your hand, and letting the cake drop out. Peel off parchment paper and brush each cake with 2 more tablespoons of curing solution. Let cool overnight on a rack.

The next morning, brush each cake with another tablespoon of curing solution, being sure to coat bottoms and sides of cakes. Let dry about 20 minutes before wrapping tightly with plastic wrap. If you have curing solution left, continue to brush cakes every few days until the solution is gone, always being careful to rewrap cakes tightly.

MAKES 6 CAKES OF 4 SERVINGS EACH.

ITALIAN SHORTBREAD WITH ALMONDS, BRANDY, AND LEMON (FREGOLATA)

❖❖❖

. . . .

Our Italian shortbread is more than a cookie and less than a cake — a real toasty-brown, peasant-style dessert. Though it can be cut into wedges, the shortbread is meant to be broken into rough pieces and served with fruit, cheese, and wine. For a picnic or as part of a dessert buffet, it will bring raves.

This recipe uses an 8-inch tart pan with removable bottom, but the drama of the dessert only increases with size. For a large group, use a 12-inch pan and double the recipe. **PREPARE-AHEAD/SERVING NOTES:** Tightly wrapped, the shortbread keeps well for a couple of weeks. **ESSENTIAL GEAR:** 8-inch tart pan with removable bottom

Pam (nonstick spray coating)

1 cup plus 1 tablespoon butter at room temperature

1 cup sugar

2⅔ cups white flour

1⅓ cups finely ground blanched almonds

3 tablespoons fresh lemon juice

1 tablespoon brandy

Zest of 1 lemon

Pinch salt

2 tablespoons sugar — coarse preferred (we break up sugar cubes or use Whitworth's brand Cane Demerara Sugar, as in the bread pudding on page 247)

Preheat oven to 350°F. Generously coat an 8-inch tart pan with removable bottom with a nonstick spray coating.

Place butter and sugar in a food processor bowl equipped with a steel blade and process until mixture is creamy. Add flour, almonds, lemon juice, brandy, lemon zest, and salt. Process just long enough to thoroughly blend. Spread mixture into the prepared pan. Refrigerate 15 minutes. Then, using a frosting "comb" or the tines of a table fork, cut concentric ridges into top of dough. Sprinkle with coarse sugar. Bake for 20 minutes. Lower heat to 300°F and continue baking — about 45 minutes longer — until shortbread is golden brown. (Since you want the shortbread quite crunchy, do not underbake.)

Remove from oven and let cool on a rack before removing from pan.

SERVES 4 TO 6.

APRICOT AND SOUR-
CHERRY BREAD PUDDING

◆◆◆

· ·

This pudding was inspired by our truly exceptional apricot preserves. We added the dried sour cherries for the superb flavor and texture they promise almost any dish. **PREPARE-AHEAD/SERVING NOTES:** Serve the pudding hot out of the oven, or rewarmed, or at room temperature, or even cold. It keeps well for three days. Because of its prepare-ahead ease, we recommend the pudding as a breakfast or brunch sweet, as well as for dessert. **ESSENTIAL GEAR:** Shallow baking pan (9 by 13 inches)

1 cup dried sour cherries

8 dried apricots, quartered

6 eggs

3 cups half-and-half

1 (10-ounce) jar Pasta & Co. Apricot Preserves

½ cup sugar

1 teaspoon ground cinnamon

2 tablespoons cream sherry or bourbon

2 teaspoons vanilla extract

8 ounces white bread (leave crusts on), coarsely crumbled in a food processor — about 3 ½ cups

6 ounces white bread (leave crusts on), cut into ¾-inch cubes — about 3 cups

1 tablespoon butter, cut into tiny pieces

½ teaspoon cinnamon

3 tablespoons sugar — coarse preferred, such as Whitworth's brand Cane Demerara Sugar (a really superb sugar for giving baked goods a crusty top)

Optional: Lightly whipped and barely sweetened cream

Steep cherries and apricots in hot water for 15 minutes. Drain well and reserve. Preheat oven to 350°F. Butter a shallow broilerproof baking dish (a 9-inch by 13-inch Pyrex dish works well).

In a bowl large enough to eventually hold all ingredients, using a rotary mixer or an electric mixer at low speed, beat together eggs, half-and-half, preserves, sugar, cinnamon, sherry, and vanilla. (There are whole apricot halves in the preserves. Break these up as much as possible in the beating.) When ingredients are well-combined, fold in crumbled bread, bread cubes, and drained cherries and apricots, until bread is well-coated with the egg mixture and cherries and apricots are evenly distributed.

Spoon mixture into the prepared baking dish. Top with butter, cinnamon, and sugar. Bake until golden, about 45 minutes. If pudding browns too quickly, cover dish with parchment paper or foil. Remove paper for the last 5 minutes of baking. If pudding has not sufficiently browned by the time it is done (and you *do* want it crusty on top), remove it from oven, turn oven up to broil, and run pudding under the broiler just until sugar caramelizes. (Careful, it burns quickly.) You may need to rotate the pudding several times.

Serve warm, at room temperature, or cold with the optional whipped cream.

SERVES 8 TO 10.

APRICOT MOUSSE

Lie when you make this and no one will guess that it isn't made with fresh apricots.

Use the Dark Chocolate Mousse recipe on page 237. Eliminate the chocolate, reduce the confectioners sugar to 2 teaspoons, substitute 1 jar of Pasta & Co. Apricot Preserves for the chocolate and 1 tablespoon (or to taste) Cognac for the espresso powder and water.

Follow the same directions, folding in the apricot preserves and Cognac into the egg and sugar mixture. Then proceed to vigorously fold in the whipped cream.

The Mousse is superb topped off with the Pasta & Co. Chocolate Sauce (page 241).

ALIX'S CHOCOLATE
LAYER CAKE

♦♦♦

. . . .

Alix Hague, one of our bakers, developed our chocolate layer cake. For a showy cake, it is the easiest one we have found. (The hardest part is washing all the dishes.) The fudgy cake is filled with chocolate whipped cream, topped with an ultra-shiny chocolate glaze, and decorated with coarsely chopped walnuts. Next time you need to make a birthday cake, try Alix's Chocolate Layer Cake.

This recipe makes a two-layer cake. However, the recipe doubles reliably, and a four-layer version is a grand sight indeed. **PREPARE-AHEAD/SERVING NOTES:** The cake holds well for at least three days. It is a party planner's dream. **ESSENTIAL GEAR:** Electric food processor, two 8-inch cake pans, baking parchment

FOR TWO CAKE LAYERS:

8 ounces semisweet chocolate (the best quality you can find; we use Valrhona or Guittard)

¼ pound unsalted butter

1½ cups sugar

6 eggs

1 teaspoon vanilla extract

1¼ cups flour

1 teaspoon salt

¼ teaspoon baking soda

1 cup finely ground walnuts, the texture of coarse flour

⅔ cup plus 2 tablespoons buttermilk

WHIPPED-CREAM FILLING:

4 ounces semisweet chocolate

1 cup whipping cream

1 teaspoon vanilla

GLAZE AND GARNISH:

1⅔ ounces semisweet chocolate

1 tablespoon plus 1 teaspoon unsalted butter

¾ cup coarsely chopped walnuts

Preheat oven to 350°F.

Cut round pieces of parchment paper to fit the bottom of two 8-inch cake pans.

Melt the 8 ounces chocolate and the 1/4 pound butter together over hot water. Set aside. Cool to room temperature.

Place sugar, eggs, and vanilla in work bowl of a food processor equipped with a steel blade and run until mixture is pale yellow (nearly 10 minutes).

In a large bowl, sift together flour, salt, and baking soda. Mix in ground walnuts.

Alternately add buttermilk and cooled chocolate to the dry mixture. Carefully fold in beaten-egg mixture just until mixed. Divide batter between the two prepared pans.

Bake for 30 minutes or until cake tester comes out clean. Cool for 15 minutes on a rack, then remove cakes from pans and finish cooling.

Melt the 4 ounces chocolate over hot water as before. Cool to room temperature. Whip cream until almost firm. Add vanilla and continue whipping until very firm. Fold into chocolate. (Theoretically, the chocolate should still be very runny when whipped cream is added. However, some of us like it when it has begun to solidify so that there are little "shards" of chocolate in the whipped cream.)

When cake layers are cool and ready to assemble, melt the 1⅔ ounces chocolate over hot water as before. Add butter. Stir until melted, and mixture is a smooth glaze.

Place one cake layer on a serving platter. Top with one-half of the whipped-cream mixture. Spread evenly across cake and set second layer on top. Pour glaze over top of the cake and spread to the edge of the top layer. Spread the rest of the whipped cream around sides of cake, meeting the glaze where it leaves off. Pat the walnuts into the whipped cream, making a 1-inch ring of walnuts around top edge of cake.

SERVES AT LEAST 16.

MAD HATTER BRAN
MUFFINS
•••

Opening our store in Seattle's financial district put us squarely in the breakfast trade. From day one, customers wanted a great bran muffin. This is it, spiked with our Grown-Up Granola (page 254). We call the muffins "Mad Hatters" because we bake them in troublesome little pans that make them stand up like top hats. This recipe, however, calls for far more practical conventional paper muffin cups and tins. **PREPARE-AHEAD/SERVING NOTES:** The batter and the streusel topping can be stored for at least a week before baking. **ESSENTIAL GEAR:** Paper muffin cups, 6- or 12-muffin tin

Ingredient Note: Just as this book goes to print, rumor (though unconfirmed) is that Kellogg Co. is discontinuing BranBuds. If this is true, we suggest replacing the BranBuds with additional Allbran.

THE BATTER:

½ cup Kellogg's Allbran

½ cup boiling water

¼ cup butter, softened to room temperature

⅔ cup sugar

1 egg

1 cup buttermilk

1¼ cups all-purpose flour

1½ teaspoons baking soda

Pinch salt

1 cup Kellogg's BranBuds

½ cup raisins, plumped in hot water for 10 minutes and well-drained

¼ cup Pasta & Co. Grown-Up Granola (purchased or made according to recipe on page 254)

Place Allbran in a medium-size mixing bowl and cover with boiling water. Let stand 10 minutes. Cream together butter and sugar until fluffy. Add egg and continue beating until incorporated. Add buttermilk to Allbran. Fold butter/egg mixture into Allbran. Add flour, soda, and salt. Stir until well-blended. Add BranBuds, raisins, and granola. Batter can be stored for several days before baking.

THE STREUSEL:

¼ cup brown sugar, lightly packed

2 tablespoons chopped walnuts

2 tablespoons raw pumpkin seeds (page 15)

2 tablespoons wheat germ

1 tablespoon butter, melted

¼ teaspoon ground cinnamon

Mix all ingredients together until granular.

TO ASSEMBLE AND BAKE MUFFINS:

Preheat oven to 350°F.

Line muffin tins with paper muffin cups. Fill each cup almost full with batter. Top with 2 teaspoons streusel mixture. Pat lightly into dough. Bake until top springs back to the touch, about 35 minutes. Remove from tins and cool on a rack.

MAKES 12 MUFFINS.

ONE MORE USE FOR PASTA & CO. GRANOLA: JUDY SCHAAD'S GRANOLA BARS

(OUR NEWEST RECIPE BEFORE GOING TO PRINT)

ESSENTIAL GEAR: A jelly-roll pan (10 by 15 inches); for thicker bars, use a shallow ovenproof pan (9 by 13 inches) and bake 1 to 2 minutes longer

Pam (nonstick spray coating)

⅓ cup butter

½ cup brown sugar

¼ cup honey

1 teaspoon vanilla

1 pound Pasta & Co. Grown-Up Granola (purchased or made according to recipe on page 254)

2⅓ cups rolled oats

Preheat oven to 400° F.

Lightly spray baking pan with Pam.

In a 4-quart saucepan, melt butter. Add brown sugar and honey. Raise the heat and cook at a constant bubble for 2 to 3 minutes, stirring constantly. Remove pan from heat and stir in vanilla. Fold in granola and oats. Stir well to distribute all the fruit and nuts evenly.

Press mixture evenly into a prepared pan. Bake in preheated oven 9 to 10 minutes until lightly browned. Remove from oven. Cool 15 minutes. Cut into bars. Refrigerate until bars are firm enough to remove from pan (about 1 hour).

MAKES 24 3½-INCH BY 1½-INCH BARS.

DESSERTS AND BAKING

PASTA & CO.'S
DOWNTOWN OATMEAL
SCONES

♦♦♦

- -

These are our signature scones. They are not like any other scones we know of. They are coarse-textured and hefty with dried fruit. And for years, customers have loved them. **PREPARE-AHEAD/SERVING NOTES:** As with all scones, these are best eaten within an hour or two of baking. **ESSENTIAL GEAR:** Electric food processor

⅔ cup dried sour cherries

2 dried apricot halves (⅓ ounce), cut into ¼-inch dice

½ cup buttermilk

1 egg

1 cup oatmeal

1 cup plus 3 tablespoons flour

2½ tablespoons brown sugar

1½ teaspoons baking powder

½ teaspoon baking soda

¼ teaspoon salt

4 tablespoons cold butter, cut into pieces

Preheat oven to 350°F.

Soak cherries and apricots in hot tap water for 15 minutes.

While fruit soaks, place buttermilk and egg in a mixing bowl. Without stirring mixture at all, add oatmeal and let soak for 10 minutes.

Drain fruit well and add to buttermilk mixture. Do *not* stir.

Place flour, brown sugar, baking powder, baking soda, salt, and butter in a food processor bowl equipped with a steel blade. Process until very well blended.

Using a circular motion, gently fold flour mixture into buttermilk mixture. Do not overstir.

Turn dough onto a floured surface and pat it into a round about 1 inch thick. The dough will be very sticky. Do *not* add flour, and do *not* knead. Lightly flour a knife to keep it from sticking to dough, and cut into 6 equal wedges. Place wedges on an ungreased cookie sheet.

Bake for 20 to 30 minutes on the middle or top shelf of the oven. Check, and if necessary continue baking another 4 minutes until golden brown.

MAKES 6 SCONES.

GROWN-UP GRANOLA

•••

. . . .

This is the very same granola we sell in our stores. We call it "grown-up" because it seems to have no resemblance whatsoever to the slew of juvenile breakfast products called granola. You can alter the granola to your taste. Some of us like it with peanuts as well as walnuts. Others prefer pecans or hazelnuts. **PREPARE-AHEAD/SERVING NOTES:** The granola keeps well for at least a month.

2⅓ cups rolled oats

⅓ cup wheat germ

½ cup sweetened Angel Flake brand coconut

⅓ cup raw sesame seeds

½ cup cooking oil

⅓ cup plus 2 tablespoons honey

2 tablespoons molasses

⅔ cup walnuts or nuts of choice

⅓ cup raw pumpkin seeds (page 15)

⅔ cup dried sour cherries (page 240)

⅓ cup currants

⅓ cup golden raisins

In a large bowl, mix together oats, wheat germ, coconut, and sesame seeds. Place cooking oil, honey, and molasses in a saucepan. Bring to a low boil and simmer for 5 minutes. Fold honey mixture into dry ingredients.

Preheat oven to 350°F. Pour granola onto a cookie sheet lined with parchment. Bake for 15 minutes. Remove pan from oven and stir in nuts and pumpkin seeds. Return to oven and bake 5 minutes. Rotate pan and bake 5 minutes more or until mixture is golden. Remove granola from oven and stir in sour cherries, currants, and raisins. Let cool.

MAKES 7 CUPS.

INDEX
♦♦♦

INDEX